Choose Costa Rica for Retirement

John Howells
& Teal Conroy

Choose Costa Rica for Retirement

Retirement, Travel, and Business
Opportunities for a New Beginning

TENTH EDITION

Guilford, Connecticut

All the information in this guidebook is subject to change.
We recommend that you call ahead to obtain
current information when making plans.

Copyright © 2013 by John M. Howells

Editor: Amy Lyons
Project Editor: Lauren Brancato
Layout: Joanna Beyer
Maps: Overview by Stephen Stringall, all others by Lisa Reneson © Morris
Book Publishing, LLC

ISSN: 1543-6411
ISBN: 978-0-7627-8102-7

Printed in the United States of America

10 9 8 7 6 5 4 3 2 1

Contents

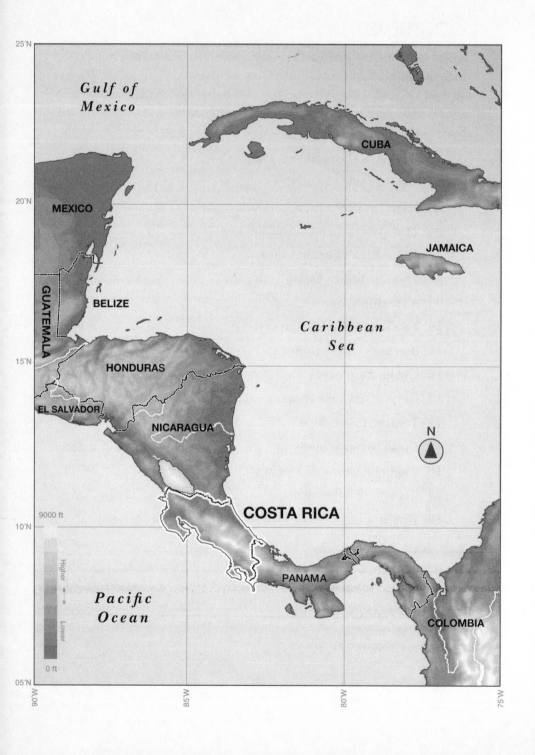

Introduction

This tenth edition of *Choose Costa Rica* is the outcome of thirty-five years of traveling in, living in, and writing about Costa Rica and Latin America in general. My bias toward the country comes through quite clearly, but I try to balance the picture by reminding readers that living in a foreign country is definitely not for everyone. It takes a special type of person to enjoy an interesting and challenging life abroad. Hopefully, this book will help you determine if you are that type of person. If you have any doubts on this topic, I urge you to read the last new chapter in this book: "Will You Love Costa Rica or Hate Costa Rica?"

My first exposure to Costa Rica came about thirty-six years ago. While researching Guatemala for a freelance travel article, my wife and I decided to go a little farther south to see what Costa Rica was all about. We expected it to be nice, but we were stunned by the country's breathtaking beauty. We were captivated by the friendliness of the Costa Rican people and loved the choice between perpetual spring weather in the highlands or perpetual summer along the Pacific and Caribbean coasts.

Like many other first-time visitors, we wanted to move to Costa Rica immediately! We spoke with fellow North Americans who were living here—some in business, some retired, and some seasonal expats, routinely escaping from frigid winter weather or spending summer breaks away from teaching school back home. We made friends with several Costa Rican families as we toured the country—from coast to coast, from top to bottom. Like many tourists before and since, we resolved that we would embark on a new beginning in paradise—if not immediately, then eventually.

We bought our first Costa Rican home in 1993. It was a condo in Rohrmoser, a popular neighborhood not far from the center of San José, and a dozen blocks from the US Embassy. Then in 1996, we bought a building lot in a friendly Pacific beach community and proceeded to design and build our own Costa Rican house. Our second house we constructed in 2005. However, to enjoy the best of both worlds, we've maintained our original home in California, on Monterey Bay, and travel back and forth several times a year. We take pleasure in friends and social connections in both locations, and feel very lucky to enjoy such a delightful lifestyle. A bonus is that Costa Rican swaps are extremely popular with home-exchange enthusiasts, so we have no problem trading residences with people in foreign countries. (Our favorite home exchange was a fascinating six weeks in the south of France, in a three-bedroom home with a swimming pool and a view of the Mediterranean.) This book is intended not only for retirees. It's also for those who would like to start or manage their own business. The book is for those nearing retirement age who are casting about for ideas for the future in today's uncertain world. It's a guide for those individuals who manage to have part or all of the year free for doing exactly what they feel like. It's for the professor on sabbatical, the schoolteacher on summer vacation, the construction worker with chronic winter unemployment, as well as the business executive who can take a leave of absence. This book is also for self-employed individuals who can trust their businesses to others while they enjoy life now instead of waiting for a "someday" that may never come. *Choose Costa Rica* is especially oriented toward those who seek a "new start," who might wish to invest time and resources into launching a new business career as well as enjoying a fascinating lifestyle in an exotic foreign country.

Although this is partly a travel book, the emphasis is on "how to do it" rather than "where to stay." A hotel, bed-and-breakfast, or restaurant may be mentioned from time to time but only as an adjunct to the narrative and should not be taken as a personal recommendation.

After reading through this book, maybe you'll understand why Costa Rica has such a good reputation among North Americans and Europeans. You might even find a niche there for you and your family. A word of caution: Costa Rica isn't for everyone. There are those who can't resist comparing conditions in Costa Rica with those in the United States or Canada. Remember, Costa Rica is still a developing country. There's a world of difference. For those of us who love Costa Rica, we thank our lucky stars for the difference.

About prices quoted throughout this book: They are accurate as of the time of writing, based on the current dollar exchange rates in Costa Rica. At the end of 2012 the Costa Rican currency, the colón, was worth about 500 colones to the dollar. (More about money exchange rates later on.)

Note: Unless otherwise stated, all phone and fax numbers in this book are in Costa Rica, and to connect, you must dial the proper access and country codes. Within the country, there are no area codes. For details, see "Dialing in Costa Rica" in chapter 5.

1

The Switzerland of the Americas

Just about every Costa Rica guidebook feels obligated to describe Costa Rica as "The Switzerland of the Americas." Never mind that Costa Rica is as much like Switzerland as a Chihuahua is like a Pomeranian. (They're both small.) So I suppose this book is obliged to make the same comparison. At first glance, the one thing Costa Rica and Switzerland have in common is that they are both small countries. Actually, Switzerland is a little smaller than Costa Rica—one of the few countries with that distinction.

Costa Rica is lushly tropical and continuously swathed in luxurious green vegetation. A place where coffee, sugarcane, and mangoes thrive, and where snow never falls. The exact opposite is Switzerland's snowcapped peaks with high meadows and rugged mountain terrain. Yet the more one travels in Costa Rica, the more apparent certain parallels with Switzerland become. Both are peaceful, progressive countries where democracy and stability are hallmarks. Although Costa Rica's tropical beaches are incongruent with Swiss landscapes, Costa Rica's mountains, in their own tropical way, rival the beauty of the Alps.

Even closer similarities between Switzerland and Costa Rica appear in their political philosophy and economic structure. Both countries are places of small farms and small businesses, with an air of prosperity and a feeling of equality among citizens. Both countries have renounced aggressive militarism, diverting resources instead toward education, medical care, and other services that benefit society in general. In short, both places are affluent, happy, and tranquil. Both are locations where North Americans can feel at home, safe, and welcome.

Obviously, Costa Rica is nearer to the United States and Canada, making it much more accessible for North Americans than Europe. Costa Rica also enjoys a much lower cost of living than Switzerland. Although Costa Rica's cost of living appears to be increasing over the past five years, it's actually a result a devaluation of the US dollar against *all* foreign currencies. It isn't that Costa Rican prices are going up so much, as it is the value of the American dollar going down!

A big plus for North Americans: Costa Rica has a climate that can be enjoyed year-round by those of us who hate wearing snow boots and earmuffs. The country's higher elevations (commonly known as the Valle Central, the Meseta Central, or the Central Valley) enjoy spring-like temperatures year-round. Brightly colored flowers seem to glow in the crystal-clear atmosphere. The countryside is so fertile that fence posts sprout and become trees despite the farmers' best efforts. Crossing over the mountains, you drop down to tropical lowlands where you'll find plantations of coffee, macadamia nuts, black pepper, and other exotic crops for export. (Macadamia-nut plantations are exceedingly rare in Switzerland.) Beaches flank either side of Costa Rica, dotted with small communities where North Americans and Europeans live in communion with surf and jungle. Switzerland, of course, is totally landlocked.

A UNIQUE HISTORY

Costa Rica stands out in this hemisphere in many ways, but its biggest contrast is with its Central American neighbors. When you drive across the border into Costa Rica or when you step off an airplane arriving from another Central American country, you know immediately that Costa Rica is a special place. Relative affluence stands out in contrast to the grinding poverty of other Central American nations. Income, wages, and standard of living are the highest of any of the countries in the Northern Hemisphere, with the exception of the United States and Canada.

Citizens of neighboring countries envy Costa Rica's benevolent and democratic government. They point to Costa Rica as an ideal goal. My wife and I recall being in Nicaragua in early January 1977, several weeks before the uprising that eventually overthrew the Somoza dictatorship. When a group of students in Managua somehow discovered that I was a writer, they surrounded us, demanding that we write something about their upcoming revolution. One student said, "Tell Americans that we are *not* against the United States! On the contrary, we want to be just *like* the United States! Look, if Costa Rica can be prosperous, democratic, and free, why can't Nicaragua be the same?"

The students had hoped to start the uprising to coincide with Jimmy Carter's inauguration. When I asked why, they explained, "Because, when President Carter was running for election, he promised he would never deal with brutal dictators. Since our Somoza is a brutal dictator, President Carter will no doubt send US marines to help us."

I tried to explain to the students that although Somoza was indeed a brutal dictator, the US government considered Somoza to be *our* brutal dictator, which made him okay. That idea was dismissed by the students. The rest is history. The United States supported Somoza until the day the dictator finally fled for his life to South America.

Clearly, there's a world of difference between Costa Rica and other Central American countries. How did this happen? Why does Costa Rica have so much less poverty and a large middle class in comparison with neighboring countries? Answers to these questions can be found in a series of historic events—some accidental, some planned. Let us do a historical review:

In 1502, when Columbus happened upon Costa Rica during his last voyage to this hemisphere, he anchored somewhere near the present-day port city of Limón and dispatched an expedition ashore. Thinking he had found an island, Columbus waited on the ship for a report from his landing party. His explorers returned with news of an inhospitable jungle and impossible swamps, plus ferocious natives who owned but a few paltry ornaments of thinly pounded gold (probably trade goods from Panama). In short, the Caribbean Coast offered little to excite the imagination of these avaricious explorers.

According to legend, Columbus gave his new discovery the name *Costa Rica* ("rich coast") to impress the king of Spain. The explorers sailed away as soon as the ships were repaired, without any thought of colonization. The Caribbean Coast was left virtually ignored by Europeans for several centuries. In contrast with the rapid colonization and development of other parts of the Americas, Costa Rica grew very slowly.

It was the custom for the Spanish Crown to grant huge tracts of land to the conquistadores as a reward for their services. Natives were considered a part of the land, and although not exactly slaves, they essentially belonged to the enormous haciendas: They were forced to work as peons for the aristocratic conquerors. In places like Peru, Mexico, and Guatemala, the Indians meekly accepted their new rulers and continued working the same lands as before, paying tribute to new overlords.

However, the Indians of Costa Rica (like their cousins in North America) proved to be determined, fierce fighters who resisted the idea of accepting subjugation. Experts in defending their heavily forested territory, the natives simply withdrew farther into the jungle when defeated. They clearly weren't interested in tilling fields for the pink-faced, bearded intruders. Archaeological evidence suggests that at least some tribes might have been headhunters, similar to the Jívaro tribes in Ecuador, whose warriors dangled their enemies' shrunken heads around their necks as ornaments. In short, these people were unlikely candidates to willingly become docile servants and field laborers.

This left the newcomers in a position they hadn't counted on. Instead of being lords over huge estates and overseeing gangs of laboring peons, the conquistadores were forced to work the land for themselves. A disappointment, to say the least. The colonists had to resort to manual labor in order to eke out a marginal existence from small, family-run farms. From the beginning, all were equal in their struggle for existence. Even the royal viceroy had to raise chickens and tend his own garden to avoid starvation. Small wonder that many early settlers and would-be exploiters moved on to easier pickings.

Over the ensuing centuries, Costa Rica remained a backwater of Spanish colonization, all but forgotten. Undisturbed, the colony grew in its own way, ignoring the ineffective Spanish governors sent by the royal court of Madrid. Costa Ricans lived quiet and simple lives, isolated and unaffected by events in other colonies. In fact, when Spain granted independence to the Spanish colonies in 1821, Costa Rica was the last to know (and probably cared the least). For all practical purposes, the region had always been on its own. Independence was no novelty.

A bit of historical trivia: Most people assume that Latin America's struggle for independence was a revolution against the king of Spain. Not true. In 1810, when the Mexican and South American revolutions began, the mother country of Spain was occupied by the French army commanded by Napoleon Bonaparte. The Spanish king and the royal family were imprisoned in France. Napoleon's brother, Joseph Bonaparte, occupied the throne of Spain, and the country was under French martial law. Therefore, the revolution was against *France*, not against Spain! However, after the king of Spain was restored to his throne some years later, the revolutionaries decided that independence was not such a bad idea, after all!

Coffee Economy

Fortunately, Costa Rica's first president turned out to be a progressive thinker, a visionary who wanted to see the country develop socially and economically. He was convinced that growing coffee for export could be a major economic breakthrough, a key to modernization. Coffee profits could build roads, schools, and cities.

Since the country was scantily populated, more people were needed to grow coffee in order to fulfill the president's dream. Consequently, free land was offered to anyone willing to cultivate coffee trees. Since coffee production is ideally suited to small, family-operated farms, European families began immigrating to take advantage of Costa Rica's opportunities. They came from Italy and France as well as Spain. Instead of huge plantations owned by a few wealthy families, as in other Central American republics, hundreds of small farms sprang up, selling coffee beans to merchants who processed and exported the product. This created a tradition of independence and equality, with a preponderance of middle-class farmers and a few moderately wealthy, coffee-exporting families. The spread between rich, middle class, and poor was much narrower than anywhere else in the hemisphere and remains so to this day.

Troubled times in Europe during the last half of the nineteenth century sent new waves of economic and political refugees to the Americas. This was their chance for a new beginning. The standing offer of free land to grow coffee was irresistible. These refugees, instilled with contemporary Europe's liberal intellectual and political philosophy, contributed substantially to the notions of freedom, equality, and individual rights that were already in place.

This is not to say that Costa Rica didn't develop a wealthy oligarchy of elite families whose positions rested upon their control of coffee exports. But because of their tradition of being "self-made" families and their respect for hard work, their mentality was different from that of the arrogant Spanish conquistadores who worshipped royalty and privilege, and who considered manual labor to be beneath their dignity.

Free and compulsory education was an early development, starting in 1869. This established a tradition of literacy that ranks Costa Rica high among other developing countries of the world. A university was founded in 1844, staffed in part by intellectuals who fled Europe's political and economic maelstrom of that era. These and other modern European traditions developed in Costa Rica in stark contrast with the medieval, feudal heritage of Mexico and other Central American countries.

Dismantling the Military

A truly significant event that totally separated Costa Rica from the ranks of other Latin American nations occurred in 1948. The ruling party decided not to recognize the results of an election by refusing to give up power. The defeated president ordered new elections because of the closeness of the vote and accusations of fraud. A crisis of democracy threatened. Pepe Figueres, a charismatic member of one of the wealthy families, stepped forward to lead an uprising against the government and its illegal attempt to use the military to hold on to power. The result of this successful revolution (the first and only in Costa Rican history) was a decision to abolish the army and replace it with the Guardia Civil, a civilian-controlled police force that augments the local police. In many smaller towns the Guardia Civil is the only police force.

This was a brilliant and bold step. Barracks were turned into schools. Ex-soldiers were given jobs building roads. Money that would normally be absorbed by military corruption was devoted to highways, education, and medical care. Today a huge percentage of the national budget goes to education and culture. Public money pays for four universities, three symphony orchestras, and several autonomous state publishing houses. Of the gross national product, about 10 percent is spent on medical care. Costa Rica has an average of one physician for every 700 inhabitants.

Some North Americans shake their heads in dismay at the lack of a standing army. They ask, "Without a military, how can you defend your country from aggression?" The answer is simple: The function of a Central American military has never been to deter aggression. The military's duty is to protect the country's politicians from irate citizens. Soldiers are there to keep people in line, to maintain privileges for the military and the country's financial elite. Democracy doesn't stand a chance when army officers nominate candidates, and armed soldiers threaten voters, conduct elections, and then count the ballots. Are we surprised when generals are elected president?

Throughout this book you will see Costa Ricans referred to as *ticos* and North Americans as *gringos*. These terms are commonly used in Costa Rica and are not meant to be disrespectful (this will be explained later on). These nicknames actually carry an affectionate connotation, since both groups like and respect each other.

A WELCOMING DEMOCRACY

Many North American expatriates will tell you they decided on Costa Rica for a new beginning in life because they feel at home here. We find it easy to make friends among the sizable community of fellow countrymen who have planted roots in Costa Rica. It's a place where North Americans feel comfortable living in ordinary middle-class neighborhoods instead of being forced to huddle together in wealthy and fortified enclaves of other expatriates for mutual support. That's not to say Costa Rica is crime-free (is there such a place?). Yet compared with other foreign retirement destinations in this world, Costa Rica gives most people a sense of well-being and safety. More about this later.

Costa Rica is a country where your conscience isn't continually assaulted by grinding poverty, malnourished children begging in the streets, or social injustice. Juvenile gangs and graffiti are the exception, not the rule. It's a country of full employment; just about anyone who wants a job can find one, and wages are the highest of any country between the Panama Canal and the US border.

In my opinion, every country appears to have its own personality. The Costa Rican personality resembles that of North Americans in many ways: how they view the world, their social behavior, and their value systems. *Ticos*—as they call themselves—are open, friendly, and egalitarian. Most North Americans feel right at home in Costa Rica. Those newcomers who don't fit in are commonly those who are uncomfortable because the cultural environment, customs, and everyday routines are so different than where they came from.

Because of these ingrained attitudes, Costa Rica has avoided problems that have mired other Central American republics in quicksand of turmoil and tragedy. Costa Rica's devotion to democracy and peaceful cooperation with neighbors has enabled the country to retain its enviable position as a showcase of prosperity, respect for law, and personal freedoms.

Honest Elections

More than a century-and-a-half tradition of free and honest elections forms the basis for today's political life. Instead of frequent military takeovers so common in Latin American countries, Costa Ricans change their government via the ballot box. Although members of the same affluent families often compete in the elections, they are civilians, intellectuals, and, for the most part, working for the good of the country as a whole, not just for one particular class.

Election Day is arguably one of Costa Rica's most important holidays. It's a riotous celebration with a joyous spirit that goes far beyond mere politics. Voting is mandatory—nonvoters are supposed to pay a token fine—but few citizens would think of passing up the fun and excitement of an election. Typically, about 60 percent of eligible voters cast ballots (that's probably double the percentage in US elections.)

In weeks prior to Election Day, all parties campaign vigorously. Homes everywhere display the flag of their preferred party. People proudly pin political flags to their clothing. When an automobile drives by flying a political flag, people either cheer enthusiastically or boo good-naturedly, depending on the flag's colors. On election day, many stores and businesses, and all bars, are closed. Until recently, liquor and beer could not be sold on Election Day, the day before, or the day after. The law had no real effect, because everyone stocked up on liquid refreshments beforehand, to be consumed on the day in question. The law was recently repealed, and will probably mean no change to the level of celebration.

Traditionally, public transportation is supposed to be free on Election Day. Buses, taxis, and even private cars are expected to stop when someone indicates he or she needs a ride to a polling booth. This is in theory. I doubt that many buses and taxis actually honor the tradition, although cars will often stop for anyone who waves and asks for a ride in whichever direction the driver is headed. After all, this is a fiesta!

It's interesting to note that many Costa Ricans, when they move from their hometowns to another part of the country, do not change their voting registration to their new address. Elections are considered an opportunity to return to their hometowns to vote, to visit friends and family, and to party at the same time. Reunions and celebrations are a vital part of Election Day.

Voters must dunk their thumbs into indelible ink to prove they've voted (and cannot vote again). This purple digit is worn as a proud badge of civic duty. Automobile drivers honk their horns and wave their discolored thumbs in the air as they drive along the streets, to show everyone that they have voted, while shouting, "Have you voted yet?" Sometimes there are so many horns blowing on Election Day that it sounds like New Year's Eve at midnight.

As a result, Costa Rica is a country intensely dedicated to principles of equality and democracy. All segments of the political spectrum, from extreme right to far-out left, are represented—any and all parties are totally legal. The crucial point is this: The electorate has a free choice, even though fringe parties rarely garner more than a small percentage of the vote. Voters can vote right, left, or center, choosing whichever party presents the best ideas. Because citizens can change their government at will, Costa Rica is virtually revolution-proof.

The end result is a free, prosperous, and peaceful country.

High Standard of Living

Please don't misunderstand: I'm not implying that Costa Rica has no poverty or that Costa Rican workers are highly paid compared with industrialized countries. Yet compared with Mexico, Central America, and most South American countries, workers here enjoy excellent working conditions, living wages, and government guarantees of fair treatment from employers. Even those at the poverty level live far better than in most other developing countries and better, in my opinion, than millions of people living at the poverty level in the United States.

Welfare is an unknown concept in Costa Rica, partly because family and friends are always there for backup in case of disaster. Jobs are plentiful and unemployment a fraction of that in most highly developed countries. Food is abundant; medical care and education are virtually free for working families. Agriculture here depends on illegal aliens from Nicaragua to harvest crops and tend banana plantations; Costa Rican workers prefer not to do this kind of backbreaking work. (Does this sound familiar to Californians and Texans who depend on illegal Mexican immigrants for *their* crops?) Open-air markets have a tradition of giving excess food to the poor, with vendors handing out unsold merchandise to those in need.

Although wages are higher here than in neighboring countries, they appear to be extraordinarily low to us *Norteamericanos*. How can workers be expected to survive on as little as $80 to $100 a week? The answer is that even though the cash salary is small, fringe benefits connected with the job make a big difference. In addition to their cash salaries, workers are guaranteed benefits such as sick leave—at the rate of 50 percent of their salary—from the first day of illness up to a lifetime of disability. Workers receive a month's pay as *aguinaldo*, or Christmas bonus, every year and a minimum of two weeks' paid vacation every year. Women receive six weeks' maternity leave (at full salary), and all receive a Social Security pension upon retirement. It isn't necessary to put aside money for the children's college tuition, because education is virtually free, a basic right provided by the government. Since medical care is free, a worker can spend his or her entire salary on living expenses without having to put a portion aside for those inevitable medical emergencies or illnesses of the end-of-life years.

These benefits are guaranteed by law, and all Costa Ricans know exactly what their rights are. Since there's usually a shortage of help in many regions of the country, anyone who really wants to work can find a job. As a result, many employers pay above the minimum wage in order to attract competent workers. This is in contrast with other Latin American countries, where the minimum wage and the maximum wage are considered one and the same.

When you measure these benefits and put a cash value on them, you'll agree that Costa Rican workers are ahead of many North Americans. In the United States a woefully inadequate medical-insurance monthly premium can cost a family as much as a typical Costa Rican worker earns in two months! Since few low-paid US workers can afford medical insurance, one short visit to a hospital can push them over the financial edge. Sick leave? In the United States only large, affluent companies can afford such extravagance. Paid vacations are not mandatory in the United States; they're granted at the discretion of an employer. In Costa Rica, paid vacations are the law.

I'm always amused when I hear ultraconservatives point to Costa Rica's health-care system as evidence that the government is socialist. They overlook the fact that if universal health care makes a country socialist, the

United States would be one of the only *non*-socialist countries in the world! So where does the money come from for Costa Rica's health care, pensions, sick leave, and such? It comes out of workers' wages in the form of Social Security contributions and matching funds paid by employers as part of the wage package.

You'll see few if any street people, panhandlers, or beggars on Costa Rican streets. Children never beg. You cannot visit some Latin American countries without a flock of hungry-looking kids trailing you. As a friend observed, "Among the world's poor, Costa Rica's poor are probably the world's most affluent."

LARGE NUMBER OF EXPATRIATES

Costa Rica has a high percentage of North Americans (and foreigners in general) who are "starting over" or living part-time in this exotic semi-paradise. You'll find these newcomers scattered all around the country—almost every nook and cranny has a few of us living there—instead of everyone concentrated in enclaves or colonies, as is the case in other foreign countries.

Nobody knows exactly how many North American citizens reside in Costa Rica at any given time. Most reliable sources estimate between 20,000 and 30,000 North Americans live in Costa Rica—some full-time, others making their homes here seasonally. Exact figures are impossible to come by because the embassy doesn't keep track of US citizens in the country. Canada does register citizens living abroad, but most Canadians are hesitant to stay out of Canada more than six months at a time because they can lose Canadian health-care benefits. The percentage of Canadian versus US citizens is difficult to state with precision, but you can be confident that plenty of Canadians are represented.

A few North Americans live in other Central American countries—Guatemala, Honduras, Belize, and Nicaragua—but their ranks are scanty compared with those in Costa Rica.

Costa Rica graciously welcomes seasonal residents, retirees, and business investors, placing fewer restrictions on newcomers than most other foreign countries. Government rules and laws make it easy to own property or start a business. In fact, you can do both, even as a tourist or part-time resident. To live in Costa Rica permanently as a *pensionado* (retiree), you need to show proof of $1,000-a-month retirement income from Social Security or some other totally guaranteed retirement income benefit. Although living on $1,000 a month is possible, at least on a basic level, it isn't recommended. Even though $1,000 is more than twice what a skilled Costa Rican worker earns in a month, the average US or Canadian retiree would need to acquire an enthusiastic appetite for beans and tortillas and be willing to trade his or her automobile for a bicycle.

Until you qualify for residency, working could cause you trouble with *Migración* (immigration). To live in Costa Rica for an extended period of time, it is required that you qualify for and at least apply for residency. The only form of residency that permits you to legally work in Costa Rica is *permanent residency*, which can take several years to obtain. If you can show that your job is such that Costa Rican workers aren't prepared to handle the work, however, this can be circumvented.

Those too young to receive a guaranteed company pension or Social Security can still qualify for permanent residency in Costa Rica by showing they have enough income to prove they aren't indigent. The amount required is $2,500 a month (which also covers a spouse). This can be proven by depositing a certain amount of dollars in a Costa Rican bank (at the time of writing, $150,000) and showing proof of withdrawals of $2,500 a month, which have been converted to colones. That doesn't mean you need to *spend* $2,500 a month. You can deposit the money right back in your bank if you want to. (Details are discussed in chapter 17.) You can check on the status of any changes in retirement regulations at www.discoverypress.com/update.

Although a steady devaluation of the US dollar on the world market has caused the cost of living in Costa Rica to rise somewhat, a retired couple can easily cover basic living expenses on an average US Social Security check: around $1,500 a month. On that amount you should be able to afford to support an inexpensive car, a part-time housekeeper and gardener, and dining out whenever you feel like it. Just consider the lifestyle you would lead in the United States on that amount! You might be looking for part-time work to make ends meet. I personally know people who manage to get by in Costa Rica on less than $900 a month—and others who spend $3,000 and feel they are economizing.

Salaries in Costa Rica are traditionally adjusted twice a year to compensate for inflation. In June of 2012, the adjustment to Costa Rica's minimum wage structure resulted in a very small increase. However, for the first time in recent memory, the increase not only reflects the economy's inflation, but also a devaluation of the US dollar on the world market.

Until 2007, the dollar's value, instead of increasing every six months to adjust for the Costa Rica's inflation, at one point *dropped* from 522 colones to 490! This reflected a 9.3 percent *decline* in the value of the US dollar. Remember, a decline in the dollar's value amounts to an increase in prices in Costa Rica's economy. It isn't so much that goods and services cost *more*, it's just that the dollar buys *less*. American inflation has caught up with Costa Rica's inflation!

A PERFECT CLIMATE

Two other conditions make Costa Rica a special destination for part-time or full-time living. The first is the almost perfect weather. Being located relatively close to the equator, Costa Rica's temperatures remain constant year-round. (Contrary to popular belief, the weather does *not* become hotter as you near the equator. It simply levels out, with less extremes in high and low temperatures.) At these latitudes, climate is determined by elevation rather than by the season. That is, at sea level the climate is perpetual summer. Daily highs are in the mid-eighties to low nineties. (Although I'm sure it happens, I've never seen the thermometer hit 100 degrees at sea level.) Nighttime lows at sea level are usually in the low seventies, just right for sleeping under a light bedspread. That's year-round.

At altitudes over 3,000 feet (900 meters), you enter a climate of perpetual spring. Daytime highs are usually in the mid- to upper seventies, while evening temperatures usually drop into the mid-sixties. Sweaters often feel comfortable after sundown. Yes, this is in the tropics, and yes, these temperatures are year-round!

The second special condition is Costa Rica's favorable investment climate. Instead of placing barriers to prevent foreigners from going into business, as do most other countries in the world, Costa Rica encourages foreign investment. To lure investors, the government offers tax incentives and duty-free imports. Again, you don't have to be a citizen or even a legal resident to own property or conduct a business. You can even own a business on a tourist visa! Not many desirable countries permit you to do this. As a nonresident, however, you are restricted to management chores. It is preferred that tourist-owners not tend bar, wait tables, or make beds in their bed-and-breakfasts. Anyway, who would want to do this when hiring employees is so economical? More about this later.

PLANNING YOUR VISIT TO COSTA RICA

One publication I strongly recommend for anyone considering Costa Rica for anything more than a short vacation is San José's English-language newspaper, the *Tico Times*. If you read every issue from front to back, including the advertisements, by the time you actually get to Costa Rica, you will know so much about the place that you will feel as though you are returning home. The classified ads keep you up to date on rental costs, housing prices, and what secondhand furniture and appliances sell for. Display ads tell you what you should pay for a hotel room or a bed-and-breakfast. You'll find the best places to dine as well as where to go for a beach excursion. The news columns are well written, with complete and unbiased news of what's happening in Costa Rica as well as in neighboring countries—news not available in US or Canadian newspapers. Featured are articles relating to foreign residents, governmental actions, or changes in law that may affect them, as well as news of social activities and club events. An extensive letters-to-the-editor section prints opinions of tourists and residents alike, telling of exceptionally nice places to go and which places are rip-offs, giving opinions about the country, kudos and complaints, political views, and just about anything else you can imagine.

Having presented these enthusiastic recommendations to subscribe to the *Tico Times*, I have to report that the newspaper ceased *printed* publication as of the end of September 2012. After fifty-six years of supplying English-language news for Costa Rica's expat community, the paper gave in to the pressure of high publication costs and the competition by online newspapers, the same way as printed media is disappearing throughout the world. (As an ex-newspaperman, this is a disheartening event, yet what can we do, except mourn?)

That is the bad news. The good news: The *Tico Times* is available on the Internet (www.ticotimes.net) so you can still browse current news. Or, for a nominal price, you can subscribe to the entire online edition and download and save each edition to your computer for future information and research (in Adobe Acrobat format). By all means, start your online subscription several months before you leave for your first Costa Rica visit.

A second essential for your first visit is a good travel guide: *Choose Costa Rica* is not intended to be a travel book. This is a guide to retirement, long-term living, and investment in Costa Rica. US and Canadian bookstores are loaded with excellent Costa Rica travel guidebooks packed with information about obligatory places to visit, detailed descriptions of the locations, choices of hotels and restaurants, and what to do when you get there.

A final essential for your trip is a sense of adventure and an ability to go with the flow. Things are going to be somewhat different in Costa Rica, as you will learn by reading this book. Folks who love Costa Rica are those who savor the differences, who find inconveniences amusing, or at least tolerable. Those who can't stand Costa Rica are those who are disappointed because everything isn't exactly as it was back home.

Easy Access

To enter Costa Rica, you simply show your passport and are automatically granted a ninety-day visa. It couldn't be easier. Your passport must have at least three months to go before the expiration date. Technically, you are supposed to carry your passport with you at all times, but it's okay to carry a photocopy of the page with your photo and another copy of the page with your entry stamp, so it can be determined exactly when you entered the country. Be aware that although a passport copy is acceptable, the police have the right to accompany you to your hotel to see the original. (This only happens when someone is suspected of a serious wrongdoing or of using a touched-up photocopy.) Be careful not to lose your passport—it's a bummer to have to go to the embassy and apply for a replacement before you can return home. I would highly recommend carrying your original passport when driving a vehicle, in case you get stopped by traffic police.

Your tourist visa that you receive when entering the country is good for ninety days. It's possible to apply for a ninety-day visa extension through the Department of Immigration (some travel agencies claim to be able to do this for you). However, many people take the option of leaving the country for seventy-two hours, visiting the beaches of Nicaragua or the islands of Panama for a three-day vacation. When they reenter the country, they are granted another ninety-day visa. This makes a stay of six months possible, allowing plenty of time to investigate and tour all the nooks and corners of Costa Rica to see whether it would be an appropriate place to retire or go into business.

Theoretically, this "seventy-two-hour turnaround" was intended to be allowed once in a six-month period. That is, after the second visa, you should remain out of the country for three months before reentering the country. Although still on the books, this rule hasn't been enforced for many years (if ever). Hundreds (if not thousands) of foreigners have lived in Costa Rica for years, leaving the country every three months to renew their visas. They are referred to as *perpetual tourists*. However, you should be aware that there *could* come a time when the law is enforced, or at least interpreted differently. At that point you might consider applying for residency, especially if you own property. It would be tragic to be barred from reentering the country to visit your home! Occasionally, the ministry of tourism threatens to crack down on perpetual tourists but rarely takes action except in the case of a few undesirables. Of course, being in the country with an *expired* visa, even one day over the allowable ninety days, could get you into trouble. You should take this rule seriously. Otherwise, when you return, it's possible that your tourist visa could be for only a week, rather than the expected ninety days! Don't misunderstand, I am not encouraging anyone to violate immigration rules; I am merely reporting how the laws have been enforced over many years, probably many decades. My personal opinion is that the government recognizes this group of North Americans as law-abiding, peaceful residents who benefit the economy by spending millions of dollars here. However, the government's attitude is always subject to change, just as the government itself is subject to change

One more caution: A foreigner who tries to exit the country without paying a traffic ticket might not be allowed to leave until the ticket is paid! This could cause a huge problem when trying to board your airline flight! Maybe even miss your connection. There's always been resentment about car rental tourists getting away with not paying tickets, but a recent rise in the cost of traffic penalties encouraged the government to go after those who refuse to settle up. So make a trip to the bank and pay for your traffic violations before leaving for Nicaragua for your seventy-two-hour sojourn, or before heading for the airport!

every four years. Therefore, I encourage anyone who intends to live in Costa Rica for long periods of time to apply for permanent residence. (See chapter 17 for details.)

Finally, I urge that you make no decisions about permanent moves, such as buying property or making business investments, without spending several months "on location," getting to know the country and the community, meeting your potential neighbors, and learning what Costa Rica is all about. Before making any financial moves, find a good lawyer, one recommended by residents in the North American community. Above all, don't hand your money to someone simply because he or she speaks English, comes from Akron or Atlanta, and has an honest face. Honest faces and firm handshakes are the marks of successful swindlers! Costa Rica has suffered its fair share of sweet-talking *gringos* with designs on your pocketbooks. There's something about a foreign country that tends to bring out latent larceny in some people. Later on in this book, we'll discuss ways to protect yourself from being swindled.

Retirement Tours

Although travel in Costa Rica is easy and plans can be very casual, some folks prefer to take a guided tour to the more popular areas for relocation. An organized tour is more efficient and saves time because the tour guide knows exactly where the expatriates prefer to live, and the guide will be able to introduce you to North Americans who have made the move to Costa Rica.

One tour that comes highly recommended is conducted by Christopher Howard, who has been a resident of Costa Rica since 1980, appeared on the *Today* show, and authored several guidebooks about Costa Rican living. His in-depth tours take you to the Central Valley and the central and southern Pacific regions of the country. All tours include a two-day seminar on every subject related to moving here. Mr. Howard recently published the book *Guide to Real Estate in Costa Rica.* Visit his website and blog at www .liveincostarica.com.

Another Costa Rica tour operator, George Lundquist, features a retirement tour called "Expose Me to Life for the Non-Rich in Costa Rica." His four-day tours take guests to some nontraditional retirement locations as well as some of the standard places. He places an emphasis on retiring on Social Security checks. George's website is www.costaricaretireonss.com.

Internet Research

The Internet is an invaluable planning tool. If you are one of those anti-technology holdouts living in the dark ages without a computer and Internet connection, allow me to strongly recommend that you get one right away. With today's simplified web browsers, anyone can learn to tap in to this information with an hour or so of instruction. The amount of information on Costa Rica available on the Internet is almost unbelievable, and it grows even more comprehensive by the day. Many expats in Costa Rica don't use answering machines; if friends or family up north call when nobody is home, long-distance charges apply when the answering machine kicks in. An e-mail message serves the same purpose. Not only that, e-mail is a great way to keep in touch with family in the States or friends in Scotland without expensive long-distance charges.

Even better than a traditional telephone, a computer program known as Skype provides a free way to communicate with friends in any nation in the world, provided they also have Skype installed on their computers. Simply connect with your friend's computer and talk as long as you like, for free. If you use an inexpensive little video camera, your phone call will also be a video call! The sound and video quality are excellent. If your friends don't have a computer, you can use Skype to call their land telephone for next to free. For example, to call a California telephone from our Costa Rican home, the charge is 2.3 cents a minute (compared with 50 cents a minute by long-distance telephone). There is no charge to download Skype to your computer. You can find the program to download at www.skype.com.

I recommend taking a laptop for your Skype connections, since you can easily carry it on the plane and keep it with you as you travel about the country. If you don't have a laptop, a regular desktop computer can be purchased in Costa Rica. The government places low or no import duties on computer products. Prices are somewhat similar to what you would pay in the States.

A Google search will return scads of websites with regional descriptions of Costa Rica, real estate for sale, homes for rent, and online expatriate groups. If you want to correspond directly with folks living in Costa Rica or others who are considering moving there, you'll find forums and bulletin boards where they post their e-mail addresses. You should try to make some Costa Rica friends before you ever leave for the airport.

A valuable Internet resource is the website of the **Association of Residents of Costa Rica (ARCR).** We highly recommend ARCR as the place to apply for residency and buy group health insurance, and for newcomers as well as residents to solve problems. The bulletin board has extensive archives of past messages. The website is www.arcr.net.

A search for Costa Rica blogs will return a flurry of websites as well, full of experiences of North Americans who have relocated to Costa Rica. These may be great source of advice for potential visitors who might be interested in relocating in paradise. Some blogs are also designed to promote business interests, but the basic information is there. Just a few websites, off the top of my head, are listed below:

Costa Rica Living (www.groups.yahoo.com/group/costaricaliving.com) is a popular expatriate website. The forum allows expatriates living in the country to keep in touch with each other socially, with news of expat gatherings, luncheons, and other events, both scheduled and impromptu. They exchange information about where to procure hard-to-find items and are generous when answering questions from those wanting to know more about Costa Rica. Occasionally you'll find arguments and conflicts with the participants, and sometimes the forum is under attack from "trolls" (people who don't live in Costa Rica, but enjoy stirring up trouble). That's just part of the fun.

Retire for Less in Costa Rica (www.retireforlessincostarica.com) is a blog by Paul and Gloria Yeatman, a couple from the States, outlining their experiences while settling into residency in Costa Rica, specifically in the San Ramon area. It's very well-done and informative.

BoomersOffshore.com (www.boomersoffshore.com). Too young for to qualify for Social Security, way too young to qualify for Medicare, a baby boomer couple with a bleak financial future made a major decision to pull the plug on this thing they call "work." This blog outlines how they cashed out and retired early in Costa Rica.

WeLoveCostaRica.com (www.welovecostarica.com) is a website by Scott Oliver, a British expatriate, who has done extensive Costa Rica research, and profiles established as well as newcomer retirees. The website gives reviews of numerous Costa Rican communities that welcome newbie expatriates to their midst as well as objective information about living and retiring in Costa Rica.

2

What's Costa Rica Like?

Costa Rica is the second-smallest country in Central America, comprising around 20,000 square miles. Many sections are almost unpopulated, mantled with rain forest, dense jungle, and rugged mountain landscapes. Costa Rica is so small that you can have breakfast at a restaurant on a Pacific Ocean beach and drive leisurely across the country in time to have an early dinner at a restaurant on an Atlantic beach. At its widest point, Costa Rica is 174 miles wide; at the narrowest, only 100 miles.

Yet the country doesn't appear small. Certainly not from the viewpoint of tourists driving rental cars over slow roads, winding uphill and down. Every turn in the road brings a new vista, another scene to contemplate, another curve to watch out for cattle on the road and traffic cops armed with radar guns.

Travel articles and guidebooks traditionally describe Costa Rica as being the size of West Virginia. We can also say that Costa Rica is about half the size of Kentucky. If these figures make the country sound small and insignificant, we can balance the equation by pointing out that Costa Rica is twice as large as Israel and Albania. It's also larger than Belgium, Holland, or Switzerland, plus many countries you and I can't even pronounce.

Few countries of any size offer such a wide diversity of scenery and climate or the variety of flora and fauna. Probably no other country in the world dedicates such a large percentage of its territory to national parks and wildlife refuges. About 27 percent of Costa Rica's land is thus protected. These preserves range from cloud forests to tropical beaches, from volcanic craters to jungle swamps and inland waterways. The national park system is a major attraction for tourism.

When you hear friends remark that they were disappointed in Costa Rica, there's a good chance their visit was a ten-hour stopover on a cruise ship. Cruise ships here disembark at one of two shipping ports, one on the

Pacific and the other on the Caribbean, where major scenic attractions are industrial warehouses, tank trucks, and storage sheds. These typical port towns do not leave a favorable first impression on tourists. (To say the least.) So the cruise director loads passengers onto buses and zips them away to the city of San José or to a scenic jungle park for a short visit and then back to the ship in time for dinner. Small wonder cruise-ship visitors cannot understand why people praise Costa Rica.

Costa Rica's bewildering assortment of wildlife includes 850 species of birds—more than in the entire continent north of Mexico. Representative mammals are monkeys, coatis, jaguars, and ocelots, as well as sloths, tapirs, and agoutis. One evening down on the Pacific Coast, a large anteater ambled in front of our car, its long snout almost touching the ground in front and an equally heavy tail drooping behind, looking very prehistoric. Turtles, colorful frogs, and toads of all descriptions abound, as do crocodiles and iguanas. Snakes? Of course. They range from huge boa constrictors to tiny coral snakes. Experts say there are more varieties of butterflies in Costa Rica than in the entire African continent. More than 2,000 species have been collected so far, and more are being discovered. The number of orchids and bromeliads boggles the mind. This is truly a naturalist's paradise.

Many tropical countries offer beaches and vacation accommodations, but nowhere else in the world can a tourist find such a combination of beaches, mountains, friendliness, and tropical wonder that's accessible year-round.

The Costa Rican government recognizes these unique assets and actively involves its citizens in both the preservation and the exploitation of nature at the same time. How do you protect as well as exploit the environment? Just one example: By hiring local people to guard and preserve endangered-turtle-nesting beaches, jobs are created. Beach villages then become tourist attractions, complete with motels, restaurants, and shops, thus creating even more jobs. Visitors from all over the world can now visit cloud forests, turtle-nesting beaches, and nature preserves—in comfort. In the process, tourists leave much-appreciated foreign currency with Costa Rican businesses and banks.

North Americans and Europeans are scrambling to join this bandwagon and, with government encouragement, are investing heavily in tourist businesses, particularly in motels, restaurants, and endeavors of a like nature. Some enterprises become instant successes, with full bookings and plenty of business. Despite occasional slow spells, Costa Rica's commerce and tourism have forged ahead through the past decade and continue to be healthy and grow into the new century. (Details about starting and operating a business in Costa Rica are presented in chapter 11.)

A COUNTRY OF CONTRADICTIONS

Before readers are left with the impression that everything is perfect in paradise and that Costa Rica is the best of all worlds, let's examine some contradictions.

The first contradiction: Even though the Costa Rican government is totally committed to preserving the environment and tries to control illegal deforestation, it also permits foreign companies to bulldoze forests in order to make more banana plantations and tourist resorts. The government puts large tracts of land into biological and wildlife reserves, forest reserves, national parks, and Indian reservations, yet at the same time, farmers and agribusinesses cut down forests on private tracts almost at will. The economy destroys in the name of progress, while the government tries to preserve in the name of conservation. But at least the government does try, and its efforts are improving.

Another contradiction: The growth of ecotourism in Costa Rica brings hundreds of thousands of visitors to enjoy the ecological wonderlands. But large numbers of visitors tramping through delicately balanced wilderness systems threaten to destroy the very ecological treasures that lure them to Costa Rica in the first place. The government raised admission fees to national parks in an effort to cut traffic to some extent. Some say the increase was merely to bring in more revenue, which may well be true, but it did indeed lower the number of visitors and traffic in national parks. The fee increase had a beneficial side effect in directing more business toward private ecological parks and developments.

Yet another contradiction in Costa Rica is the high incidence of petty crime among such a peaceful population, particularly in larger cities. In fact, a major criticism this book has received in the past is that it does not place proper emphasis on the crime rates. I have to admit that I've had a tendency to overlook this issue, in part because I feel that the problem is lightweight compared with the crime situation in most other foreign countries. Violent crime in Costa Rica is almost insignificant when matched with the crime rate in many US communities of similar size. On the other hand, there are some localities with a relatively high crime rate (just as in any country). We'll discuss crime in more detail in chapter 5.

Some will disagree, but I personally feel that Costa Rica's substandard roads, congested traffic in some areas, and serious potholes are a bigger annoyance than petty crime. I must admit, the government is trying its best to upgrade the roads and fill in potholes. A chronic shortage of funds, ever-increasing traffic, heavy trucks, and occasional intense rainfall make road maintenance difficult. The problem of potholes in rural highways and heavy traffic in the city will always be another of those fly-in-the-ointment nuisances you'll have to accept if you want to live in paradise. Nothing's perfect. When you are really deep into rural areas, your biggest obstacle to driving might be a herd of cattle being driven down the road or a sow and litter of piglets ambling across the way.

Another contradiction is the Costa Ricans' attitude toward foreigners buying prime coastal land now that the foreign population is increasing. Even though the Costa Rican people are friendly, gentle, and welcoming, you might assume they feel some level of resentment as they see foreigners bidding up the price of choice property until it is out of their price range. When they sell their agricultural properties, they are forced to move into local villages and accept employment from the newcomers. The big-money players are heavily represented by North American, British, and German buyers (more or less in that order). However, this resentment, when evidenced, is low and balanced by an appreciation of how foreign investment creates jobs and bolsters the economy.

Where my wife and I own property, local people tell us they'd much rather see foreigners own the land, because Costa Rican ranchers tend to clear-cut the forest to make room for cattle. From the cattle ranchers' viewpoint, trees don't make money until they are chopped down and sold for lumber or wood pulp. But they consider pastures with fattening cattle as renewable resources. *Tico* workers are well aware that cattle ranches create few jobs other than mending fences. On the other hand, foreign businesses, construction, and working for expat residents create employment and prosperity for all. So the bottom line is that there is surprisingly less resentment toward foreign developers than one might expect.

Visitors and foreign residents can do little to resolve these contradictions, but they need to be aware that problems do exist and may crop up in the future. The best we can do is try to minimize our impact upon the natural resources of the country. None of these problems have gotten out of hand and the Costa Rican government is constantly seeking solutions. But in any democracy, the going is slow and cumbersome. Just be aware that not everything is perfect—but for our money, Costa Rica is still paradise!

MENU OF CLIMATES

For such a small country, Costa Rica has an astonishing variety of climates. From the misty mountaintops of Talamanca and Monteverde to the dry northern Guanacaste province, from the permanent spring weather of the Arenal area to the jungle lushness of the Caribbean Coast, Costa Rica has every kind of climate one might desire. Well, except frozen snow and bitter cold; but you don't want that anyway. Yes, there are seasons, but the differences between them are measured in differences in rainfall rather than in temperature variation. Therefore, unlike many other choice world vacation spots, Costa Rica isn't a one-season destination. Almost any time of the year can be a perfect time to visit. September and October are probably the least popular months, because these are the rainiest. (Conversely, many expat residents prefer these months because there are fewer tourists.)

Costa Rican people transpose the meanings of winter and summer. To them, "summer" months are December, January, and February—the dry season. This is when children take their "summer vacation" from school. To Costa Ricans, "winter" is June through October! Conversations can become confusing when Costa Ricans and North Americans discuss the seasons, with summer and winter having opposite meanings for each. To avoid misunderstandings, I generally say "rainy season" or "dry season" instead of "winter" or "summer" so everybody knows what I mean.

The dry season, which begins around the end of November and lasts until May in many parts of the country, isn't parched and arid, as the name might imply. Occasional showers keep plants and lawns pleasantly green and flowers blooming in the higher elevations. Some Pacific coastal areas are truly dry January through May, yet much of the vegetation has adapted to this wet-dry environment and manages to stay green through the yearly drought. On the Caribbean Coast and in the northern areas around Lake Arenal, "dry season" is just a figure of speech; rain knows no seasons here.

A common misconception is that "rainy season" means continuous downpours. Typically, even in the rainiest parts of the country, the day begins with glorious sunshine. Blossoms seem to glow in the sparkling-clean air; birds sing happily. Then clouds roll in after lunch. Rain, sometimes heavy, falls between 2:00 and 4:00 p.m. (In some places you can almost set your clock by it.) The downpour sends people indoors for a couple of hours (an ideal time for a nap). Then sunshine returns, and the world is once again refreshed, ready for another glorious sunset. Rain often returns in early morning, from 2:00 to 4:00 a.m., followed by a gloriously colored sunrise. Seldom does it rain every single day; and several days in a row can be perfectly dry and full of sunshine.

To further complicate matters, what is true of the mountain valley environment around San José isn't necessarily true on the Caribbean side, which can be flooded with sunshine while the capital is awash in *aguaceros* (rainstorms), and vice versa. The fact is, no matter what time of year you choose to visit, you're guaranteed a generous serving of sunny weather—and possibly some rain as well.

On the northwestern Pacific side, the dry season is exactly that, with very little rain falling from early December until the beginning of May. The grass turns brown, and many trees lose their leaves, just as they do in North America in the winter. But the reason for leaf loss is to conserve water, not because of frost and freezing weather. Most trees are evergreen, but even some of these lose a portion of their leaves. It isn't as bleak as it sounds, for many of these trees replace leaves with brilliantly colored blossoms, as this is the time of year to attract bees, butterflies, and other pollinating insects.

Because most North Americans customarily think of the tropics as a place to visit during their winter season—to escape the snow and ice of their homelands—they are often surprised to find that the months of June, July, and August are the favorite time of year for many who live in Costa Rica. "You can't really appreciate this country until you've experienced our *winter* months," says my friend Graham Henshaw, an expatriate from England. "When the rains start in May, the grass and trees change to a bright emerald color. Flowers that bloom only in July and August are absolutely stunning. That is my favorite time of year."

TEMPERATURES AND RAINFALL
FOR SELECTED COSTA RICAN LOCATIONS

Avg.	Jan.	Feb.	Mar.	Apr.	May	Jun.	Jul.	Aug.	Sept.	Oct.	Nov.	Dec.	Annual
				(In degrees Fahrenheit and inches)									

Alajuela

	Jan.	Feb.	Mar.	Apr.	May	Jun.	Jul.	Aug.	Sept.	Oct.	Nov.	Dec.	Annual
Highs	81	83	85	85	82	81	81	81	80	80	80	81	81
Lows	62	62	63	63	64	64	64	63	63	63	63	63	63
Rain	0.3	0.5	0.6	3	11	11	7	10	1	14	20	1	92

Golfito

	Jan.	Feb.	Mar.	Apr.	May	Jun.	Jul.	Aug.	Sept.	Oct.	Nov.	Dec.	Annual
Highs	91	92	92	91	90	89	89	90	89	89	89	90	90
Lows	71	72	73	73	73	72	71	71	71	71	71	71	72
Rain	6	6	8	11	19	18	18	22	28	28	23	12	199

Cahuita

	Jan.	Feb.	Mar.	Apr.	May	Jun.	Jul.	Aug.	Sept.	Oct.	Nov.	Dec.	Annual
Highs	86	86	87	87	87	87	86	86	87	87	86	86	86
Lows	68	68	69	71	71	71	71	71	71	71	69	69	69
Rain	13	8	8	11	11	12	17	13	6	8	16	18	141

Nicoya

	Jan.	Feb.	Mar.	Apr.	May	Jun.	Jul.	Aug.	Sept.	Oct.	Nov.	Dec.	Annual
Highs	91	93	95	96	91	89	89	89	87	87	87	89	87
Lows	69	71	71	73	73	71	71	71	71	71	69	69	71
Rain	0.2	0.4	1	3	11	13	10	12	16	16	5	1	89

Manuel Antonio

	Jan.	Feb.	Mar.	Apr.	May	Jun.	Jul.	Aug.	Sept.	Oct.	Nov.	Dec.	Annual
Highs	87	87	89	89	89	87	87	87	86	86	86	86	87
Lows	69	69	71	71	71	71	69	69	71	71	71	69	71
Rain	3	1	2	7	16	17	18	19	21	26	16	7	153

San José

	Jan.	Feb.	Mar.	Apr.	May	Jun.	Jul.	Aug.	Sept.	Oct.	Nov.	Dec.	Annual
Highs	73	75	77	78	78	78	77	77	78	77	75	77	77
Lows	59	59	60	60	62	62	67	62	60	60	60	59	62
Rain	0.4	0.2	0.5	2	9	12	9	10	13	13	6	2	77

Even on the dry Guanacaste coast, you'll find microcosms of green environments tucked away in the interior valleys, where sporadic rains are coaxed from the westerly Pacific winds. Farther south along the Pacific Coast, the dry-season rainfall is even more frequent, keeping things pleasantly green during the driest months. The weather chart in this chapter provides statistics on the microclimates of Costa Rica. You will find an interesting interactive weather map on the Internet at www.discoverypress.com/weather.

INSECTS AND THE TROPICS

An odd thing about the weather checkerboard of Costa Rica: Contrary to what one might think, the more humid areas are not necessarily the most insect-plagued. Of course, bring your insect repellent, but I'm convinced that you need it less in most places in Costa Rica than you do in the American Midwest, Florida, or most certainly in many Canadian locations. Along the forested Pacific Coast and the Nicoya Peninsula—where the insect varieties are amazingly abundant—mosquitoes and flies pester you far less than in the dry regions of Guanacaste. On the humid Caribbean Coast, where rain can fall almost any time of the year and where bugs can get so large you'd think they'd been taking steroids, household cockroaches and flies are not nearly as plentiful as I've seen in Houston or New Orleans. (We've seen many interesting beetles but surprisingly few ordinary cockroaches in our Costa Rica travel and homemaking.)

In many parts of Costa Rica—especially in the most tropical locations—insects such as mosquitoes are so rare that many local residents don't bother with screens on their windows. This is partly because the forest's acidic water runoff in jungle streams and pools does not allow mosquito larvae to hatch. Of course, the rainy season in some areas will make a liar of me, so it would be best to carry repellent. This is particularly advisable when staying in one of the areas where dengue fever has been reported (mostly around the outskirts of Puntarenas and near Liberia). There's a vigorous campaign continually under way to eliminate the mosquito that spreads the flulike ailment. Although it is potentially dangerous for those who contract the ailment more than once, very few deaths have been recorded in Costa Rica from dengue fever.

Why flies and mosquitoes are scarce might still seem puzzling. I'm convinced the deciding factor is because the natural environment in Costa

Rica is largely intact. Natural enemies of pests such as flies and mosquitoes haven't been eliminated by pesticides, chemicals, and other methods, as they have back home. By day, birds of all descriptions flit back and forth, snacking on insects, keeping them in balance with nature. Many birds consider houseflies to be special treats. By night, squadrons of bats keep up the good work, finishing off mosquitoes before they get a chance to do much damage. According to one naturalist, a small bat can catch about six hundred mosquito-size insects per hour, and a large colony of bats will consume thousands of pounds of insects every night. (Costa Rica has more than thirty species of bats, thank you very much.)

Meanwhile, lizards, geckos, and chameleons patrol the walls and corners of houses, cleaning up cockroaches and water bugs before they have a chance to infest the kitchen or make a condominium out of your bathroom. The fearsome-looking praying mantis sometimes prowls about the edges of rooms, snapping up bugs that the lizards miss. Ugly as the mantis is, we love 'em!

Attack of the Army Ants

Folks living in the tropical lowlands have additional help in keeping their homes bug-free. From time to time, our Costa Rica house is invaded by army ants. Black and about a quarter of an inch long, the ants come marching in broad formation up the concrete columns to our veranda. They spill over the floors in a busy wave of housecleaning, removing moths and other night-flying insects that committed suicide against the porch lights the previous night. They scour the baseboards, corners, and ceilings in search of bugs, beetles, and insect eggs. Scorpions flee in terror; they have no defense against army ants—if they tarry, they are dismantled and served as snacks. Even snakes fear the ants. We simply stay out of their way or prop our feet out of range on a footstool while we read a novel, until their twenty-minute cleaning expedition is finished. We say good-bye and thank them as they continue on their way to their next housecleaning duties.

To our dismay, when our housekeeper sees army ants coming, she runs for the insecticide can and sprays profusely. This stops the wave of ants immediately, and they retreat. She is totally deaf to our protests and won't stop spraying until the ants completely disappear.

Actually, I'm exaggerating somewhat. (My wife has asked me a thousand times to stop exaggerating. Or maybe it was a million times!) The truth is, these army ant invasions don't happen all that frequently, maybe every other month or so, depending on where you live. If they happen to arrive while you are out shopping, you'll miss them. But they are spectacular.

During a visit to the town of Cahuita, on the Caribbean Coast, I was about to enter my tourist cabin when I encountered an enormous beetle. It was the size of a large teacup, shaped like a giant ladybug, and the color of an olive drab army helmet. Feeling brave, I gingerly picked it up by its back, correctly figuring that its wicked-looking legs couldn't reach around the shell. I carried it to a nearby restaurant and proudly displayed my beetle to the people sitting at the bar, figuring that I'd raise a few eyebrows. The bartender looked at my discovery with a bored expression as he remarked, "Yes, those little ones are females."

It turned out that I was holding a rhinoceros beetle, possibly the largest bug of the entire insect world. They tell me the male, which I never happened to confront, grows to a length of ten inches, sports enormous golden horns, and is colored in brilliant metallic hues. Harmless, though. According to one source, it feeds on decaying wood in the forest. My fingers were never at risk!

CENTRAL AMERICAN EARTHQUAKES

All along the mountain chains that stretch from the tip of South America to Alaska, you will feel earthquakes. As a Californian, I've become accustomed to them and seldom experience more than a slight feeling of excitement when windows start rattling and my desk sways. We Californians expect to have several minor quakes a year and a big one every twenty years or so.

So it should come as no surprise that Costa Rica has its share of shakes and tremors. The really big ones here are usually spaced by decades. Yet, Costa Ricans are just as calm about earthquakes as are most Californians. After all, compared with those 1,836 tornadoes that slammed the midwestern and eastern parts of the United States in 2011, claiming 549 victims, an occasional California or Costa Rican earthquake seems relatively mild.

The most recent Costa Rican earthquake (the second strongest in Costa Rica's history) occurred in September 2012. The strength was 7.6 on the Richter scale. In this most recent earthquake, the only fatality was one fifty-year-old woman who died of a heart attack. On the other hand, when a 7.0 quake struck near Port au Prince, Haiti (just a couple of years ago),

220,000 people were estimated to have been killed, and more than 300,000 people left homeless.

Why the difference? It's partly due to Costa Rica's strict construction codes. For eighty years or so, the government has prohibited adobe construction and tile roofs (which have a tendency to immediately bury inhabitants). Walls of cement block have to be reinforced with steel bars. Heavy tile roofs have been replaced with lightweight aluminum, galvanized sheet metal, or sometimes special plastic looking like tile panels. Wood construction doesn't tend to collapse and bury people; it usually twists and shakes, while people have a chance of getting outside the structure unharmed.

The last Costa Rican earthquake over 7.0 before this hit the Caribbean Coast near the city of Limón in April 1991. Forty-seven people were killed and 109 injured, with 7,439 damaged homes. Most of the damage was to buildings that were either built before the earthquake specs were in place or a failure of crude wooden construction. However, by the beginning of the next tourist season, most of the damage had been repaired, hotels were operating, roads were open to traffic, and tourism was going full blast.

3

What Are Costa Ricans Like?

Most travelers will agree that every country has its own distinct personality. Native citizens of each have unique ways of behaving and viewing the world. My favorite story to illustrate differences in national personalities is called *Traveler's Heaven and Traveler's Hell*:

"Traveler's Heaven is when you are greeted by the British, the French do the cooking, Italians plan the fun and games, and Germans keep order. But Traveler's Hell is when you are greeted by the French, the British do the cooking, Italians keep order, and Germans plan the fun and games!"

Americans and Australians, for example, are stereotypically outgoing, friendly, and loud talkers. Russians are pictured as dour and morose, with no sense of humor. British are said to be terrible cooks. Of course these are stereotypes, and we all agree that it isn't fair to apply stereotypes. (Except in the case of the Brits, who do tend to boil everything they can't fry.) Yet there is more than a kernel of truth here. The reasons for a nation's personality differences often can be explained by the historical development of each country.

In South America, for example, Argentina has a personality that reflects the heritage of its large Italian immigration, while next-door Chile was influenced by English and German newcomers who joined the original Spanish settlers. The result is an outgoing, vivacious, and self-confident Argentine personality compared with Chile's more reserved, polite, and introverted temperament.

Costa Rica's distinct personality also is a product of history. In chapter 1 we discussed Costa Rica's isolation during the early Spanish years and how, during the early days of the republic, Costa Rica invited Europeans from all nations to immigrate and start coffee farms. Italians, the French, and refugees from other European countries joined Spaniards in the land rush, each nationality bringing its customs and personalities to blend together into Costa Rica's unique European–Central American culture, thus creating the *tico* personality of today.

One way *ticos* differ from residents of some other Latin American countries is tolerance toward other religions and other points of view. Costa Ricans are predominantly Catholic but without the zeal and rigidity often found in other Catholic countries. This, too, has a historical explanation. In the early days, many villages were so isolated that the Church either couldn't afford or didn't bother to build a house of worship. Priests visited villages on rare occasions, sometimes never. The result was a view of religion as something remote and almost irrelevant (except for the joyous celebration of each village's Saints Day, which routinely involves happy dancing and drinking!). Even today, churches in many small villages are attended only by visiting priests. This situation creates fertile ground for the establishment of evangelical denominations. Some villages have evangelical Protestant churches only. An example of Costa Rican religious views: Three-fourths of couples prefer civil wedding ceremonies, with only one-fourth of young couples tying the knot in church in front of a priest or preacher.

Yet curiously, one of the country's most important celebrations is on August 2, when thousands of Costa Ricans end a pilgrimage walk of several days to pay homage to the *Virgen de los Angeles* statue in Cartago. Throughout the country, Catholics, Protestants, and agnostics alike enthusiastically celebrate their villages' religious fiestas with dances, bullfights, parades, and fund-raising events. It's more like a carnival than a religious observance. By the way, do not miss attending these celebrations! The local people appreciate *gringos* joining in and will welcome you with enthusiasm. You'll have a great time.

WHY TICOS?

Throughout this book you'll see the term *tico* used when referring to Costa Ricans. This is the appropriate nickname for a Costa Rican citizen, just as *nica* is a Nicaraguan, and *gringo* describes North Americans in general (as well as any foreigner whose natural language is English). Costa Ricans call themselves *ticos* when distinguishing themselves from foreigners, instead of the more cumbersome *Costarricenses*. Personally, I much prefer the term *gringo* over the dictionary-correct *Estadounidense* (which most of us couldn't possibly spell, much less pronounce, even on a bet).

The nickname *tico* comes from an archaic practice of using the sound *-ico* on the end of a word as a diminutive instead of the normal *-ito*. For example, whereas a Mexican would say *momentito* for "just a tiny moment," some Costa Ricans might say *momentico*. Thus, a kitten would be a *gatico* in Costa Rica but a *gatito* in Mexico. Note that not all Costa Ricans use this ending, but enough do to keep the tradition alive.

This isn't something that originated in Costa Rica; the use of *-ico* was common in sixteenth-century Spanish literature. However, it dropped out of style sometime after Costa Rica was settled. The country's limited connection with Spain didn't allow Spanish vernacular to stay current.

THE TICO PSYCHE

An outstanding difference between the psyche of Costa Ricans and other Latinos is the way they view the world and their place in it. Because of a long tradition of democracy and equality, the country has developed an egalitarian society similar to the United States and Canada. Unlike many other Latin American countries, the spread between Costa Rica's rich, poor, and middle classes is narrow. The middle class is large and relatively prosperous; the upper class is small and only moderately wealthy. This is a country where you can see the president and his wife pushing a grocery cart in a supermarket. People here feel an extraordinary sense of equality: They look you in the eye and shake your hand, fully convinced that everyone is on the same level.

Because *tico* attitudes are similar to the North American viewpoint, we feel comfortable when socializing with our Costa Rican neighbors. However, there are some subtle differences in the *tico* psyche that need to be understood. First of all, it is considered ill-mannered to be loud, brash, argumentative, and overly competitive, as Americans tend to be. (The exception, of course, is when *ticos* are playing soccer or driving an automobile.) In fact, they dislike confrontation or making someone feel bad so much that they'll do anything to avoid giving you bad news. When your contractor tells you that the transformer for your new home didn't arrive today but might be coming *mañana*, he may be avoiding the bad news that it could be a week, or a month, before you have electricity. Costa Ricans want to tell you what you would like to hear if at all possible. If it's not possible, they avoid talking about it so you won't feel bad.

In line with the hesitation to give bad news is a tendency to avoid saying a definite "no" to a request or business proposal. If saying no might make a *tico* appear rude, or might hurt your feelings, he becomes vague. So when doing business, remember that you can only count on an outright "yes" or "no" as being definitive. A hesitant "yes" or "maybe" could mean anything.

Another interesting trait is the reluctance to accept blame. When our maid drops a plate on the floor, she says, *"Se quebró el plato,"* or "The plate broke itself." I once tried to convince an electrician that he had installed my telephone incorrectly. (The problem was obvious: He had shorted the wires by pounding a staple across the cable shroud.) He insisted that the problem was a temporary glitch at the telephone exchange. "Pretty soon they'll find their mistake and fix it." He installed a new cable at my insistence and according to my directions, after which the phone worked. "You see?" he crowed in triumph. "While I was putting in the new cable, the telephone company found their mistake and fixed it!" I agreed with him so he could save face.

Something I do *not* believe is the often-heard claim that *ticos* deliberately mislead you about directions rather than admit that they don't know the answer. For example, some claim that when asked directions, *ticos* might give any response, pointing whichever direction they think you might like. I've often wondered where that notion came from. I have never, in all my years of traveling anywhere in Central America, had *anyone* do that. (I ought to know, because without street signs, I have to ask for directions frequently.) When *ticos* don't know the answer to a question, they simply say so, like anyone else. On several occasions when the people I asked for directions didn't know, they would flag down a passing automobile to ask. Giving misleading directions would be the height of rudeness and a violation of *tico* etiquette.

The well-known *mañana* attitude of Latin America is present in Costa Rica, but not nearly to the extent as in some other Latino countries—at least in my experience. Our workers are usually always at the job on time and work hard while they are there. (They also quit exactly on time.) The exception to this rule is on Monday mornings after a Sunday fiesta celebration. Nobody expects all of their workers to show up on time or without hangovers on those Monday mornings. Or to be really capable of work, for that matter. (They love fiestas!) Guests to your dinner party will be late anywhere from thirty minutes to an hour. Your auto mechanic will be an hour late changing your oil, but seldom a day late.

In several ways, *ticos* are very much like us, except that they speak more softly and seem more stoic about the world's problems than some of their Latin American counterparts. They laugh just as much as we do and share the same sense of humor. The best part of all: They really like North Americans, because our personalities mesh. Most of us who live in Costa Rica reciprocate this instant friendship; we like *ticos,* too.

COSTA RICAN SPANISH

One of the ways to get the most out of living in a foreign country is to learn to speak the language. In Costa Rica, speaking Spanish is neither essential nor necessary because you'll have many English-speaking neighbors, both expats and *ticos,* but learning to communicate in Spanish will open many doors. Acquiring fluency helps you make Spanish-speaking friends and become comfortable in your new environment.

I have a couple of suggestions. First, get over the notion that you can "pick up Spanish" just by being exposed to people speaking Spanish. It doesn't work that way. It takes study and hours of conversation with Spanish-speaking people. Stick with it and speak Spanish at every opportunity, and you'll find yourself enjoying the process. Just about all *ticos* have studied English in grammar school, the same as you may have been exposed to Spanish in high school. (This doesn't mean that *ticos* remember any more English than you remember Spanish!) Yet you can build fluency and confidence by throwing in an English word or two when you can't remember or haven't learned the proper word. (They won't always understand the word, but there's a good chance they might.) If you have a background in Spanish, either from high school or college classes, you shouldn't have too much difficulty with the standard Spanish spoken in Costa Rica.

Nevertheless, there are some differences you should be aware of. Because of Costa Rica's early isolation from mainstream Spanish colonies, the country maintained archaic words and idioms that long ago faded from

Spanish spoken in neighboring colonies. Furthermore, within Costa Rica itself, pronunciation and local accents developed in isolated parts of the country when communication between regions was severely restricted. For example: Before the railroad was constructed to transport coffee to Limón to be shipped to Europe, an oxcart journey took nearly two weeks. (Today it's a two- or three-hour drive.) So it isn't surprising that local idioms and accents developed in isolation throughout the country.

These accents vary from being so slight that it takes an expert to distinguish them, to being all but unintelligible for those trying to learn Spanish. The differences are similar to the way English words are pronounced in Minnesota, as compared to the way they're pronounced in Alabama. This is most noticeable in Guanacaste (northwestern Costa Rica). Like the Alabama accent, the Guanacaste accent is the result of dropping consonants and slurring vowels together. This lingo is similar to that spoken in Nicaragua (not surprising since Guanacaste originally was part of Nicaragua). Once you get used to this blending of sounds, it becomes clear.

Even though, in some isolated parts of Costa Rica, people tend to use colloquial expressions when speaking Spanish, they are aware of the problem and can easily switch to standard Spanish when talking to beginners. They simply repeat their words with a more careful pronunciation and avoid using local slang—just as they learned to do when they were in grade school.

One outstanding difference between *tico* Spanish and standard high school Spanish might puzzle those who have studied the language back home. Instead of using the traditional polite *usted* and informal *tu* forms of Spanish, which are normally taught in our high schools and universities, Costa Ricans use the archaic Spanish *vos* instead of the more common *tu* for the familiar first person singular. Originally, *vos* was the polite form of Spanish first person singular, and *tu* was familiar. Then somewhere in the late sixteenth century, the use of *vuestra merced* ("your grace") became the polite form, later shortened to *usted*. This downgraded the formal pronoun *vos* to informal use, and the pronoun *tu* was used only when speaking to inferiors or animals. Later, the use of *vos* was totally dropped and *tu* once again became standard for informal speech in Spain. However, the first Costa Rican immigrants from Spain arrived *before* that switch in grammar occurred and therefore retained the old custom. To make things more confusing, the *tu* form is sometimes used as a form of intimacy between lovers.

Verbs have a different declension or word ending when using *vos*. Unfortunately these grammatical verb forms aren't usually taught in US schools, even though the *voseo* mode is used by several million people in the Western Hemisphere. (Yes, they teach the *vosotros* form, but that is plural and is used mostly by Catholic priests when addressing a congregation.) It takes some time to become comfortable with the *vos* form; in the meantime, play it safe by using *usted*. Look at the chart below and note the differences.

	Usted Form	**Tu Form**	**Vos Form**
Do you want?	*¿Quiere Ud?*	*¿Quieres tu?*	*¿Queréis vos?*
You speak . . .	*Usted habla*	*Tu hablas*	*Vos hablás*
You are . . .	*Usted es*	*Tu eres*	*Vos sos*

You'll also encounter some interesting differences between *tico* expressions and Spanish usage in other countries. Some are quite charming. For example, in most Spanish-speaking countries, the term for "you're welcome" is *por nada* ("it's nothing") or *no hay de que* ("don't mention it"). Costa Ricans feel that those expressions are somewhat impolite. To say "you're welcome," they say *con mucho gusto,* which translates as "with much pleasure." (Now, is that polite or what?) Of course, they're used to hearing *gringos* use the other expressions, so they won't be surprised when you say *de nada*.

Instead of greeting friends with *"¿Como está usted?"* ("How are you?") they'll often ask, *"¿Como amaneció?"* ("How did you wake up this morning?").

Another curious custom: For some reason *ticos* feel that asking for something using the verb *dar* (to give) is impolite. Instead of *Dame una coca, por favor,* meaning "Give me a Coca-Cola, please," they consider it more polite to use the verb *regalame,* which means "give me" but also could mean "make me a gift of . . ." So to be polite in a *tico* sense, you might say, *"Regálame una coca, por favor."* A *tica* friend told of her first visit to Mexico and of ordering a cup of coffee in a restaurant by saying *"Regálame un café con leche, por favor."* The waitress was obviously embarrassed when she said, "I'd love to give you some coffee, but the owner would be angry with me if I did!" My friend giggled about this, saying she hadn't realized that she could be misunderstood.

One uniquely Costa Rican term, solidly ingrained into the language, is *pura vida*. I suppose this would translate as "it's a great life," but in effect it means "okay," "cool," "all right," or sometimes an emphatic "aw-right!" Instead of asking "Would you like anything else?" a clerk in a store might say, *"Pura vida?"* A gas-station attendant might ask, "Is your oil *pura vida,* or should I check it for you?" When you greet someone with *"¿Como está usted?"* the answer is often, *"Pura vida!"*

A couple of strictly Costa Rican expressions initially puzzled me and could be puzzling to those learning the language. This is a tendency to begin sentences with the words *vieras que,* or simply *vieras.* Literally it means something like "You see" or "You know." Also used in the same way is *digamos* ("let's say . . ."). Since the sound *d* is often softened or dropped entirely, it often comes out *"igamos."*

Remember that slang changes over time. Many years ago I ran across a series of tapes with *tico* slang expressions, bought them, and put them away, vowing some day to master *tico* slang. Twenty years later I actually began to study those tapes. Armed with this knowledge of *tico* slang, I ventured forth to display my proficiency and was shocked to see smiles and laughter. Then I realized that over the years, this slang had fallen from favor. I was saying things like "Twenty-three skidoo!" or "Groovy!" or "Far out!"

For those who would like to study Costa Rican slang, a Google search will return several websites devoted to this. One can be found at www.discovery press.com/slang.html. A word of warning: Those who have learned and used Spanish slang in another country should be careful when using it in polite company in Costa Rica. Some expressions that might be clever and inoffensive in Mexico, for example, could mean something obscene or insulting in Costa Rica, and vice versa.

4

Why Choose Costa Rica?

Ask the question, "Why did you choose to relocate in Costa Rica?" and you'll receive almost as many different answers as there are expatriates living here. Typically, the process of choosing Costa Rica for a new beginning starts with a vacation visit. People are curious about this small Central American democracy. They've heard of lush rain forests, lofty mountains, marvelous wildlife, and gorgeous beaches. Costa Rica's welcoming expat community and friendly natives make tourists feel at home. Before the vacation is over, the possibility of living in Costa Rica on a permanent vacation begins to look very attractive.

Costa Rica's unique selection of climates is a definite drawing card, with fugitives from bitter-cold winters or suffocating summer heat finding welcome relief from weather extremes. "I grew up in Kansas," one retiree explained. "We had blizzards and frozen ground in the winter, then 110-degree days trapping us indoors in the summer. Where we live now, on the hillside above Escazú, we only need one set of clothing—for spring weather."

Some who succumb to Costa Rica's attractions are much too young to retire, either mentally or physically. Their goals often include some kind of business enterprise they've always wanted to try. This is their chance to do what they *want* to do rather than what they *have* to do, or what they are *told* to do. Later in this book we have a chapter on doing business in Costa Rica and why some make a success of it and others do not.

To most retirees, business sounds like work. Work is exactly why they are retiring in the first place! Yet lying around the swimming pool or hanging out on a beach isn't exactly what they have in mind. An alternative is volunteering in some worthwhile activity. Perhaps at the local library, teaching English to children. Maybe helping preserve turtle nesting grounds, or working with one of the many North American social clubs and organizations throughout the country. The need for volunteers is constant. Besides self-satisfaction, you immediately become part of a social group of like-minded compatriots and friends.

Some relocate to Costa Rica simply for the enchanting experience of living in a foreign country, learning a foreign language, making friends in a totally different culture, and learning how other people live. This includes creating an active social life among fellow countrymen, with clubs, evening get-togethers, and travels throughout the region. Costa Rica's relative affluence and absence of obvious poverty make retirees feel comfortable while experiencing the stimulation of foreign retirement. The fact that Americans genuinely feel welcome makes it easy for retirees to settle almost anywhere they choose, not necessarily confined to expatriate gated communities.

Most people do a lot of research and spend some time in the country before making a solid decision about moving here. But not all do. When asked how she and her husband made the decision to move to Costa Rica, one lady said, "We probably did things differently than most sane people do. We decided to move here without even visiting. We had traveled in Mexico, and everyone we spoke with compared Costa Rica favorably. In fact, some people liked Costa Rica better than Mexico. We decided we could handle Costa Rica without testing the waters first. Our initial plan was to spend a year in Costa Rica, rent furnished homes, learn the language, and take our experiences back home when it was over. However, our children were enjoying school here, so after one year into it, we expect to be here for a long while."

MONEY MATTERS

When the first edition of *Choose Costa Rica* came out two decades ago, one of the themes was the delightfully inexpensive cost of travel and retirement. In those days, a couple could easily retire in Costa Rica on average US Social Security benefits (about $800 a month or $9,600 a year). At that time, a part-time housekeeper earned about $1 per hour, a full-time gardener $180 a month. Gasoline cost about the same as in the United States: $1.60 a gallon. It was economic paradise for North American retirees. I hope everyone realizes that times have changed. Prices in both countries have increased exponentially. But Costa Rican prices, compared with US and Canadian prices, appear to be rising much faster. Every six months, the dollar buys a little *less* for expats than it did in the previous six-month period. Does that sound strange? Let me explain.

Costa Rica's currency is called the colón. As with many foreign currencies, the colón's value fluctuates against the US dollar according to global financial trends. For years, colón exchange rates have been routinely adjusted to compensate for inflation every six months. For example, in 1992 the exchange rate was 138 colones to the dollar; fourteen years later, in mid-2006, the colón's value was about 520 to the dollar. That's a devaluation rate of about 12 percent a year—not as bad as it sounds, considering that Costa Rican banks are known to pay as much as 17 percent interest on colón certificate-of-deposit accounts.

For years, the twice-a-year adjustments kept prices in dollars fairly even, although prices in colones kept rising. For example: In 1992, Costa Rican restaurants priced a bottle of beer at 138 colones (or one dollar). At that time, in the US, a bottle of beer in a restaurant would have cost two dollars. Later, in 2006, the price of a beer in a Costa Rican restaurant was priced at 520 colones. Since 520 colones equaled one dollar, the beer was still one dollar a bottle, fourteen years later! (My wife can tell you, whenever I give a lesson in economics, I use the price of beer as an example.)

But something happened around the early part of 2007. The international value of the dollar *stopped* appreciating against the colón. The dollar's value stagnated until, at one point in 2012, the dollar had dropped *below* 500 colones. That's *less* than the dollar was worth six years earlier! Foreign residents complain bitterly about this, yet they forget that the cost of the beer in a typical American restaurant has risen from $4 to $5. It's still only $2 in Costa Rican restaurants.

LOW COST OF LIVING?

There are two reasons why I'm reluctant to emphasize Costa Rica as inexpensive. The first reason: Some folks might be encouraged to move to Costa Rica simply because they want a cheap place to live. Those who choose Costa Rica for this reason are continually comparing prices and conditions. They tend to ignore the climate and gorgeous tropical ambience. They complain bitterly when conditions are substandard in comparison with back home: roads, bureaucracy, the *mañana* syndrome, and so on.

They feel cheated to discover that many items cost almost as much here as in their hometowns—some imported goods and gasoline even more! Focusing on this aspect of Costa Rican living makes some newcomers bitter and resentful, convinced they've been cheated somehow.

Let's face facts: There always have been localities in the United States where you could live almost as inexpensively as in Costa Rica. Many rural communities in Arkansas, Alabama, and Oklahoma have a cost of living similar to that in Costa Rica. Yet, do they offer a comparable quality of life? Ever try to surf on an Oklahoma beach?

The second reason: I hate to see people relocate to Costa Rica because they are having a difficult time making ends meet back home. When they arrive here, too often they come without sufficient backup funds to cover those emergencies that inevitably occur. You'll not find any "safety nets" in Costa Rica: no welfare, no food stamps, no emergency room health care. And, they cannot expect assistance from the expatriate community. That's one reason the government insists on your proving a sufficient income before granting permission to immigrate.

It's always amusing to hear tourists—and even an occasional resident—complain about high prices in Costa Rica. For some reason, people assume that property, goods, and services ought to be dirt-cheap in a developing Central American country like Costa Rica. One evening, my wife and I happened to be dining next to a couple from New England who were first-time visitors to Costa Rica. They expressed disappointment with Costa Rica as a place to retire. When asked why, they replied that they felt that Costa Rica was not the beautiful and interesting place described in magazines and guidebooks. (They didn't know that we were authors of a guidebook.)

Dumbfounded by their answer, I politely inquired how long they had been in Costa Rica and where they had visited. They admitted that they had just arrived a few days earlier and that their travels were limited to taxi rides around the San José region.

"Okay, we realize there must be more to Costa Rica than the San José area," the husband explained. "But we were under the impression that everything is cheap here. That's not the case. For example, we see houses advertised in the *Tico Times* priced almost as much as back home." They admitted that they hadn't actually looked at many of the houses. They had expected to find a nice home for around $30,000.

Their concern over high prices amused us. They were enjoying a delicious sea bass dinner priced at $10, including dessert. They were drinking Costa Rican beer priced at $2 a bottle. They were staying at a nice bed-and-breakfast for about $40 a night. To be polite, we agreed with the couple; Costa Rica probably wouldn't be the ideal place for them to retire.

Although I have a hard time imagining a quality place in the United States or Canada that makes Costa Rica look expensive, my routine reply to bargain hunters is: "If rock-bottom prices are your priority, look at Mexico, Guatemala, or Nicaragua." Many developing countries offer cheaper living than Costa Rica. But is the quality of life the same? Is the weather as nice? Are the people as friendly?

The bottom line is: You're in for disappointment if you expect to pay $5-a-day wages for your gardener or maid or purchase ocean-view property at Texas Panhandle prices. If you anticipate luxurious $10-a-day hotel rooms and lobster dinners for $3, this might be the time to stop reading this book.

Affordable, Not Cheap

In general, I estimate most Costa Rican prices (for food, rent, clothing, etc.) to be about the same as in many rural communities in North America. Of course, imported goods can be much more. The hotels expatriates patronize usually range from $35 to $65 dollars a night, often including breakfast. These aren't luxury establishments by any definition, but they clearly offer far more than budget hotels do in the United States or Canada for the same price. Backpackers are delighted to find rooms for $10, since they don't mind sharing the bathroom and don't demand ironed bedsheets.

Go to just about any nice restaurant in Costa Rica and check the menu. Few entrees are priced over $12. A juicy steak goes for about $14, pasta Alfredo for $8. If the entree exceeds $15, you're probably ordering lobster or jumbo shrimp. (For some reason, jumbo shrimp is expensive in Costa Rica.) If you're into *tipico* Costa Rican food, you can order a *casado* for about $5—a delicious plate of beans, rice, fried banana and yucca, and salad, with your choice of chicken, fish, or pork chop. My favorite *tico* restaurant serves a delicious butterflied pork chop half the size of a dinner plate for about $4.50.

Let's forget about hotel prices and restaurant costs; they don't figure heavily in most long-term residents' budgets. More important is comparing the cost of everyday living here with the lifestyle the same amount of money provides in North America. You would be hard-pressed to find another place in the United States or Canada with so much to offer for such a reasonable outlay—without ice and snow, and without 100-degree summer days as a bonus.

Can You Live on Social Security?

The answer depends on the size of your monthly check. Current US Social Security benefits for a couple averages around $1,500 a month. (That would be $375 a week.) Assuming no extraordinary expenses, most people would have no problem maintaining a comfortable lifestyle on that amount. After all, $375 is about the *monthly* income of a typical Costa Rican family! Consider this: The salary of a Costa Rican college professor or a business executive is around $800 dollars a month. Therefore, for most Costa Ricans, $1,500 a month is an *extravagant* amount of money!

Yes, you can get by back in the United States on $1,500 a month—provided you live in an inexpensive part of the country—but it would require some creative budget trimming, especially in northern locations where winter heating bills can average over $350 a month and air-conditioning expense is not much less during summer months. (Almost no Costa Rican homes have furnaces or air conditioners.)

Numerous surveys here show that most expatriate couples report spending between $1,500 to $2,000 a month in Costa Rica to maintain an acceptable lifestyle. This would involve comfortable living accommodations, an inexpensive auto, and a part-time housekeeper and gardener. Clearly, the standard of living on budgets like these will be much higher than one could ever hope for in the United States or Canada for the same outgo. Some people spend a lot more, but their living standards are much higher as well.

Of course, a number of North Americans who live here draw *below*-average Social Security benefits. I personally know of one couple that gets by on $900 a month. Even though this is almost twice the average income of a Costa Rican worker, it would require considerable downscaling on the part of most North Americans to make this work. It certainly wouldn't be what my wife and I would consider an ideal lifestyle. More about this later.

One way of economizing is by living in ordinary rather than deluxe housing. In many foreign countries, North American residents feel they must live in certain "safe" areas, gated communities for which they pay premium prices. Because Costa Rica is not a highly stratified society, North Americans feel comfortable living in almost any middle-class neighborhood or small villages where there are other expats in residence. This translates into a wide selection of rents and housing prices. While you can pay $1,500 a month to rent in a luxury section of Escazú, you can often find a small place for $700 a month in a nearby neighborhood. You can usually find affordable accommodations in very livable areas such as Alajuela or San Pedro.

Low-Budget Example

This may sound repetitive, but I feel it's important to emphasize: In no way would I encourage anyone with a *limited budget and no backup funds* to move to Costa Rica simply because of the relatively low cost of living. That would be an invitation for disaster. At home, low-income people qualify for Medicaid, welfare, food stamps, and other public programs. Safety nets such as these do not exist in Costa Rica. However, if you have sufficient funds to cover emergencies and money to splurge for luxuries on a regular basis, you are encouraged to investigate further.

One of my favorite examples of living in Costa Rica on a restricted budget was our friend Tom Stafford, from California. Like several million other US retirees, Tom was drawing Social Security benefits of less than $700 a month. Although he had accumulated a modest nest egg as a backup, Tom knew he had to live conservatively, preferably within his Social Security income.

Tom explained: "The decision to live in Costa Rica was made after my third trip to Costa Rica. I began to scout out a piece of land with the idea of building a home. When a friend bought a few acres north of San Ramón, I threw in with him, buying a one-half-acre plot for my house. I decided on a prefabricated Swiss chalet-style log cabin that seemed to fit me like a tailored suit. While only 750 square feet, it has a commodious loft and plenty of beautiful land all around it."

Tom pointed out: "My transition to '*tico* provisional' was not all that smooth. Without the generous help and advice of friends I made along the way, it might not have happened at all. One piece of advice I would give to anyone thinking of coming here is: Meet a lot of people—both expats and *ticos*—make friends with them, and follow their advice. I know it's a cliché, but there is no sense in reinventing the wheel."

For several years Tom managed to get by just fine on $671 per month (his Social Security check), but only because he owned his home, thus eliminating rent. His monthly expenses, such as electricity, water, and telephone, were very low. Public transportation allowed him to get by sans automobile. Tom said, "My budget doesn't leave much for nights out on the town or rollicking good times. But after two years, I'm convinced I made the right decision."

At the conclusion of last visit, Tom said, "I often sit on my upper veranda in the morning—looking out over a vista my friends in California would pay a million dollars for—and I ask myself: 'Tom, what the hell did you do right to deserve this?'"

As we drove away from his charming little home, we couldn't help but wonder: How would Tom be making out in Los Angeles, California (instead of Los Angeles, Costa Rica), in his struggle to survive on $671 a month? Yes, millions of US residents are forced to get by on Social Security as their sole income, but with what level of dignity?

More to the story: After a while, Tom made friends with a widowed Costa Rican neighbor. They married and led active and full lives together, enjoying a large family of in-laws and nearby relatives. Unfortunately, after ten years of a full and happy retirement, Tom suddenly passed away.

Could that experience be duplicated on $671-a-month income? Well, for Costa Ricans, that would be a nice income—almost double the income working-class families enjoy. Yet it would take a special personality, with Tom's envious spirit of adventure, to consider this an ideal lifestyle.

COSTA RICA SOCIAL LIFE

When asked why they decided to live in Costa Rica, most people begin by describing Costa Rica's gorgeous weather and magical tropical surroundings. They'll rave on about favorite beaches, mountain retreats, cloud forests, and restaurants. But oddly enough, when you ask people to pinpoint the most important factor in making the decision to relocate to Costa Rica, most people admit that lovely surroundings are only part of it. When you pin many people down, they'll agree that a very important factor in enjoying Costa Rica is the numerous friends and acquaintances they've made and their active circle of expatriate comrades.

It's interesting to observe how North Americans who live in a foreign country—any foreign country—tend to cling together, to form close social groups. They reach out to draw newly arrived English-speakers into their midst. Since the pool of English-speakers is limited, each addition to their circle of friends is valued. People with almost nothing in common—who wouldn't even nod at each other back home as they passed on the street—become great pals in a foreign setting. In Costa Rica, newcomers are eagerly sought after. The friendliness varies with the number of expats living in the locality. The fewer North Americans in the neighborhood, the more friendly local expats become toward newcomers, hoping to enlarge their circle of friends.

I've found this to be true no matter which foreign country we've researched. Expatriates in Mexico, Guatemala, and other foreign locations will affirm this close camaraderie among fellow English-speakers. Foreign residents usually explain their love for their new surroundings by saying, "Everyone is so friendly here! I have more friends and companions than I ever had in my hometown. There, our closest friends were mostly people we worked with." Almost as an afterthought, they mention the exotic surroundings or affordable living costs.

This doesn't mean that you needn't work at making friends in Costa Rica. You must go halfway. If you wait for expatriates to knock down your door and drag you out to dinner, you may give the impression of wanting to be a hermit. We have those here, too.

Mixing with Tico Neighbors

The usual strategy for newcomers is to seek out a place where most neighbors are fellow countrymen who speak English and are available to guide them through the process of fitting into their new surroundings. It is usually best to become accustomed to the environment and learn at least some Spanish before settling in a *tico* neighborhood with no English-speaking neighbors.

But not everyone feels this way. The following is a favorite story of an English expat family and their adventures in total cultural immersion.

Before Laura and David Streek, of Cambridge, left England for Costa Rica with their two young daughters, they decided they wanted their Costa Rican adventure to be something special. Laura said, "We looked forward to integrating into an authentic community and society of a new country where we could lead a simpler, warmer life spent mostly outdoors. We wanted our children to experience a new culture and learn a new language." They discovered a village they liked on the Pacific Coast and decided to try living there.

Instead of joining the foreign community who lived in tasteful and comfortable homes with lovely views of the ocean, the Streek family rented an older *tico*-style house, right in the center of the village. Little stores flanked both sides of the house, and goal posts of the village soccer field were across the street. The grade school where their children attended classes was located near the sidelines of the soccer field.

Their neighbors were mostly *ticos*, with a scattering of North American and European émigrés from Switzerland and Holland, some of whom were operating small businesses in the village. They immediately set about making friends. They found it surprisingly easy. Before long, the family felt comfortable with their surroundings and became acquainted with enough of their neighbors to have a party.

Laura said, "We decided to have an open house one weekend, which begged the question: Where else in the world could you have moved to, not knowing a single soul, and within two weeks have met enough likable people to have a house party? We spent a happy afternoon of flower arranging, stringing fairy lights, and setting up the music system in readiness for the night's festivities.

"Soon after sundown, with the house sparkling in the twilight and music drifting out into the balmy air, people began to arrive. Before long the party was in full swing, with guests bringing pots of chili, dips, tortillas, crates of beer, and gifts. The porch was filled with young *ticos* and *gringos* alike drinking beers. The living room held the food, and young children danced the salsa with the more-than-willing grown-ups. The kitchen and back rooms bustled with the usual party activities. The garden was the only place one could find to sit under the stars and enjoy a conversation with new friends."

In many countries, something like this could never happen. Class lines are too rigid. But *ticos* have a strong sense of equality and think nothing of joining multicultural celebrations. Instead of meeting foreigners with an awestruck bowing of the head—as is the custom in many Latin American countries—*ticos* look strangers in the eye, shake hands, and sometimes even invite the strangers to visit their homes. That probably wouldn't happen in your hometown, would it?

The Streek family have since returned to England, to their hometown of Cambridge, but I am confident that they will always look back with fondness on their interlude in paradise. They will remember the *tico* and *gringo* friends they made while in living in the village. The children will always have the advantage of being bilingual, with a Costa Rican accent to their Spanish.

Even if your Spanish is far from fluent in situations like this, communication flows. Most *ticos* have learned about as much English in high school as you learned Spanish in high school. (They have also forgotten as much English as you've forgotten Spanish!) Yet both sides have fun talking, learning new phrases in the other's language, and becoming friends.

Making friends among the *tico* community is a rewarding experience. However, you should resist the temptation of moving to a totally "non-*gringo*" community, far from other English-speaking neighbors. The fact is, most newcomers need a circle of English-speakers to round out their lives. They find that even though communication skills with *ticos* are okay, many common elements of understanding are lacking. After a while there's a craving to talk politics, to discuss movies, or to reminisce over the "good old days." You'll receive blank stares from your *tico* friends when you start speculating about the Chicago Cubs' chances for the pennant or whether Senator Phoghorn can be reelected. In short, the average newcomer to Costa Rica needs both *gringo and* Costa Rican friends. Happily, this is possible. Newcomers are attacked with aggressive friendliness.

CLUBS AND ACTIVITIES

There's no excuse for being lonely in Costa Rica: too much to do, too many people to meet, too many places to go. Take some Spanish classes, attend a meeting of Republicans Abroad or Democrats Abroad, do some volunteer work, learn to play tennis or bridge. You'll meet more friends than you've dreamed of, and you'll live the rich life you moved to Costa Rica to find.

The biggest mistake some make is not keeping active. Some newcomers will take a drink or two when things get too quiet for them; next thing they know, they're drinking too much. If you haven't already acquired interests to keep you busy in your new location, check out the *Tico Times* "Club Directory" section and look at the broad range of invitations. (If you can't find a group of friends who are involved in your favorite activity, chances are your favorite activity is illegal, immoral, or boring!) Volunteer work is another satisfying way to make friends and become involved in fun activities; this can be much more satisfying than sitting around a bar until closing time.

An example of a volunteer project, one of which my wife and I are very proud: Establishing a public library in a Guanacaste village. Local expatriates contributed funds to purchase several shelves of reference material as well as books that are fun to read for adults and that will enhance the local children's interest in education. A Costa Rican businessman donated ten obsolete typewriters to the library, and we accumulated ten used computers. Knowing that touch-typing was virtually unknown in the country (most everyone uses the "hunt-and-peck" system), we insisted that students learn to type thirty words per minute on the typewriters before they could go on the computers. We taught word processing and Excel bookkeeping spreadsheets to prepare students for business career possibilities. The program became wildly successful. Not only did children sign up, but we were flooded with applications from the children's mothers as well as other village women who were eager to learn skills that paid better than cleaning houses for *gringos*.

Within about six years, the library accumulated enough donations to build a beautiful new building on land donated by the village. The library now has a dozen new computers for teaching marketable skills to teenagers and adults. Several rooms are filled with fiction and nonfiction shelves in both Spanish and English for *gringos* as well as *ticos*. Just a slight exposure to volunteer projects like this increases a retiree's social circle immensely! Not to mention the effect on local children and participating adults.

Recently, two incidents gave my wife and I the feeling of being richly rewarded for our library involvement. One afternoon, when shopping in a supermarket complex (clothing, dishes, cosmetics, etc., in addition to food), we found one of my former computer students in charge of the cosmetics and women's wear department. She proudly showed us her computer and bookkeeping system. Later on that same day, we had occasion to visit a pharmacy to fill a prescription. There we were greeted by another smiling face of a former student. She introduced me to her business partner (her mother) and explained how she received pharmaceutical training at the public college (an hour bus trip from the village). Without computer training, she would never have qualified for the class. With her degree, she had opened the small pharmacy with her mother's help. A decade ago, the only job options for these women would have been making beds in a motel or cleaning houses for expat retirees. (To read more about this project, visit the Nosara Library's website: www.discoverypress.com/library.)

BEING SINGLE IN COSTA RICA

As you'll notice, much of the advice, experiences, and examples of living in Costa Rica given in this book seem directed toward married couples. The fact is, you'll find an unusually large number of single people happily residing here. Some have never married, some are widowed, and many are divorced. A single man I interviewed, when asked why he was single in Costa Rica, observed, "I never understood what complete happiness meant until I got married. Then it was too late. So after the divorce, the first thing I thought about was leaving the country! There's something romantic about the name 'Costa Rica,' so I just knew this would be a great adventure."

Single Men

I've known a dozen or more fellow countrymen who married Costa Rican women. A common explanation goes something like this: "Actually, I planned to stay for only one month, but before I knew it, I met this nice-looking lady, and now I'm married again!" When I asked an ex–New Jersey-ite why he married a *tica*, he explained, "The thing is, Costa Rican women are different in many ways. It's not just that they are pretty and maybe younger. That's not what it's all about. We come here looking for something we feel we lost somewhere back along the years. What I found is someone who treats me as if I were special, and as if I were twenty years younger. She doesn't nag or complain because I'm not perfect. She is much more than a wife; she is my best friend."

This is not a one-sided proposition. Having a *gringo* husband offers advantages for the Costa Rican woman, too. From her perspective, the groom's Social Security check is more than enough to maintain an enviable standard of living. The groom is expected to provide not only for his new wife, but also support the children from her previous marriage. This typically includes paying tuition for private schools and sometimes college in the States. The husband usually finds himself responsible for his new in-laws as well. When Mámi wants a new refrigerator or Pápi needs a new set of dentures, guess who is expected to pay?

Now, having created all these cheery and optimistic scenarios about *gringo* men marrying *ticas,* let me follow up with a few words of caution. As a friend once pointed out, "My trophy girlfriend was more expensive than I ever dreamed possible." Because she never insisted on marriage, my friend didn't give any thought to legalities and assumed himself to be single. To his dismay, it turns out that when a couple lives together for a length of time, ostensibly three years, the woman acquires all the rights of a legal marriage. So when they broke up, his girlfriend went to court and was awarded the house he had purchased, plus support for her three children from a previous common-law marriage (which she had neglected to mention) until they reached the age of eighteen.

I have heard of other situations where a wife claimed spousal abuse (falsely, according to the husband, but who knows?). The wife had her husband permanently barred from entering the home he had bought, and she was granted monthly support payments. Costa Rican judges are reputed to routinely favor the wife's interests over the husband's, and even more so in the case of a *gringo* husband. These stories are legend in Costa Rica, although I'm sure that happy arrangements far outnumber the scams. Nevertheless, I strongly suggest that anyone contemplating a marriage (or a long-term cohabitation arrangement) consult a *good* attorney before obligating oneself or investing in real estate that could be contested. I've been told that prenuptial contracts and proper real estate documents can provide protection.

Gringo Gulch

Single *gringo* males tend to congregate in an area of downtown San José that I call Gringo Gulch—around the odd-numbered *avenidas* and *calles.* A concentration of inexpensive hotels and *gringo* bars attract a large number of recently arrived single or divorced fugitives from northern climes. They hang out in these bars of sometimes-questionable repute, where they drink Pilsen beer and exchange lies about their romantic conquests, their financial successes, and the injustices of their divorce settlements. Most habitués of Gringo Gulch are transient and ephemeral. Within a few weeks they either move on to discover the real Costa Rica or return home with exaggerated tales of their adventures in Central America.

The majority of these Gringo Gulch habitués are of Social Security age, looking for that one last go-round. Some are hoping to find a woman to become a life partner. Surprisingly enough, some actually find one. The fact is, *all* women who visit the *gringo* bars aren't necessarily prostitutes. Sometimes they're simply working women hoping to meet a wealthy foreigner to marry, someone who will "take me away from all this." (*Wealthy* being defined as someone with a monthly Social Security check. With that income, the woman can quit her job and support her children in style.)

A word of caution to would-be *gringo* Don Juans: Be careful after dark, and avoid the *zona roja* (red-light zone) as the evening gets late. Some street girls here are rather skilled thieves. Your wallet can disappear quickly while you are basking in sweet talk from one of these women. Often their scam is pretending to be overwhelmed by a man's sex appeal. While several enthusiastic girls hug and caress the delighted gentleman, others are helping themselves to the contents of his pockets. It's almost always a nonviolent robbery; the victim doesn't realize he's been had until he tries to pay for his next drink. (Sorry, I have difficulty feeling sorry for his loss.)

Although an occasional visit to downtown San José bars can be entertaining, it's all too easy to make hanging out there your social life to the exclusion of all else. (Of course, that's a hazard anywhere in the world.)

If you're single and looking for someplace to go and people to meet, simply surf the *Tico Times* online to the "Calendar" section. You'll find a page and a half of listings: classes, art exhibits, concerts, lectures, dances, theaters, political clubs, sports, and every possible activity you can imagine—great places to meet people and make quality friends. There's no excuse for being bored in Costa Rica.

Single Women

We know numerous single women and single mothers who are quite happy with their move to Costa Rica. We've also known several single women who tried Costa Rica and found they couldn't stand living here. My observation is that single women (or married, for that matter) tend not to enjoy Costa Rica as much as men.

My wife explains it this way: "Men enjoy sitting in a fishing boat under a blazing sun or surfing from daybreak to sundown. They love to hang around *tico* bars, drinking beer, gossiping, and trading stories—as well as checking out the local babes." (My wife harbors the ridiculous suspicion that female companionship is at the top of the agenda for men traveling alone.)

The fact is, single women socialize differently than single men. Women can easily become bored with the typical macho scene. Single people we know (men and women) who have made successful and happy transitions to living in Costa Rica are those who become actively involved in the social scene from the very beginning. Making friends is the key. Joining special-interest clubs, political or church groups—any situation where you come in contact with other expatriates—is the key.

A great way to make friends is through volunteering. One woman explained, "While volunteering I became involved with of a group of like-minded friends. Before long I was invited for cocktails to meet other volunteers, then a dinner party, and other social gatherings. My circle of acquaintances kept widening, until today, I have more friends than I've had in my entire life." Women with children find volunteering at school puts them in social contact with parents of their children's classmates. Almost every community has volunteer opportunities for newcomers.

I have no firm statistics, but I'm firmly convinced that among expats, eligible single men outnumber single women by a large percentage. That's the good news for single women who might want to socialize with men friends as well as women friends. Of course, just as it was back home, "eligible" bachelors are vastly outnumbered by those who are single for very good reasons. (Their ex-wives could have interesting tales to relate in this regard.) Nevertheless, we've seen many happy and successful marriages among North Americans who met in Costa Rica (as well as a few disasters).

Single women soon discover that many Costa Rican men like to fancy themselves as prototypes of the "Latin lover." A Brazilian friend once explained: "When I was young, my father took me aside to tell me the facts of life. He said, 'My son, in this world you must understand one thing. You *cannot* expect to go to bed with every woman you meet. But, of course, you *must try!*' That's the essence of a "Latin lover." The stereotype is a playboy supporting one or more mistresses and continually trolling for more conquests. To a small extent this could be true among the more affluent Costa Rican business types (same as anywhere else in the world), but the average eligible *tico* bachelor, the type most single women will meet, doesn't earn enough to even dream of supporting a mistress. He has a tough time scraping together enough money to keep gasoline in his car's gas tank.

Although we've seen some successful romances develop between foreign women and *tico* men, more often than not, cultures clash and the relationship falls apart. Again, I have no statistics on this; it's just our observation of couples we've known. Typically, the *tico* husband becomes deeply disappointed when his wife will not, or cannot, provide enough income for the husband to enjoy the luxurious life to which he had expected to become accustomed. Therefore, no matter how much an expat woman loves her intended, it's important to consult a competent lawyer to ensure that in case of a marriage crash, the groom can't walk away with assets of the bride—particularly if they plan on investing in property after the marriage, when community property issues can arise.

For a good book about a single woman's experiences in Costa Rica, I recommend *Butterfly in the City*, by Jo Stuart. Jo is a friend and a columnist for the online newspaper *A.M. Costa Rica*. When I asked for Jo's take on single women in Costa Rica, this is how she replied.

"John, you have just about covered the waterfront on the subject. However, I can add a bit about San José's friendly and safe casinos (just as in the States, women—especially older women—seem to enjoy the slots). I like to play roulette so I notice the women are there as well as men. I have never felt uneasy or out of place in a casino here, and the bathrooms are always the best equipped in town. (By the way, I am in accord with your wife on the subject of men and companionship.)

"Your advice about joining clubs and volunteering is the best advice to give, and Costa Rica, especially the Central Valley, has much to offer a single woman. If one picks a club or volunteer group doing what she enjoys, she immediately is in contact with like-minded people. This applies, as well, to political and religious groups.

"Costa Rica, generally, is a welcoming place for gay men, so women can enjoy the company of an interesting, compatible male with no strings attached. I think older women appreciate the opportunity. You also have captured the essence of the relationships between *ticos* and expat women. I have heard of situations that ended badly for the woman, especially in the case of an older woman with a comfortable income.

"I have several women friends who live on the east side of the city, get around by bus, and take advantage of the free or almost free courses for seniors at the University of Costa Rica. For those who enjoy music and theater, attending a symphony at the National Theater or a play in English at the Laurence Olivier are easy things for a woman to do alone, or with a female friend." (To find out more about Jo Stuart's book, e-mail jocstuart@gmail.com.)

GAYS AND LESBIANS IN COSTA RICA

We've interviewed several gay couples who have lived in Costa Rica for some time, asking about their acceptance by rank-and-file *ticos* and their expatriate neighbors. Most experiences have been positive. There does seem to be a certain amount of disapproval of public displays of affection between gay couples, as if it's okay to be gay, only don't flaunt it. The indignation demonstrated in some other parts of the world is rarely encountered in Costa Rica. In the final analysis, *ticos* seem to view homosexuality as mildly humorous and an inescapable fact of life, rather than something that raises hostility.

5

Living in Costa Rica

Used to be, we could easily distinguish between "first-world" and "developing" nations by the standard of living and the type of government. First-world countries enjoyed individual freedom, democracy, and, most important, a viable economy where people lived dignified lives and enjoyed economic security.

Developing countries were none of the above. More often than not in Latino countries, the ruling elite would be a group of wealthy families with a well-armed military to enforce order, using terror to keep working-class citizens in line. Thankfully, over the past thirty-plus years, conditions have changed for the better in most developing countries in this hemisphere. Some, such as Argentina and Chile, have achieved living standards not too much different from North America. Brazil has also entered the realm of exceptionally robust world economies and increasing standard of living. Costa Rica will probably never progress that far, yet the potential is definitely here.

Costa Rica never went through the repressive conditions described above. It started out as a democracy and has never experienced a military dictatorship. The overall standard of living in Costa Rica is admired and envied by neighboring countries. Costa Rica is different. After all, it's a place where you can drink the water and eat the food without risking your health. It is where your conscience isn't continually assaulted by beggars and abject poverty. Furthermore, it's a place where the government isn't run by a bunch of uniformed thugs.

For these reasons, we North Americans find adjusting to Costa Rican living conditions rather easy. Of course, there are differences in lifestyles, but instead of being traumatic, in most instances the variations are charming. Whether you will enjoy living in Costa Rica depends on your approach to life and your expectations. If you expect people to conform to your ideals and you want conditions to be exactly as they were in your hometown, you are bound to be disappointed. Costa Rica is, after all, a foreign country. That's exactly why so many *gringos* choose to live here. We enjoy living in a foreign country.

In this chapter we'll look at some everyday living conditions that make Costa Rica different.

COURTESY AND CUSTOM

Costa Rican social behavior is a curious mixture of old-world, European formality and a special *tico* style of relaxed interaction. You shake hands politely when being introduced or when meeting an acquaintance on the street, women as well as men. Women may also greet other women friends with a kiss on the cheek; with close friends a woman may do the same with a man, but only if they know each other well. Usually touching cheeks without the kiss is the custom. Exaggerated hugging and kissing, while common in the United States, is not approved of here. Men, when greeting truly close friends, will give an *abrazo*—a quick hug and pat on the back—or perhaps lightly clasp the friend's wrist or forearm instead of shaking hands.

"Getting down to business," as we North Americans are apt to do, without any preliminary greeting and small talk, is considered somewhat rude in Costa Rica, but not terribly so. Costa Ricans know how we North Americans are, so they never make a big deal out of it; they realize that "business" is the custom in our countries. To be polite, you might spend a few moments inquiring about someone's children or spouse, perhaps giving a compliment about the person's clothing, noting the weather, or anything else you might think to say before talking business. Doing so gets things off to a smoother start.

Costa Ricans have a delightful habit of issuing off-the-cuff invitations to visit them at their homes for dinner or for cocktails, but you should always wait for the invitation and not just drop in. An exception to this is when someone moves into the neighborhood or when you move into a new home. Then it's considered polite to knock on the door and introduce yourself.

A crucial point to remember: In social or business transactions, *ticos* just cannot handle confrontation. Unlike the people of some countries, where arguing, shouting, and mock displays of anger or emotion are the accepted norm, Costa Ricans are appalled at such behavior. It's considered not only rude but also degrading. Confrontation is foreign to the culture.

I know a New Yorker who lost an excellent gardener when his *gringo* temper flared momentarily. Chuck's employee had planted some flowers in the wrong place. As usual when making a point, Chuck raised his voice and waved his hands in the air to signify his displeasure: "No, no! Not here! I wanted the flowers over *there*!" The astonished gardener loaded his tools in his wheelbarrow and left the property, never to return, despite pleas from the homeowner's wife, who tried to explain: "That's just Chuck's way. He doesn't mean anything by shouting."

LATIN AMERICAN TIME

A difficult notion to understand is the way Latin Americans view time. When invited to a social event in the United States or Canada, it's considered ill-mannered to arrive late. Not so in most parts of Latin America. Should you receive an invitation for dinner, say, at 6:00 p.m. and actually arrive at that time, you are likely to embarrass your hosts. She is probably in the shower, and he still at the office. Guests are expected to arrive late. It doesn't matter, because dinner isn't served until 8:00 or 9:00 p.m., anyway. (A second thought here: This isn't necessarily true in Costa Rica's countryside, where folks are used to rising when the sun rises, having lunch at noon, and going to bed well before 9:00 p.m.)

When keeping appointments with your lawyer or businesspeople, you can arrive at the office fifteen minutes late without worrying about it. You'll probably have time to catch up with the latest goings-on in the world by reading *Newsweek* and *La Nación* while waiting for your appointment. The lawyer will probably be an hour late anyway.

Most Costa Ricans share this cavalier view of time—not, however, to the extremes found in Mexico and most other Latin countries. Still, after several decades of exposure to Latin American time, I've never understood it and never will. When my contractor says he will be at the house at 8:00 a.m., I sometimes ask, "Is that *tico* time or *gringo* time?" The reply is usually a sheepish grin and, "Better make that nine o'clock." (I can't really count on nine o'clock either—my contractor doesn't wear a wristwatch.)

On the other hand, my personal experience with Costa Rican employees is that they're usually on time. I'm always surprised to see them arrive at the job a few minutes early, start to work on time, and—after a morning and an afternoon break—go home on time. Maybe this is because I pay higher than the going wage scales, but I am convinced that the Costa Rican work ethic is unusually positive, at least for Latin America.

HOUSEHOLD SERVANTS

The notion of having housemaids and gardeners seems a bit wild for many of us when we first move to Costa Rica. (The last time we hired a cleaning lady in the United States, she charged $16 an hour and wouldn't do windows.) But in Costa Rica servants are affordable. It makes sense to hire a housemaid and a gardener, at least on a part-time basis. *Ticos* are generally hardworking and honest, so if you can afford $3 an hour for part-time help, you can have someone working around the house who won't complain about doing windows.

Most North Americans report that they pay more than minimum wage; doing so keeps their employees happy and loyal. Although servants are affordable, you must be aware of the laws covering their benefits. By law, not by custom, you are responsible for things like vacations, Christmas bonuses, Social Security, and severance pay. Wages are indexed twice a year, according to inflation. You are responsible for knowing about the benefits and paying them on time. These rules are discussed thoroughly in chapter 12. Don't hire a servant until you've read the rules!

One way to avoid the problem of being legally incorrect when hiring servants is to contract with a property manager. In addition to paying your monthly bills, taxes, and insurance, the property manager sends a housekeeper and/or gardener to your home as often as needed. This way, your domestic workers do not work for you; they work for the manager. Therefore, it is the manager's responsibility to take care of employees' monthly obligations, such as keeping track of holidays, paying Social Security, insurance, and pension payments at the proper local office. With your property manager in charge, you needn't worry. However, you should make sure that your manager is actually doing all of this, because you could be liable in case of a problem. Of course—depending on your contract with your manager—terminating a long-term employee could involve severance pay.

COSTA RICAN FOOD TREATS

You'll find every type of restaurant you can think of in Costa Rica, from steak and lobster to Chinese to McDonald's hamburger emporiums. But for really authentic Costa Rican food, you need to go to *tico*-style restaurants where they serve *comida típica* ("typical dishes"). *Comida típica* is home-style cooking as found in *tico* homes throughout the country. This cuisine relies on simple ingredients such as rice and beans, free-range chicken, and tasty, lean pork flavored with plenty of garlic. One of my favorites is *arroz con pollo* (chicken with rice) piled high on a dish, steaming with the savor of cilantro and diced peppers. It is often served with shrimp and calamari instead of chicken. Try the *sopa negra* (black-bean soup), topped with chopped green onions, crumbled white cheese, and a fresh egg poached in the thick broth, plus a dollop of *natilla* (a thick sweet cream).

You might be disappointed with Costa Rican beef steaks, however. They don't exactly come from Black Angus; more likely from one of those large, homely, bony, grass-fed creatures from India, called Brahmas. The meat can be tough and dry, more suitable for hamburgers than steaks. That's not to say you can't find good beef; you just have to go to a good butcher shop or order a rib eye in an expensive restaurant.

In the larger cities, you can find interesting dining places ranging from elegant French restaurants to superb pizzerias. Some excellent Chinese restaurants will surprise you with dishes that are quite different from what you are used to back home. Their style of cooking is a cross between traditional Asian and tropical American. Some terribly mediocre Chinese restaurants are also to be found (ask friends for recommendations).

One very common Costa Rican food—served everywhere for breakfast, sometimes for every meal—is *gallo pinto,* which inexplicably translates as "painted rooster." This is a mixture of cooked rice and black beans—sometimes mixed with cilantro and chopped onions—fried together until the rice turns a purple color. Mixed with eggs and topped with *salsa Inglesa* or *salsa Lizano,* it makes a filling breakfast—nutritious but boring when served every morning.

In small restaurants away from the city, a typical menu item is a *casado:* a large plate with beans, rice, fried *plátano* (a green cooking banana), and some sort of meat, chicken, or egg. (*Casado* means "married man." Why the meal is called this is a mystery.) *Olla de carne* is a tasty meat stew with vegetables such as chayote, squash, yucca, and *plátano.*

Another favorite is empanadas: fried dumplings filled with meat or cheese, sometimes sold by children, who carry them around in galvanized buckets. A *tortilla Española* in Costa Rica is an omelet made with chopped potatoes or yucca root. Mexican-style corn tortillas are popular in the countryside and are simply called tortillas; these are far more common than the egg-and-yucca variety.

Bocas

A delightful custom in Costa Rica is the serving of *bocas* (free appetizers) with drinks in bars. The treat could be a small dish of chicken and rice, or perhaps a chicken wing, a piece of fried fish, or *chicharrones* with yucca— whatever the exotic specialty of the house happens to be. *Bocas* aren't served as frequently as they used to be, especially in bars mostly patron-ized by *gringos,* since we don't expect them. But *tico* bars often sustain this custom, so when you see someone else being served a treat, don't hesitate to ask. You may have the chance to sample a raw turtle egg—bars are just about the only places where you can legally find them. They are served one to a shot glass, with a little hot sauce. You do a bottoms up and chew it to taste the yolk. Some people love 'em; my wife wouldn't touch one with a pointed stick. *Note:* Some bars have *bocas* but no longer give them away. You have to pay a small amount, 50 cents or so, but they are worth it!

Bocas aren't just served in bars; they play an essential role when enter-taining guests. Informal "*boca* parties" are a popular substitute for more formal dinner parties. Guests are expected to bring their favorite *boca* to share with other guests, thus eliminating the need to cook and serve din-ner; people help themselves. When you have no way to make *bocas* (if you are a tourist staying in a bed-and-breakfast, for example), a bottle of Cen-tenario rum or good wine is a substitute, or if you prefer, a takeout pizza cut into small pieces. Friends compete for new and unusual recipes for tasty *bocas.*

Gratuities

Restaurants are supposed to add a 10 percent service charge to the bill— then it's up to customers if they care to leave something extra. Some res-taurants cheat and don't give tip money to employees, so leaving an extra 10 percent tip on the table after paying the bill ensures that the waitstaff at least gets something—and guarantees special service next time. Away from the city, many restaurants don't add tips to the bill; it's customary to tip 10 to 15 percent in these cases. Barbershop and beauty salon personnel expect a 10 to 15 percent tip. My last haircut cost the equivalent of $5, and I tipped a generous $2.

By law you must give a Christmas bonus to your maid, gardener, and other employees. This bonus is called an *aguinaldo* and consists of one month's pay, prorated on the number of months worked. This Christmas bonus is not a gift or a tip but a legal requirement. An extra present to special employees is considered thoughtful and generous.

If you are a guest in someone's home where there are servants, it isn't necessary to tip them unless they've done something special for you, such as laundry, ironing, or running errands. If a friend lends you the services of her maid, it's customary to tip generously and to pay for her taxi or bus fare home. Hotel chambermaids like to be tipped just as they do back home.

COOKING AT HOME

For those staying for longer than a vacation, an apartment or house with a kitchen is a wonderful way of enjoying Costa Rican cooking and experimenting with the unusual tropical ingredients available in the markets. Around the San José area, every neighborhood has at least one supermarket, supplemented by weekend *ferias* (open-air markets). Many neighborhoods and most small villages have *pulperías* (rustic convenience stores), where you can buy items you forgot at the other markets.

Some major supermarket chains are: Auto Mercado, Periféricos, Pali, and Mas X Menos. By the way, the *X* in Mas X Menos is pronounced as it would be in a mathematical equation: In English we would say "two times two," while Costa Ricans would say *"dos por dos."* Since the Spanish word *por* can also mean "for," the literal meaning of the store's name, *Mas por Menos,* is "more for less." (Yes, I know, it would be less confusing if they simply followed American custom and gave supermarkets names like "Safeway" or "Albertsons," but this is, after all, Costa Rica.)

Open-air markets are held on weekends, the major ones being Saturday in Escazú, on the south side of the main square; Saturday in Pavas, about five blocks from the main shopping center; and Sunday in Zapote, next to the Bull Ring. Heredia's farmers' market, also on Saturday, is perhaps the best known of all, with local families selling produce grown in their backyards. Heredia's main market, open daily, is a wonderful place to browse for food, clothing, tools, furniture—anything you can imagine.

Costa Rica's selection of fruits and vegetables is sometimes bewildering for North Americans. In addition to delicious pineapples, strawberries, melons, and other produce we recognize, you'll find chayotes, *pejebayes*, *palmitos*, *plátanos*, and other strange-looking items that will soon become standard ingredients of your menu. A common substitute for potatoes, the yucca root, in my opinion, tastes much better than ordinary spuds. Exotic tropical fruits such as *guayabas, tamarindo,* and carambolas are exciting to experiment with and make delicious *refrescos* (blended drinks). One of my favorite *refrescos* is made by blending fresh cacao nuts (the source of chocolate) with *horchata* (a rice-flour and sugar drink). My wife prefers a *batida* of fresh papaya, milk, and ice, whipped to a milk shake–like consistency.

Some fruits are so exotic they border on fantastic. Sporting shells, spines, and barbs, they look like something from a science-fiction book cover. Especially interesting is the *marañón* fruit, the source of the common cashew nut. The nut itself grows at the end of an edible orange or yellow fruit that can be eaten raw or, more often, made into a *refresco* by blending it with sugar and ice cubes. The cashew nut itself is encased in a rubbery shell that is primed with cyanide. That's right, *cyanide*, which makes the shell bitter and somewhat poisonous. We have to marvel over the wonderful way nature designed this fruit as an efficient way to disperse its seeds. In the wild, monkeys, parrots, and other creatures pluck the fruit and carry it away to be consumed. When they finish eating the sweet fruit, they drop the bitter-tasting seed on the ground, where it produces another tree.

Costa Rica is a cattle-growing country, and beef is plentiful, although as mentioned earlier, it's not the same quality as we are used to in North America. But the quality of pork and chicken here is excellent, mostly because they are raised differently. Instead of being tightly penned or caged and force-fed to put on weight, the animals usually run loose, foraging for food as well as being fed at the farmhouse, living a natural, albeit sloppy, existence. Pork is lean with a firm texture. Eggs—especially those from free-range hens rather than crowded egg factories—are delicious, having a brighter-colored yolk and a better flavor than we're used to up north.

With an ocean on both sides, Costa Rica, of course, enjoys a wide selection of seafood. Since shipping distances from either ocean involve just a few hours, the sea harvest arrives fresh. Almost any kind of fish and shellfish you can imagine is available, plus some you can't imagine. You might want to try some of the shellfish and conch that thrive only around the Costa Rican shores. My favorite is a shellfish known as *cambute,* similar to conch shellfish found in the Florida Keys. Like abalone, the *cambute* has to be pounded before cooking, and it tastes very much like the almost extinct abalone.

Imported foods can be somewhat expensive. Partly because of shipping costs and partly because of foreign-exchange differentials, North American and European products can be costly. Central American substitutes are often as good and locally grown. For my money, fresh foods are always much better than canned or packaged food.

GREAT COFFEE

Some of the best coffee in the world grows on shaded mountain slopes in Costa Rica. These exceptionally rich-tasting beans are in demand by coffee wholesalers, particularly those who boast that their products are "mountain grown." To substantiate such a claim, at least 60 percent of the coffee has to come from mountain farms in places like Guatemala, Colombia, or Costa Rica. Curiously, Costa Rican coffee is exceptionally low in caffeine. Retailers blend it with high-caffeine (and less expensive) beans from Brazil and Africa to bring the jolt up to what we coffee drinkers expect. In Costa Rica you have the advantage of brewing coffee from 100 percent Costa Rican beans. If you need more caffeine, drink another cup! We sometimes purchase coffee beans directly from the roaster and take them home while they are still hot. The use of instant coffee (a barbarous practice) hasn't caught on here. A *café con leche* with just a dash of sugar makes a wonderful starter for breakfast and is great for washing down savory *gallo pinto* and warm tortillas.

Costa Ricans have an interesting way of making coffee that gives a characteristically rich flavor to the brew. Instead of using a percolator or an automatic coffeemaker, *ticos* use a wire or wooden stand holding a cloth strainer bag, shaped like a sock that hangs over a waiting cup. They place two teaspoons of coffee into the bag and pour boiling water over the grounds, letting it drain into the coffee cup below. For each additional cup of coffee, another teaspoon of ground coffee is added. The result is a flavorful, velvety drink that grows richer with each cup made. The grounds aren't discarded until the sack is full of grounds or until the end of the day, whichever happens first. "The aroma and essence of the coffee is much better if it isn't boiled," explained a *tico* friend. "We call our coffee-making system a *chorreador.* It brings out the flavor without acid bitterness. This method requires more coffee grounds, but since coffee is inexpensive, we use nothing but the best."

FURNISHING YOUR HOME

At one time, when foreign retirees received their residency papers, they had a onetime right to import household goods duty-free, and the right to bring in an automobile every three years and thus avoid enormous customs taxes. This was a valuable consideration, since high import duties in those days made electrical appliances, televisions, video recorders, and the like very expensive in Costa Rica.

To the dismay of future *pensionados,* this benefit was repealed several years ago. However, duty-free imports on household goods aren't nearly as important today as they once were. Supply has caught up with demand; you'll have no problem finding a wide variety of furniture at reasonable prices. The amount of money you'd have to pay just to have that bedroom suite and living-room furniture shipped from Topeka or Toronto would pay for furnishing your home in Costa Rica with brand-new merchandise. Furniture stores have great selections, and you can visit small, family-operated factories and have pieces custom-made for about what you'd expect to pay for retail back home. Also, furniture made here in Costa Rica is designed for a tropical climate, whereas some furnishings made in the United States can be unsuitable or susceptible to mold or insect damage.

Household appliances such as refrigerators, washing machines, and TVs can be purchased from local dealers without waiting for months, as was the situation before. Import taxes on these appliances have dropped dramatically. For example, recently my wife and I built a new home and bought a washer and dryer for almost the same price as they would have cost in California. Our *tico* neighbors, by the way, were astounded that we would waste money on a dryer when we could simply hang the wash on a line and let the sunshine dry it in an hour for free. But being spoiled *gringos*—too impatient to wait for the sunshine and too often forgetting about the drying clothes until after the next rain shower wet the clothes down again—we felt we couldn't live without an electric dryer.

TELEVISION AND OTHER MEDIA

A few years ago, in order to watch baseball or football games, you had to wait for a videocassette to be mailed from the States. Today there are several cable TV services in the San José area, plus satellite dishes throughout the country. On our San José cable system, we enjoyed abundant programming direct from the United States: two TV stations from Denver, one from Atlanta, and one from Chicago. Several international channels delivered programs coming from South America, France, and Germany as well. We found that watching CNN, CBS, and NBC nightly news on our cable TV made up for not having a daily newspaper delivered to our door.

Note that I describe our TV cable system in the past tense; where we live now, on the Pacific Coast, cable is unavailable and normal reception is confined to a few weak channels. (That's the price you pay for living away from the big city.) The answer for those who need to watch CNN, the World Series, and Home Box Office movies is satellite-driven DIRECTV, with an almost unlimited choice of channels. Reception is as good as it gets, and monthly charges are about what you would pay in the States. Depending on the neighborhood you choose to settle in, you'll probably have a choice of several TV cable and satellite servers. It's best to inquire among your neighbors for their recommendations.

In San José and many of the surrounding cities, you'll find stores selling English-language paperback books and magazines. You can often find daily editions of major US newspapers in bookstores. These papers are a bit expensive—they arrive by airplane—but at times North Americans become starved for a big-city daily newspaper. Today, it's easier to keep up with major newspapers, and very likely your hometown newspaper, via Internet. Every morning with my coffee, I read the front pages of the *New York Times,* the *Washington Post,* and the *San Francisco Chronicle* (including the comics). As far as I know, all Costa Rica daily newspapers are online, so every morning I browse *La Nación* and *Diario Extra,* as well as the English-language papers: *Tico Times, Inside Costa Rica,* and *A.M. Costa Rica* for Central America news. And they are all free.

MONEY MATTERS

Costa Rica's currency is the colón, which was valued at 500 to the dollar in 2012. The exchange rate between the colón and the US dollar varies depending on the world value of the dollar and the inflation rate in Costa Rica.

Some people feel uneasy when inflation continually deflates a nation's currency. The important point is whether the exchange rate between Costa Rican colones and US or Canadian dollars is in line with reality and not arbitrarily set by the government (a practice that continually leads to disaster in other Latin American countries). Many people, even some economists, tend to assume that when the exchange rate is stable, inflation is under control and all is well. That's not necessarily so. When exchange rates are steady, yet prices of goods and services rise in the host country, your dollar loses value every day. A currency holding its own against the dollar isn't necessarily a sign of a healthy economy. It could be an artificial manipulation of currencies that masks serious problems.

Dealing in Dollars

You often hear people say, "You can use dollars just about anywhere in Costa Rica." This is not necessarily so. Yes, businesses that deal with expat residents and visitors commonly accept US dollars. Cabdrivers, restaurants, supermarkets, and other businesses that routinely do banking several times a week, or daily, usually have no problem with dollars. They simply deposit them into their accounts. But for smaller restaurants, and businesses with low turnover, accepting dollars would mean having to make a trip to the bank, standing in line, and waiting for a turn at the teller's cage just to cash your $5 bill. It just isn't worth it.

Credit cards are usually accepted in larger restaurants and businesses with high-volume trade. But smaller establishments often refuse to take credit cards. Two reasons for this: One, a bank service charge is deducted from each transaction, so the restaurant loses money when accepting a credit card. Another reason: Until recently in some regions of the country, credit cards couldn't be used because there was a shortage of telephone connections to validate them. Businesses got along just fine by accepting cash, so today some are reluctant to change just because telephone connections make credit cards possible.

When bringing foreign currency into the country, be sure to inspect each bill carefully for rips or tears. Banks and businesses often refuse to accept any foreign currency if it's torn ever so slightly. Never mind that a 10,000-colón bill you get from the bank teller might look like a dog's breakfast; if that US $50 bill you have isn't pristine, you'll end up taking it back to the States with you. One scam is for a waiter or shopkeeper to take your good $50 bill, then return with a torn bill and ask you for something smaller, hoping you won't notice the tear. The bill is okay, but you'll have to take it home to spend it.

A continual problem is the importation of counterfeit US $100 bills from Colombia—so many that shopkeepers sometimes refuse to accept big bills. One place where you might get stuck (so I've been told) is at a gambling casino because in the unlikely event that you win big, the house tries to get rid of the phony bills they previously got stuck with by slipping them to happy *gringo* winners. This could be an urban legend, but it's worthwhile to be suspicious. You can check the authenticity of a $100 bill by holding it up to the light and looking for distinctive watermarks.

COSTA RICAN BANKING

In many ways Costa Rica is a modern country, but for some inexplicable reason a visit to the bank can be an *Alice in Wonderland* experience. It can take forever to do a simple transaction such as exchanging dollars or traveler's checks into colones. Opening a bank account can be a real adventure. Many amusing stories circulate regarding opening an account. Since many banks have no English-speaking tellers, non-fluent applicants are wise to bring along a *tico* who can help out. There do not seem to be common requirements, even among branches of the same bank.

When I accompanied a friend to help her open a savings account, her letters of recommendation were rejected because the clerk insisted on letters from people who had lent my friend money. So she had her friends rewrite the letters to indicate that she had borrowed money. We went to another branch of the same bank and tried again. This time the clerk didn't even ask for letters, just the check for deposit and her passport! I understand that some banks insist on notarized copies of your residency permit, your passport, and documentation of your corporation (if any), as well as a letter from your attorney. Again, it is an *Alice in Wonderland* experience.

Having said this, my last experience, six months ago at Banco Nacional, was surprisingly easy. This may be because the bank teller knew me.

All I had to show was my passport and a telephone bill with my name and address on it. However, under pressure from the US government's anti-money laundering campaign, banks are asking more questions and presumably passing the answers along to the US law enforcement agencies. We can probably expect more intrusive legislation as time goes by. The days of using Costa Rican bank accounts for hiding assets from the IRS may become a legend of the past.

Although each bank handles things a little differently, doing ordinary transactions sometimes involves standing in one line where the clerk checks your passport, examines the bills or checks, fills out forms in triplicate, and pounds everything in sight with a rubber stamp. Then you move to another line and wait until a second clerk fills out more forms in quadruplicate and does more rubber-stamping. One thing to remember: Lines are going to be much longer on days following holidays, when banks have been closed for a day or so, and on the days when pensioners receive their Social Security checks. Some banks provide separate lines for pensioners, which helps considerably. To be fair, the banks do seem to be gaining efficiency, and the lines are becoming shorter. This is especially so with the appearance of several reliable US-based banks, such as Scotia and Cuscatlán. Bank accounts can be in either colones or dollars. An unpleasant and basically unfair bank practice is holding US-dollar checks from foreign banks for up to a month before crediting them to your account. For a variety of reasons, most expats also maintain their home bank accounts when they move to Costa Rica. For one thing, your checks could be tied up for a couple of weeks or more before you can withdraw the cash. With your money deposited in a US or Canadian bank, you can use your ATM card almost anywhere in Costa Rica to withdraw cash as you need it. Some expatriates don't even bother with *tico* banks, relying on ATM machines exclusively. Some banks charge a fee for ATM withdrawals. Local businesspeople who get to know you will often accept your US or Canadian bank checks. They know they're good, and they don't worry about a long wait because there's always a large balance in their bank accounts anyway. Our local grocery store, where we are well known, cashes our US checks up to $100 anytime we need money.

One of the benefits of Costa Rica's Internet revolution is the ability to pay your bills back home through your hometown bank's website rather than attempting the impossible task of sending a check to your creditor.

Between the Costa Rica post office and your US bank is a long and uncertain trail. The time for a check to make the journey to your creditor varies from a span of two weeks to never. The late fees and interest charges can add up quickly. Make arrangements to pay your bills back home via the Internet, and have the bank show you exactly how to make the transfers. You'll never be sorry.

Banks are also where you can usually pay traffic tickets and utility bills and sometimes make Social Security payments for your maid and gardener. Since each transaction requires a flurry of forms, rubber stamps, and calculations, you can count on spending a lot of time in Costa Rican banks. Because of the time-consuming process of dealing with banks, insurance payments, and government bureaucracy, some *ticos* earn their living by standing in line for you or by knowing whom to contact and when. They are called *tramitadores* (from the verb *tramitar,* meaning "to transact," "to take legal steps"). Your friends and neighbors can recommend a reliable *tramitador* to make your life easier. Many people become close friends with their *tramitadores,* dining with them and exchanging presents at Christmas. With banks becoming more sophisticated, and businesses providing online Internet payment facilities, the role of the *tramitador* is becoming less important and will probably be ancient history before long. (If not already.)

Criticize the banking system as we do, the fact is that government banks are financially sound. A few years ago BancoAnglo, one of the big three government-owned Costa Rican banks, was forced to close its doors because of mismanagement and reckless speculation. The situation closely paralleled the savings-and-loan debacle at that time in the United States. Costa Rican investors didn't panic; they simply took their passbooks to any one of the other national banks and exchanged them for new passbooks from that bank. Nobody lost a nickel (or a colón). By the way, the Costa Rican bank officials responsible were immediately arrested. Now just consider how many US savings-and-loan wheeler-dealers were even scolded, much less shown the inside of a well-deserved jail cell.

Costa Rica went one step further: The government decided that those who borrowed money and didn't pay it back were equally guilty. The borrowers claimed that they lost the money, but it was surprising how quickly many "bankrupt" businesspeople *found* millions of dollars to repay their loans rather than go to prison. Is there a lesson here?

Not all banks are government-owned. Several private banks deal with the public, usually in a more efficient manner, at least as far as the amount of time you spend in line in front of a teller's cage. But there are two problems with private banks. One is that deposits are often backed only by the bank's reserves. In some cases, limited government funds are available in the event of default. The second problem is that some private investment companies that appear to be banks are outrageously fraudulent; their reserves siphoned into private accounts in the Bahamas. Before you invest in a private bank, investigate its past performance and talk to your lawyer about its reliability. If the bank just opened last March and the main branch is a post office box in the Bahamas, you just might be suspicious.

Interest Rates

At the time of this writing, the rate of interest being paid on time deposits of colones is between 7.5 percent and 11 percent. Dollar accounts pay about the same as CD rates in New York, about 1.5 percent. While 7.5 percent is a much better return on your colón deposits than dollar accounts, you must consider the possibility of the colón returning to its traditional inflationary trajectory. You are gambling that the colón will maintain an advantageous exchange rate against the dollar. If the value of the dollar remains stagnant, you'll do fine. But if for some reason the dollar resumes its advantage over Costa Rican currency, the colón's value could drop.

A special cautionary note: Private investment funds in Costa Rica are famous for failures and outright fraud—especially those that advertise extraordinarily high interest rates. For years some investment funds were paying 3 percent per month to investors. That's right: *36 percent per year!* This book has been warning readers about these scams for twenty years, yet it was difficult to convince investors who were blinded by lucrative monthly payments. Many expats were living on the income from their savings. After all, $100,000 invested brought in $3,000 a month—a terrific income here in Costa Rica! Tragically, the bubble burst when the largest investment company became snarled in a government investigation. Several other Ponzi-scheme companies fell like proverbial dominoes, with the scammers skipping out with whatever was left of investors' money. Some investors hold out hope of eventually recovering at least some of their money. I sincerely hope this happens, but the chances look very slim.

MISCELLANEOUS INFORMATION

Think Kilometers!

Distances in Costa Rica are measured in meters and kilometers (*kilómetros*), not in yards or miles. It's not difficult at all, so get used to it. It works like this: A meter is approximately the same length as a yard, and 100 meters or 100 yards is the approximate length of an average city block, same as in the United States or Canada. So when someone says "fifty meters," you simply visualize half a block. A kilometer is 1,000 meters, which equals ten city blocks. Now isn't that a much easier way of visualizing distance, than trying to remember that a mile is 5,279 feet, or 17.6 city blocks?

Why is it important to think kilometers rather than miles? Because when traveling in Costa Rica, *all* road signs are in kilometers, *all* road maps use kilometers for distances and directions, *all* speedometers of rental cars are calibrated in kilometers. So when you ask directions, the reply will be in meters or kilometers. *Ticos* and expats alike think and talk in kilometers, never in miles. They will give you a blank stare if you ask, "How many miles is it to the next gas station?"

Golf Courses

When I first started writing about Costa Rica, golf courses were almost non-existent. This disappointed many tourists who feel that a vacation isn't complete without a few rounds of golf. For golfers looking to spend a long time or to retire in Costa Rica, the near absence of golf was a severe drawback.

Why the scarcity of golf courses? It's partly a matter of economics. During the rainy months, when golf course maintenance is limited to cutting grass, golf-playing tourists are few and far between. In the dry season, when plenty of tourists are here, sufficient irrigation water might not be available. Another factor is that golf is not a *tico* tradition. The main sport here is soccer, a team sport, with strenuous running, kicking, and body contact. The excitement is contagious, with everybody cheering wildly for his or her team. *Ticos* have difficulty understanding golf as a sport. What they see is a few lackadaisical people fooling around with clubs. Someone hits a ball, then rides a sluggish cart to where the ball lands, and then whacks it again. Nobody cheers. Nobody gets excited. There aren't any spectators. It doesn't make sense to *ticos*. To them, soccer is more like a real sport.

Golf Courses

Cacique del Mar. Playa Hermosa, Guanacaste; eighteen holes, par 72; members and guests only.

Cariari Golf Club. General Cañas Highway, near San José; eighteen-hole championship course; hotel guests, club members.

Costa Rica Country Club West. In the San José suburb of Escazú; opened 1944; nine holes; members and guests only.

Four Seasons Hotel at the Papagayo Peninsula. Eighteen-hole golf course; guests and members only.

Golf La Ribera public driving range. In La Ribera de Belen near the water park Ojo de Agua.

La Roca Beach Resort & Country Club. North of Caldera on the Pacific Coast; eighteen-hole, par-72 championship course; members and public.

Los Reyes Country Club. San Rafael de Alajuela, near San José; nine holes; members, guests of certain hotels.

Los Sueños Marriott. Playa Herradura. Eighteen-hole, par-72 championship course; hotel guests and public.

Marriot Hotel Golf Course. Nine-hole course reserved for hotel guests.

Meliá Conchal Golf Club and Resort. Playa Conchal, Guanacaste; nine holes, with another nine holes scheduled; par-72 championship course; hotel guests and public.

Monte del Barco. Resort north of Liberia, Guanacaste; eighteen holes; members and public.

Parque Valle del Sol West. San José suburb of Santa Ana; nine holes; additional nine holes could be added; public at present.

Rancho Las Colinas Golf and Country Club. Located near Flamingo, overlooking Playa Grande in mid-Guanacaste, is the newest course in Costa Rica.

Rancho Mary La Cruz. A half hour north of Liberia; nine holes with another nine holes planned for the near future. It will be an eighteen-hole par 72; members and possibly the public.

Tango Mar. On the tip of Nicoya Peninsula; nine-hole, tough executive course, par 31; hotel guests only.

Tulin Resort. South of Jacó Beach; eighteen-hole par 72; members and public.

Since only a few *ticos* play golf and there weren't enough tourists and year-round *gringos* to play golf, investors were hesitant to build new courses. For years the Costa Rica Country Club nine-hole course and the Cariari eighteen-hole layout were about the only golf courses in the country, and both were private. If you were addicted to golf, you were restricted to living in the Central Valley and you had to join a club.

Because of the increase in long-term foreign residents and the large increase of tourism, the situation is changing. As of summer 2012, at least fifteen golf courses were in operation. Some are for members and guests only, but eight or more are open for public play. As tourism increases and more and more full-time *gringo* residents are moving to Costa Rica, more courses will be opening. See the "Golf Courses" sidebar for a partial list of golf courses open or due to open soon in Costa Rica.

Gambling Casinos

For those who love the sound of a roulette ball bouncing along the wheel or the riffling sound of cards being shuffled, you'll find no lack of action in Costa Rica. Most gambling casinos are in the San José area, with casinos in hotel lobbies. Sometimes it seems like a miniature Las Vegas. Occasionally gambling casinos are found upstairs over nightclubs or restaurants.

While I sometimes like to gamble, I also like to have a chance of winning. I have the distinct feeling that gaming in the average Costa Rican casino is not really gambling, merely donating to the profitability of the establishment. My understanding is that house rules make it highly unlikely that you will break even, much less win. Some games aren't standard ones that can be easily understood, even though they might seem similar to poker or blackjack. Play is similar to Las Vegas or Reno, but the rules and payoffs are different—sometimes confusing—stacking the odds in favor of the house.

Another disquieting thing about gambling in Costa Rica is that there is almost no government regulation. I doubt very much that the house cheats. It doesn't have to cheat since the odds are so much in its favor, but there is little or nothing to prevent cheating from happening.

Having bad-mouthed Costa Rican gambling casinos, I now have to admit that several friends disagree with me. They claim that the odds and your chances of winning are pretty much the same here as in Las Vegas or Atlantic City. I'll suspend further judgment until such time as I win something.

Holidays

Sometimes it seems as though every time you go to the bank to conduct business, it's closed for a holiday. Costa Rica celebrates more than twenty national holidays with nine of them paid holidays for workers. Plus uncounted numbers of local fiestas that call for closing the bank. Of course, your workers will assume every holiday is an excuse to take the day off (paid or unpaid).

Watch the *Tico Times* for announcements of upcoming holidays, and plan your official business accordingly. The country's biggest celebration starts a couple of days before August 2, when thousands of people walk along the highways in a pilgrimage to Cartago to honor the national saint, the Virgin of Los Angeles. Drive cautiously at this time.

Traditional Costa Rican Holidays

(Boldface dates indicate paid holidays for workers.)

- **January 1**   New Year's Day
- March 19   Saint Joseph's Day
- **April**   Holy Week Holy Thursday
- **April**   Good Friday
- April   Easter
- **April 11**   Juan Santamaría Day
- **May 1**   Labor Day
- **June (third Sunday)**   Father's Day
- **July 25**   Annexation of Guanacaste Province
- August 2   Virgin of Los Angeles Day
- **August 15**   Mother's Day
- September 9   Children's Day
- **September 15**   Independence Day
- October 12   Columbus Day—Discovery of America
- October 12   Limón Carnival
- October 31   Día Nacional de la Mascarada / Halloween
- November 2   Day of the Dead

- December 8   Immaculate Conception
- **December 25**   Christmas
- December 26   Great Horse Parade—Paseo Colon, 2nd
                                Avenue, San José
- December 25 to January 1 Feria de Zapote. Town fair with rides,
                                bull chases, food stands, concerts, etc.

RELIGION

Costa Rica is predominantly Catholic but also has a sizable Protestant population. In the village near our home, I would estimate that 20 to 30 percent of the residents are Protestant, yet villagers seem extraordinarily tolerant and accepting of other religions. Yes, there can be rivalry between Protestants and Catholics in local politics, with the Catholic priest trying to get as many of his parishioners appointed to town councils and committees as possible and the Protestant preachers doing quite the same. However, I feel it's more of a prestige thing, because the pressure is low-key and everyone works together—at least on the community projects in which I've been involved. Priests often wield political influence in a community, which can dismay some Americans—until they recall that fundamental Christian leaders back home refuse to accept a church-state separation and are continually hip-deep in local and national politics.

All in all, *ticos* are rather casual and tolerant when it comes to religion. Nobody seems to care what religion you may follow or may not follow. Church attendance also seems to be casual. It's interesting to note that while abortion is illegal, birth control doesn't seem to be an issue here. Apparently abortion is common and rarely if ever prosecuted. Posters in government health clinics urge the use of contraceptives, and my understanding is that morning-after pills are readily available at most drugstores without prescription.

Common-law marriages are frequent in Costa Rica, especially in rural areas, and are regarded as perfectly normal. Couples often live together their entire lives, raising children and grandchildren without any thought of formalizing their relationship. This practice was probably due to the absence of priests in the countryside to perform marriages. Unlike in some Latino cultures, lavish wedding ceremonies aren't important traditions.

CRIME AND PERSONAL SAFETY

I'm always amused when friends visit us in Costa Rica and express dismay when they see wrought-iron bars on our windows. "Is crime so bad here," they ask, "that people must live behind bars?" This question surprises me because bars on Costa Rican windows seem as logical and natural as window screens in Atlanta or storm windows in Cleveland.

Maybe that's because my family moved to Mexico City when I was a youth, a place where homes traditionally have bars on their windows, so I suppose I grew up with the custom. The fact is, in most Latin American countries—from the Río Grande to Tierra del Fuego—homes aren't considered complete without a set of wrought-iron bars. To me, a Costa Rican home looks naked without them, like a Cape Cod home without shutters or a Southern mansion without a portico and columns. When the first Spanish colonists came here five centuries ago, they brought iron bars with them. Roman settlers brought window bars to Spain 2,000 years ago; for all I know, the Romans picked up the custom from the Greeks, or maybe the Egyptians.

My wife and I recently made a point of checking European homes for iron bars, having spent a few weeks traveling in Spain and Italy, and participating in a lengthy home exchange in southern France. Without exception, every home in the residential neighborhoods we encountered had bars, heavy shutters, and sometimes both. After all these centuries, security is still fashionable in southern Europe. In England and northern Europe, homes almost never have bars, although shutters are quite common. The original colonists who settled on the North American continent came overwhelmingly from the British Isles and northern European countries, where bars were never in vogue.

Do window bars deter professional burglars? Not really. Not any more than locked doors prevent burglaries back home. Bars and locks simply keep out honest people. However, they do discourage amateur burglars and remove temptation from neighborhood kids. Frankly, I feel quite snug and secure with bars on our windows. By the way, Costa Rican burglaries while a house is occupied are unusual. It's much easier to wait until the homeowners are out having dinner or visiting San José to do your thing.

Unfortunately, some folks cannot accept the idea of sleeping behind bars, as if they were in jail. I know of several newcomers who stubbornly rejected the notion. They built lovely homes in the same style as in Florida or Los Angeles, with windows unencumbered by protective bars, and unprotected outside doors with windows placed conveniently for someone to reach inside to open the door. Most of them get away with it, but a few are horrified to return home after a movie or dinner with friends to find the TV and the microwave missing.

Not Crime-Free!

Like every country in the world, Costa Rica has crime. That shouldn't surprise anyone coming from the United States, especially from areas where crime and personal safety have become a high-priority concern. Take a look at some low-income US neighborhoods: The bars you see on windows and doors clearly aren't meant to be traditional. They are grim attempts to protect occupants from violent crime. The alternative to bigger and stronger bars is moving to a safer place with lower crime rates, perhaps rural Kansas—or small-town Costa Rica (that's our solution).

I personally see crime as another one of those annoyances we have to put up with if we want to live here—a nuisance, like potholes. To avoid destroying my car, I have to drive carefully to miss potholes. That's an annoyance. To avoid crime, I have to be careful where I park my car and where I keep my wallet. That's an annoyance. So far I've rarely been affected by crime, but potholes have eaten several of my tires and trashed my car's springs and tie-rods.

Several expats have criticized me for my relaxed attitude toward crime in Costa Rica. Yet, throughout our more than twenty years of owning homes in Costa Rica, we've never had problems with house break-ins (thanks to iron bars and our selection of reasonably safe neighborhoods). Once a former tenant (an American surfer) entered our house—using a copy he had made of our keys—and walked away with a laptop. (Since he was *gringo*, we can't hold that against Costa Ricans.) We've also had several tenants skip out without paying the rent or running up huge long-distance bills while calling friends in the States. But again, they were *gringos*.

Perhaps my wife and I are just exceptionally lucky. Our worst experience: having luggage stolen from our unlocked car. Two suitcases and a laptop had been left in plain sight one afternoon, while we dined in a Chinese restaurant. I consider this crime to be my fault, for leaving the car unlocked with tempting valuables there for the taking. It was an invitation. My unhappy camper friends become furious at my acceptance of the inevitable. "It's never the *victim's* fault," they shout. "The fault is the *inbred dishonesty* of Costa Ricans!"

My attitude is: Thieves do not steal because of inbred dishonesty or because they are poverty-stricken. They steal because it's easier than working and pays much better. (An unlocked car with valuables prominently displayed? Why turn down an invitation?) One evening I forgot to roll up my car window, and it rained furiously that night. The next morning the driver's seat was totally soaked. Should I blame that on myself or should I blame Costa Rican weather? Although the overall rate of burglaries in Costa Rica is not much higher than in the United States, this statistic is somewhat misleading. Obviously, a higher percentage of break-ins are performed on foreign-owned homes. Burglars know that the average expat home has a nice DVD player, a TV, a microwave, and a stereo. Here again, a little precaution is in order. Besides a protective set of bars, it's worthwhile to contribute to the neighborhood *guardia,* the watchman who patrols your neighborhood on foot or by motorcycle. In some city neighborhoods, every block has one. Because of these watchmen, most middle-class neighborhoods are often as safe as similar places in the United States, where a police car cruises by maybe once a day. In rural areas you seldom find *guardias,* but there are fewer burglaries, so it evens out.

Another big difference is the lack of rampant drug addiction among Costa Ricans. You won't find an army of desperate addicts forced to steal several hundred dollars each day to support a habit. Costa Rican law discourages drugs by handing out a jail sentence of eight to twenty years for anyone involved in drug dealing. Drug use is considered serious, and mere possession of drugs can be interpreted as evidence of drug dealing. By the way, these laws apply equally to native Costa Ricans and *gringos.* That doesn't mean Costa Rica is drug-free, either. A real problem is when young *gringo* surfers partying on the beach share crack cocaine with the local kids. So far it hasn't gotten out of hand, but it is unsettling, to say the least. Marijuana is, of course, readily available, just as it is in the United States and Canada. However, this is a common plant that grows like a weed in the tropics, it is not particularly addictive, and it doesn't require stealing to support a habit; just an occasional watering and picking.

What about street crime? It's best to take basic precautions when wandering about the center of San José—or any other big city in the world, for that matter. To be fair, having a wallet lifted or a gold chain stolen are crimes that plague tourists not only in Costa Rica but anywhere tourists go. Furthermore, this kind of crime can usually be avoided by taking reasonable precautions. Residents and long-term visitors infrequently haunt bad areas of downtown San José after dark, and they know how to avoid pickpockets and the like. In my thirty-plus years of traveling in Costa Rica, I have never had my pocket picked, even though for the last twenty years, while traveling in Central and South America, I've carried a "dummy" wallet in my hip pocket (the easiest place for a pickpocket to "hit"). The wallet contains worthless foreign currency, expired credit cards, as well as a note to the thief with some insulting descriptions of the thief's mother. I still have hopes that someone, somewhere, will steal my wallet!

THE POST OFFICE

Costa Rican mail service is clearly not up to the standards we expect at home. Let's face it: In a country where streets rarely have names and houses lack street numbers, home mail delivery can't be expected to be "reliable." When a package or letter actually arrives, it's best described as a "miracle." We waited six months in vain for our first checking-account statements. Then one day, out of the blue, they all appeared at once. Instead of complaining, I was astonished that the mail carrier actually found our house. The address on the envelopes read, "300 meters north from Amistad Park, 100 meters to the east, and 25 meters to the south." (But which house?) The poor guy probably carried these bank statements with him every day for months, just in case he deciphered those directions and figured out which house we lived in. Unfortunately, the statements arrived just after we'd sold the house and closed our checking account, having decided that having a checking account wasn't all that convenient.

That's why most folks rely on post office boxes, known as *apartados*. This means a trip to the post office every couple of days, but at least there's a good chance your mail will be waiting for you. My post office box in the village near our Guanacaste home costs about $20 a year. I understand the cost is considerably higher at other post offices, and boxes can be in short supply. In this case your mail can wait in general

delivery for you to collect it. To receive general delivery mail, ask friends
to address it this way:

John Doe
Lista de Correos
Oficina de Correo Central
San José, Costa Rica

(Of course, if your name doesn't happen to be John Doe, and if your
town doesn't happen to be San José, you need to make the proper address
adjustments.)

Not too long ago, the postal system was privatized, but as far I can tell,
it hasn't made a lot of difference. The same employees are working in
the same offices, and things look normal. I still would highly recommend
using one of the courier services or certified mail if anything important or
urgent needed to be sent.

Mail for international communication is a waste of time. Airmail
between Costa Rica and the United States or Canada involves ten days each
way. That means at best a twenty-day turnaround between the time you
send a letter and the time you receive the reply. Now that Internet access is
available just about anywhere in the country (there are Internet cafes popping up everywhere), the most practical communication method is e-mail.

Courier Mail Service

When you absolutely need to communicate by regular mail or express
mail, the way to beat the system is to use one of several Miami–San José
postal services that offer same-day delivery by air courier to and from Costa
Rica. Mail going either way gets there almost as fast as if it were mailed
in the States. This is the only practical way to subscribe to magazines or
newspapers at domestic rates and hope to receive them the same season
they were published. If you live in the boonies, your mail service company
can usually forward your mail by bus for pickup at the local bus terminal.

Listed below are some popular international and local courier services. (You should ask acquaintances for recommendations.)

Aerocasillas. PO Box 4567-1000, San José; Tel. 2-255-4567; Fax 2-257-
1187.

DHL. Pavas, San José; Tel. 2-290-3020; Fax 2-290-3000.

E.M.S. Courier. Zapote, San José; Tel. 2-233-2762.

Federal Express. Cetro Comercial Yohan, San José; Tel. 2-255-4567; Fax 2-257-1187.

Jetex Worldwide Express. San José; Tel. 2-293-0505; Fax 2-293-0808.

Mail Boxes Etc. 150 meters west of the American Embassy, Pavas; Tel. 2-291-0282; Fax 2-290-0806.

Sky Net Worldwide Express. Rohrmoser, San José; Tel. 2-232-5678; Fax 232-2797.

Star Box. 5177 NW 74th Avenue, Miami, FL 33166; Tel. (305) 257-3443; Fax (305) 233-5624.

TELEPHONE SERVICE

You'll often hear people grumbling about the Costa Rican telephone company (ICE), saying that they can't wait until the entire system is placed in private hands. But I suspect most complaints come from people who haven't experienced the substandard and expensive telephone service available in most developing countries. The fact is, Costa Rica has the one of the best and most efficient telephone systems in all of Latin America, with more than a million phones for a population of only four million. The best part is that you can dial anyplace in the world from your home and connect just as though you were calling across the street. Try that anywhere else in Central America!

This says nothing about cell phones. There might be a million of them in service. The cellular fad is an astonishing change in communications. Many *tico* families have a cell phone for each family member.

Privatization enthusiasts believe that once the government is taken out of the telephone equation, rates will drop. Well, check this out: Basic telephone service is around eight dollars a month, with 150 free minutes (no long distance charges anywhere in the country). Additional minutes are 8 cents (US) a minute. Cellular telephone service is also a bargain compared with most other countries. Basic service starts at less than $10 a month, which includes sixty minutes of free use. Does anyone really believe that a privatized Spanish or German telephone company can cut rates below these levels?

The fact is: Private, foreign corporations are basically in business to make money for shareholders—that's the bottom line. A good example of this was when ICE split the service and maintenance departments into two divisions. The installation of new phones and lines was kept as part of the parent company, while the maintenance and repair services were privatized. The effect on service has been dramatic. Previously, when a tree fell across a line near our home, there would be workers repairing the damage within fifteen minutes of the break. Often, they were there before we were even aware of the problem.

After privatization, they wouldn't appear until a half-dozen or so complaints were phoned in. (Without a working telephone, this can pose a problem!) One time, our service was out for over a month, with the repair staff insisting the problem was in our house, despite my showing them the broken telephone lines laying on the ground. After another two months, I threatened to file a criminal complaint (*denuncia*) against the company. The next day, we had a connection!

Infrastructure improvement is apparent every year, with more and more isolated communities receiving not only telephone service for the first time, but—would you believe—fiber-optic lines designed for high-speed Internet connections! Ten-plus years ago, to make a phone call from the Guanacaste beach area where we live required driving to the center of the village and seeing which of the three public phones had the shortest waiting line. If we saw teenagers were huddled around one of the telephones, we'd go on to the next. Occasionally, we'd find all three phones hijacked by giggling teenagers, and then we knew we'd have a long, long wait!

A few years later, our lives began to change. ICE telephone trucks arrived, and workers began laying wires (underground, to keep falling trees from messing things up). Suddenly, *everybody* had telephones! Teenagers had cell phones in their pockets. Instead of driving from house to house to find out where Juan Fulano the gardener might be working so you could hire him to work tomorrow, you simply dialed his home and left a message with his wife. Better yet, you could call his cell phone.

Paying telephone and electric bills seems to be different in every community. You don't simply mail a check to the phone company; you need to go to a designated place to pay. This could be a grocery store, a stationery shop, a bank, or some other local business. Phone bills are rarely paid at the same place you go to pay your electric bill, your garbage collection, or your house insurance—that would be much too easy. In the city you may receive a bill by mail, but you have to personally go somewhere to pay it. Many supermarkets can accept phone-bill payments.

I have a friend who owns a small village variety store and collects telephone-bill payments for the area. She speaks almost no English but manages to do okay with *gringo* customers. However, a couple of times I've had wild-eyed *gringos* come to me crying, "Please help me, John! I just paid my bill, but that woman canceled my account anyway! She said '*Está cancelada!*'" I calm them down by explaining that the word *cancelada* does indeed mean "canceled," but it was the bill that was canceled, not the service!

CELL PHONES AND PHONE CARDS

As mentioned elsewhere in this book, cell phones have become universal. Some families have one for each member of the family. A few years ago, you had to be a citizen or a resident to get cellular service in Costa Rica. And even if you were a resident, you'd have to get on a waiting list. It's much easer today, but you may have to prove you bought your phone in Costa Rica to get it activated. But most cell phones bought outside the country won't work here anyway. You need to be able to switch the frequency to GSM 1800, and most foreign cell phones can't do that. One of the Costa Rican phone company's modernization projects was to convert pay phones to accept phone cards instead of coins. Drugstores and supermarkets usually sell these phone cards. I like to use phone cards called Servicio 197, which can be used on any telephone by dialing 197 and then the special phone number on the card. This works with all phones, public or private. The phone cards are usually available in denominations of 300, 500, or 1,000 colones. For international calls, Servicio 199 cards work the same way and are available in 3,000- and 10,000-colón denominations.

DIALING IN COSTA RICA

To reach an AT&T international operator, you dial 0-800-0114-114, no coin needed. Verizon is 0-800-012-2222; Sprint is 0-800-013-0123; Canada Bell is 0-800-015-1162; information is 113. Direct dialing from your home is not only easy but also the most inexpensive way to place an international call. You dial the country code, and then dial the number you wish to reach. For example, to dial the United States from Costa Rica, first dial 001, then the area code and local number. To call Costa Rica from the United States, dial the prefix 011, then the country code 506, followed by the local number (there are no local area codes in Costa Rican telephone numbers).

Be aware that some international collect calls can be rip-offs. The bills are collected on the US end, not by Costa Rican companies. Unhappy tourists report placing calls from Costa Rica, and being charged up to $50 for a one-minute call to the States! These distinctive blue telephones are found around the country, mostly in hotels and at Juan Santamaría Airport. Because of the locations, the victims usually are tourists and calls placed with credit cards. The callers don't learn of the astronomical charge until the credit card bill arrives, after returning to their home countries, when it's too late to do anything. I recommend using the Servicio 199 card, as described above.

Emergency calls can be made by dialing 911, just as you do back home. The fire department is 118; highway police, 117; the Guardia Civil, 127; and an ambulance (Cruz Roja), 128. To report a problem with your telephone, dial 119. For electrical problems dial 126.

THE WORLD OF THE INTERNET

The computer age has arrived in Costa Rica. Wisely, the government keeps customs duties low on items such as computers and accessories. You'll find stores everywhere selling the latest hardware and all the software you could possibly want, at prices similar to what you would pay back home. Internet cafes are everywhere; even the smallest villages seem to have them. For those of us who had to exist in Costa Rica *without* e-mail or online hometown newspapers, this trend is nothing short of miraculous. Previously we had to depend on expensive telephone calls and faxes to keep in touch with the States, or we wrote letters that took a month for a reply. Now with e-mail, we can touch base daily with family and friends, even hourly. We can do business, sell and buy stocks, or read online, all with a few clicks of the mouse. The downside is that your family and friends can forward stupid jokes and chain letters that will cause seven years of bad luck if you don't immediately forward the message to the few remaining friends who still open your e-mails.

Even though Costa Rica has Internet access, the performance and speed usually do not compare with high-speed DSL connections in the

United States or Canada. Yes, there are some so-called high-speed cable connections, but they are expensive and somewhat slow compared with US standards. Also, they are not available in many parts of the country. In some areas, a "high-speed" ISDN connection is available at a reasonable cost per month. It's not as fast as regular DSL, but it's three times the speed of a dial-up connection. That extra speed is truly worth having, not to mention the reliability of the service.

When you have no access to ISDN, your alternative is a dial-up connection through the government-owned Radiográfica Costarricense S.A., commonly known as RACSA. Home service for families and noncommercial users starts around $15 a month for an unlimited dial-up connection. This service can only be used from the specified home connection. You pay extra for the phone time, but the cost is minimal. Opening a dial-up Internet account is easy; you don't even have to go to a RACSA office. Just about any computer store has the applications and can set you up with an account and a password while you wait. You'll have to post a deposit, and you have to bring a copy of your telephone bill and your passport. Keep in mind that this account can be accessed only from the home phone number listed on the telephone bill.

If you bring a laptop with you, a RACSA Internet card is convenient, allowing you to go online anywhere you can make a phone connection. This is handy when you're only going to be in the country for a few weeks and don't want to sign up for long-term service, or when you're traveling around the country with your laptop computer. The cost of the Internet card is about $10 for a ten-hour card or $20 for a twenty-hour card. You simply dial 134, and when you connect you enter the password on the back of the card. These cards can be purchased from RACSA in downtown San José and in some computer stores around the country.

6

The Meseta Central and Beyond

Which is the best climate in Costa Rica for expat living? Temperate or tropical? North Americans living here, either full- or part-time, are almost equally divided over this question. About half settle in the temperate central highlands, while the other half prefer the tropical coasts on either side of the country. Each group can't understand why others could possibly want to live elsewhere. Costa Ricans themselves are also divided about which is best. As proof of this division, roughly half of Costa Rica's four million citizens live in the higher reaches of the country. We'll discuss living in the temperate zone first.

The central highlands—with an altitude of 2,000 to 4,000 feet (609 to 1,219 meters)—provides a year-round spring climate where daytime temperatures average around seventy-three to seventy-nine degrees, then drop down to the mid-sixties at night. People typically sleep under a light blanket. Not just in the spring—year-round.

Costa Rica's central highlands are marked by a low mountain range that begins near the Nicaragua border and marches south, where it crosses the border into Panama. This range is known as the Cordillera, a picturesque complex of ridges, valleys, peaks, and tablelands, perpetually covered with green vegetation and teeming with wildlife. The mountains vary from rounded promontories to the rugged peaks of the Talamanca Range, dominated by 12,600-foot Cerro Chirripó. Valleys and rolling tablelands are interspersed between steep hills, volcanic formations, and fertile agricultural country.

SAN JOSÉ

San José is located more or less in the center of the country, an expansive complex of small cities and towns that surround the city of San José. This can be best described as urban sprawl. San José is Costa Rica's only real city, nestled in a wide depression about halfway down the Cordillera, at an altitude of 3,800 feet (1,158 meters) above sea level. The city, with about 350,000 inhabitants, is surrounded by dozens of satellite communities and small cities such as Heredia, Alajuela, Escazú, and Cartago, all perched at various elevations on the uneven plateau. From just about any point in this area, you are treated to views of mountains and extinct volcanoes that form a half-bowl around the Central Valley (or in Spanish, the *Valle Central* or *Meseta Central*).

Twenty-five years ago, most of these towns were distinct entities, separated from others by small farms, fields, and pasture. Today the only evidence of one town being distinct from another is a city-limits sign.

Why so many prefer the Central Valley is a question answered in two words: superb climate. This is the land of perpetual spring. Yet even this weather doesn't please everyone; some prefer temperatures in the low-eighties; others feel more comfortable in the low seventies. Fortunately, in the Central Valley it's possible to "fine-tune" your weather simply by moving a few kilometers in one direction or another. A fifteen-minute drive from anywhere in the Central Valley brings you to a slightly different elevation and climate, with more or less rainfall, with warmer or cooler temperatures. It seems as if each town or community brags of having the "best climate in the world." Alajuela is proud of being a few degrees warmer than San José, while Escazú is happy about being a few degrees cooler. Poas boasts of being even cooler than Escazú, and La Garita brags about its *National Geographic* rating of one of the three best climates in the world. The wonderful thing is that all these choices, however slight, are freely available to you. (The weather chart in chapter 2 illustrates this diversity of weather.)

Metropolitan San José

As their airplane approaches the country's international airport, visitors are treated to the sight of a broad green valley flanked by steep, volcanic mountains that seem to be forever topped with fluffy clouds. The city of San José spreads out below, thinning to a scattering of towns and villages

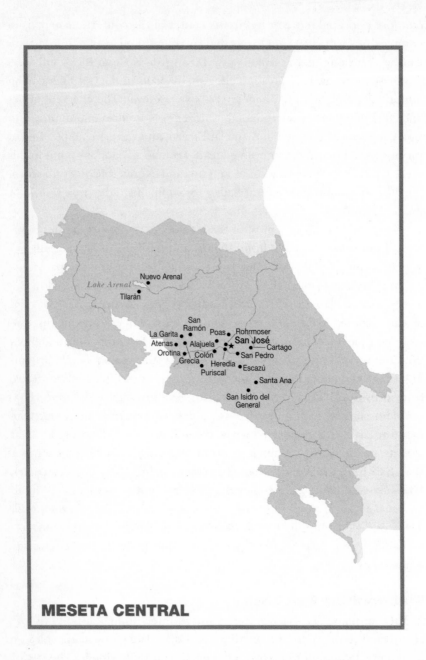

Nuevo Arenal

Lake Arenal

Tilarán

San
Ramón

La Garita

Poas

Rohrmoser

San José

Atenas

Alajuela

Cartago

Orotina

Colón

San Pedro

Grecia

Heredia

Escazú

Puriscal

Santa Ana

San Isidro del
General

MESETA CENTRAL

that eventually merge into a lush green countryside. From the air one can see homes and tidy farms lining roads and highways, showing patches of cultivated fields intermixed with wild tropical vegetation.

After passing through the easy customs booths in the modern terminal of Juan Santamaría Airport, travelers make their way toward the city of San José along a modern, divided four-lane highway. Those expecting to see the usual Central American panorama of dingy buildings, shacks, and junkyards will be surprised by tastefully landscaped grounds of light manufacturing facilities, fancy hotel complexes, offices of international corporations, and other evidence of business prosperity. A large Intel computer-chip facility is a proud addition to San José's high-tech ambience. I've heard people proclaim in surprise, "Why, it almost looks as if we are in Europe!"

The closer one gets to the center of San José, the denser the population becomes and the less it looks like Europe. Suddenly, the highway becomes a busy boulevard when it curves toward downtown and past Sábana Park. The city starts appearing more as you might expect of Central America. By the time the average newcomer reaches the heart of downtown San José, entirely too many vehicles creep along narrow streets, past hundred-year-old buildings mixed with modern ones. Dense crowds of pedestrians swarm past a confusing agglomeration of small shops, vendors, and street stands with blaring music. Typically, a feeling of disappointment sets in as the newcomer thinks, "Is this the beautiful Costa Rica I've heard so much about?"

However, it's all in the eyes of the beholder. My wife and I absolutely love visiting San José. The city becomes more attractive to us with each visit. We live hours away from the city and get enthused every time we plan a shopping excursion to San José. We look for reasons to drive or fly to "San Chepe"—as *ticos* humorously refer to San José—to see our lawyer when the business could just as well been done by telephone. (By the way, *Chepe* is a child's way of pronouncing *José*, thus the nickname San Chepe.)

Those who live here soon learn to appreciate San José for its many cool cultural events. No other place in Central America—or even most cities in the United States—offers as many opportunities for opera, plays, museums, art galleries, symphonies, and foreign artists of all kinds. Once you learn where the good restaurants are, you'll look forward to visiting often. Those who only know downtown San José can never appreciate San José's suburbs—places like Escazú, Santa Ana, Rohrmoser, Heredia, San Pedro, and all the delightful neighborhoods nearby.

San José, the capital and business center of Costa Rica, is a comfortable place despite its large population. Although downtown streets throng with shoppers and automobiles, neighborhoods a dozen blocks away can be tranquil residential areas. San José doesn't suffer from the widespread slum zones that plague most Central American as well as many US cities. You'll find modest neighborhoods, to be sure, and a few run-down areas, but not the starkly depressing ghettos so apparent in most large Central American cities, or some US cities for that matter.

There is a slight smog problem in San José's downtown streets, mostly caused by belching diesel trucks, buses, and taxis. I say slight because continuous cross-breezes keep the atmosphere fresh, except in the immediate vicinity of a bus or truck. Some residents disagree with my underemphasis of San José's smog situation. But having lived in Los Angeles and visited places such as Athens and Beijing, I truly appreciate San José's usually transparent air and continual blue skies.

For some reason, people from all over the valley feel a compulsion to do their shopping in downtown San José. This is partly from habit but also because shopping is something of a social event. Every day, crowds of shoppers amble along the streets and avenues, checking out window displays, making purchases, and gossiping with friends. Most could shop in their own neighborhoods, but it's more fun this way, and here is where you will find those scarce items you need. So many pedestrians pack the main downtown avenue (Avenida Central) that the city was forced to turn it into a pedestrian mall.

Although a few neighborhoods in San José are suitable for expatriate relocation, most North Americans are predisposed to congregate in the more costly areas on the edge of the city or in neighboring suburbs. This is understandable since we tend to be much more affluent than Costa Ricans and can better afford upscale neighborhoods. The western edge of downtown San José attracts a large number of foreign residents, particularly around Escazú, and the Sábana Park area (Sábana Sur and Sábana Norte), the upscale neighborhood of Rohrmoser, and some areas of Pavas. Better supermarkets, nicer restaurants, and amenities such as tennis clubs and attractive parks make this a very livable part of the city. The *Tico Times* classified section frequently lists homes and condos for sale or rent in Pavas and Rohrmoser. Rents for condos or apartments typically start around $400, and homes can go as high as $2,000 a month for a really nice place. Still farther out, toward the airport, is Cariari, a luxury area with a golf course and country club.

Directly across the valley, the developments around Bello Horizonte match Rohrmoser for elegance and expensive housing. Just to the east of downtown San José, Barrio Escalante is an affordable neighborhood of stately older homes. This was the "in" place for wealthy *ticos* years ago and is now in the process of adapting to middle-class families. Still farther out on the eastern edge of the city, Los Yoses and San Pedro supply moderate to expensive housing, with some of San José's most exclusive neighborhoods. San Pedro provides a university atmosphere, with many rentals available at student-budget levels. For the height of luxury housing and opulence, some neighborhoods around Curridabat cannot be topped. One area, known as "Embassy Row," has many stunning homes and mansions, some housing foreign embassies.

By shopping around you can usually find housing that will fit your pocketbook and lifestyle. Remember that ads in the *Tico Times* are directed toward North Americans who can afford to pay more. For less-expensive places, check the classified ads in *La Nación;* that's where *ticos* find their rentals. San José has several apartment complexes renting furnished places by the day or week that make excellent "base camps" while one is looking for permanent quarters or trying out Costa Rica as a place to live.

Finding Your Way

Searching for an address in and around San José and its suburbs can be an exercise in frustration; few buildings or homes have street numbers. Even worse, many streets have no names, or at least no names posted on the street corners. Very confusing. Suppose you are looking for the García residence, whose address is listed as "From Caballo Blanco 250 meters west, 300 south." To understand where this house is located, you need to know the location of a store called Caballo Blanco, then go two and a half blocks (250 meters) to the west and then three blocks (300 meters) south. At that point, you need to ask someone which house belongs to the García family.

This confusion isn't restricted to residences: Businesses use the same system. On maps, advertisements, and business cards, the word *calle* is often abbreviated as "c," *avenida* as "a," and *central* as "ctl." The distance between two points is usually stated in meters (abbreviated with an *m*). But to make it even more confusing, people occasionally give directions in *varas* instead of meters. A *vara* is an ancient measurement of thirty-three inches (in English it is called a "pace"), which was in common use before Napoleon's introduction of the metric system in the early 1800s.

Examples of address insanity: The address of the Hotel Presidente would be "c ctl, a 7–9," which translates as "on Calle Central between Avenidas 7 and 9." The address of the bus terminal for Alajuela is "a 2, c 12–14," meaning "facing Avenida 2, between Calles 12 and 14."

Directions and addresses can be vague to the point of impossibility. This is particularly true away from the orderly grid of north-south, east-west streets. An address might be described as, "From the gasoline station, 100 meters north and 75 *varas* to the east." But which gasoline station? My favorite address is on a real estate agent's business card. It says "50 meters south from where the Mas X Menos supermarket used to be."

It doesn't do any good to complain; *ticos* understand the system perfectly and actually become confused when you use logical addresses. Often when I take a cab downtown, asking to go to "Avenida Segunda and Calle Primera," the driver responds with a puzzled frown. When I add "Teatro Nacional," his face lights up with understanding and away we go, headed for the National Theater, which is on the corner of Avenida Segunda and Calle Primera.

In the fall of 2012, the city of San Jose began a heroic campaign to place street signs on its downtown street corners and put numbers on the doors. Few people have confidence that this will ever work out. Residents are accustomed to the old system, and probably will pay little attention to the new signs. Adding house numbers to the address might totally confuse residents.

FROM THE CITY TO THE MOUNTAINS

Although many foreigners actually live in the city of San José, the vast majority prefer the smaller communities surrounding the city. These towns range from expensive to moderately priced places to live. For some reason, at least six small towns in the country have the same name—San Isidro—which adds to the confusion of finding your way around. San Antonio is another favorite place-name that is scattered about like leaves in the wind.

As discussed elsewhere, the explanation for identical names is that during colonization, communication was extremely difficult between communities even though the actual distances between them is not far when using modern transportation. People couldn't possibly confuse their San Antonio with another when it took two days' travel by oxcart to get to the other San Antonio.

Rohrmoser

Rohrmoser is at the upper end of the housing market in the immediate San José area and is Escazú's main competition for upscale residences. For some folks there is no competition—Rohrmoser wins hands down. Here homes and condos consistently command rents and sale prices higher than elsewhere in the metropolitan area. Unlike Escazú, Rohrmoser looks more like a modern city suburb; it has sidewalks and boulevards instead of narrow roads and streets with dirt shoulders. (For some, an advantage; for others, lacking charm.)

Homes and apartment buildings here are much newer, with some condo development and home construction still under way. Started by a German developer (thus the name), Rohrmoser begins at the end of Sábana Park and runs along both sides of Rohrmoser Boulevard until it reaches the ultramodern shopping center of Plaza Mayor. From that point west, Rohrmoser sits on the northern side of the boulevard, with the town of Pavas on the eastern side. The US embassy, incidentally, is in Pavas, on Pavas Boulevard, a place with dozens of popular restaurants and shopping.

Many North Americans live in Rohrmoser, but the largest percentage of your neighbors will be *tico* professionals who like the convenience of being close to the business center of the city. My wife and I used to own a condo in Rohrmoser and enjoyed the peaceful ambience. We could take a taxi to downtown San José in just ten minutes (traffic permitting). We would stroll from Rohrmoser Boulevard to Pavas (some four or five blocks) to dine at one of the many great restaurants and return late at night, with absolutely no feelings of insecurity. One reason we felt okay about this was the presence of watchmen on almost every block. We had full confidence in the integrity of our neighbors because most were doctors, professors, attorneys, and the like. Then one day we saw on television that a very nice home a couple of houses away from us had been rented to a gang of professional bank robbers from Venezuela. The bandits had been living there for some time while they committed a string of robberies. They were on the "most wanted" list of the OIJ (*tico* equivalent of the FBI). Despite their occupation, the culprits dressed well, kept their front yard tidy, and paid their rent on time. They couldn't have been all bad.

Escazú

Several of the more traditional communities that attract expatriate residents run in a direct line from San José westward, beginning at Escazú—only a fifteen-minute drive from downtown San José—to the town of Puriscal, about one hour from the ocean. Nestled at the base of magnificent ancient volcanic mountains, Escazú has always drawn the affluent and those seeking tranquility away from the city. Three mountains hover over Escazú. The tallest is Cerro Rabo de Mico, at 7,770 feet (2,368 meters); the most spectacular is Pico Blanco, at 7,250 feet (2,210 meters), with a dramatic, sheer rock face that has challenged the skill of many a mountain climber. Residential streets on the edge of town ascend the mountainside bravely, presenting an even better view with each gain in altitude.

Escazú used to be somewhat removed from city hustle and bustle. Needless to say, the town no longer has a "village" atmosphere. It is now a city. Originally, Escazú consisted of three separate villages: San Miguel de Escazú, San Rafael de Escazú, and San Antonio de Escazú, each having its own church and patron saint. The red-domed church in San Miguel de Escazú was constructed in 1799 and has survived numerous earthquakes since. Some of the older barrios are famous for quaint old adobe buildings that are painted with a traditional two-color motif. The design is a three-foot colored stripe painted along the bottom of the home, which was believed to ward off evil spirits and witches. I have to admit that I've encountered very few evil spirits or witches during my visits here.

The villages expanded until they formed one city with a population said to be around 50,000. San Rafael is the commercial zone, with an astounding collection of businesses, restaurants, and nightlife. Traffic along San Rafael's main streets is exceptionally heavy, with shoppers and businesspeople driving automobiles at a snail's pace in traffic.

Trendy restaurants of all descriptions abound, including European, barbecue, Chinese, and even a Cajun restaurant for the yuppie trade. Yet a block away from the main streets, neighborhoods are as calm as they were more than twenty years ago. As San José grew and spread out, artists and those in search of serenity began moving to Escazú. No longer the peaceful retreat of yesterday, the area retains a reputation as an artists' colony as well as a retirement center.

Escazú's higher elevations are ideally suited for those who think that San José's climate is too warm. Many residents consider the weather here to be as close to perfect as you can get, with high temperatures hovering in the upper seventies every afternoon of the year. A large number of North Americans choose Escazú and surrounding towns as their place for relocation. This is where the US ambassador's residence is located. Two famous country clubs provide the area with golf, tennis, and a focal point for the society set. Escazú is the center of much of Costa Rica's expatriate social life.

Escazú and its environs have a sophistication that makes them stand out among San José's suburbs as a prestige address. Although the area admittedly has some of the more expensive places to live, modestly priced homes and apartments are also available throughout the community. Those who choose to live here say they wouldn't think of settling anywhere else. "We have the best of all worlds," explained a couple who owns a small house on the slope of Pico Blanco. "We live in the country with a gorgeous view of the city below, yet we are just five minutes away from stores, restaurants, or whatever we need." They pointed out that although they are close to San José, they rarely go there on other than essential business. Well-stocked supermarkets, shops, doctors, dentists, and a first-class health clinic serve the community's needs quite well.

You'll find no real "foreign colony" in Escazú. Expatriate *gringos* tend to spread throughout the community, interspersed with *ticos* and other foreigners. Although some prefer to live in "sealed-in" developments—compounds with high walls and twenty-four-hour security—more folks live in ordinary homes or town houses. Those who choose to pay more for the security feel it is worth it, since they can comfortably leave their places unoccupied for months at a time while they return home for visits. Others rely on neighbors and friends to take care of things while they are gone.

Santa Ana

The first edition of this book described Santa Ana as a "growing village" six kilometers from Escazú, separated by fields of sugarcane, rice, beans, and hillsides of coffee. Roadside stands sold braids of garlic and onions, garden-fresh vegetables, and jars of rich local honey. (Despite Africanized bees' nasty reputations, they produce high-quality honey and more of it than ordinary bees.)

Today you'll no longer see farmland between the towns. The most important crops today seem to be condominiums, homes, and gated communities. Santa Ana has become a small city instead of a growing village. For all practical purposes, Santa Ana and Escazú are one today.

The altitude here is slightly lower than either Escazú or San José, making it slightly warmer and drier. A number of small rivers cross the rolling valley, and rounded mountains provide a scenic backdrop. All roads converge upon a central area, giving Santa Ana a true downtown center, casual yet somewhat sophisticated. High above the town, on the mountain Cerro Pacacua, a 20,000-acre forest preserve and bird sanctuary keep nature ever present in the local ambience.

A few generations ago—before it became an easy thing to drive to the beach for vacations—San José's wealthy families maintained summer homes in Santa Ana. This was the place to spend weekends and school vacations, a place for the upper crust to host parties and entertain lavishly. This old tradition left its traces on today's community, with many nice homes scattered about the area. Many rather attractive developments, complete with swimming pools, gardens, and round-the-clock security, are here.

Santa Ana is well known for polo matches and international equestrian competitions. Seasonal festivals bring an impressive parade of horseback riders, who ride their high-stepping steeds along the streets to the central plaza where the main celebration is under way. (Don't try to drive along the parade route on festival day; horses have the right-of-way.)

Santa Ana has a deserved reputation as a working artists' colony, with a number of writers and artists in residence. The town is famous for ceramics, and production of excellent pieces is a major industry, with almost thirty workshops and more than 150 local people employed in artistic endeavors. Excellent restaurants, first-class supermarkets, and shopping of all descriptions are at hand, eliminating the need to go to the crowded world of downtown San José for odds and ends. Yet when such travel is necessary, it's but an easy drive along one of the country's few stretches of genuine superhighway. What is probably the largest and most elegant shopping mall in the country sits along the divided highway between Santa Ana and Escazú. It's called the Multi-Plaza and is worth a visit.

Every community seems to have an especially popular hangout where expats gather to socialize over a few drinks, lunch, or dinner. The Tex-Mex restaurant in Santa Ana seems to be the place for this. English is spoken here by a ratio of ten to one, and the place always seems to be crowded. Another popular place, on the road between Escazú and Santa Ana, is called the Rock and Roll Pollo (*pollo* means "chicken").

CIUDAD COLÓN

Located about fifteen minutes beyond Santa Ana and twenty minutes from Escazú, Ciudad Colón is the next to last of San José's western suburbs. The town is the site of the University of Peace, sponsored by the United Nations, offering graduate courses in peace studies. A growing number of expatriates live here, a close-knit group that welcomes newcomers. The town is very neat and inviting. As far as we can tell, there haven't been any condo developments started in Ciudad Colón, but with population pressure moving from Santa Ana, condos and gated communities seem inevitable.

The word *ciudad* means "city," but that word hardly describes Ciudad Colón. This is a small community where folks stroll to the town center for shopping or to have lunch with friends. One of the restaurants we've enjoyed is a vegetarian establishment called Earthly Delights (even though I'm normally a vegetarian only between meals). There's a sense of peace and personal safety about Ciudad Colón. Although the setting is rural, it is certainly not isolated. The enormous and elegant Multi-Plaza Mall is but a short drive, and Escazú is not much farther. Frequent bus departures from Ciudad Colón take you to the heart of San José for heavy-duty shopping and browsing the interesting downtown areas of a real city.

Of all the Central Valley retirement locations, I suspect that communities from Santa Ana west to the town of Ciudad Colón and on to Puriscal have a great potential for development and property appreciation. The reason for my belief: The government has finally completed the connection from Ciudad Colón to the coastal highway. This cuts up to two hours of travel time from San José for those bound for the Pacific Coast. Finished in January 2010, the route has become so popular that the mostly two-lane pavement ends up being clogged with bumper-to-bumper traffic during weekends and holidays. Furthermore, it suffers from occasional landslides that block traffic until bulldozers clear the way. A benefit of the new route is that traffic on this highway is traffic that would otherwise clog the conventional route going to Puntarenas and north to the Nicaragua border.

Nevertheless, I'm confident the problems will be worked out, by adding lanes and shoring up weak spots in the deep cuts through hills. With Pacific beaches just an hour's drive from Cuidad Colón instead of the three hours of pre-shortcut days, it will make the area even more attractive as a place to live, and real estate could become an even better investment.

Puriscal

A few kilometers beyond Ciudad Colón, you'll find a delightful mountain town called Santiago de Puriscal, a self-contained community of about 10,000 inhabitants. Puriscal is in the process of being "discovered" by an ever-increasing number of expats who enjoy the perpetual spring climate here. It's a pleasant alternative to the heat and humidity of Caribbean and Pacific beach communities, and it's set above the smog of San José and the Central Valley. Elevations in this area range from 2,600 to 3,900 feet (792 to 1,189 meters), with homes perched on a series of ridges with spectacular views in all directions.

A massive church anchors the center of town, with a lovely park spread out in front. The church is especially interesting because it is partially in ruins, the result of an earthquake years ago and shifting ground beneath the church. The park in front of the church is a relaxing place to wait for friends and to meet expatriate newcomers. Puriscal offers a surprisingly wide selection of business and commercial services. Probably because it is farther from the urbanized areas closer to San José, central Puriscal has the look of a much larger city. You'll find three supermarkets, several hardware stores, banks, and even several Chinese restaurants.

Puriscal is widely recognized as making the best *chicharrones* (fried pork treats) in the country. During a recent visit we tried them, and I swear they are the best we've ever tasted! You really have to love a town that appreciates good food. Puriscal loves *chicharrones* so much that the people hold a special holiday in honor of the tasty, greasy snack. More than just a holiday, the Festival Nacional del Chicharrón is held over ten days and has dancing, music, sports, and exhibitions. Is that dedication, or what?

If there's something you need and can't find in Puriscal, a good highway links Puriscal to San José, a forty-minute drive or a fifty-minute express bus ride. Actually, many *ticos* commute to San José daily to work, preferring to live in a peaceful community away from traffic and bustle. A bonus of living in the Puriscal area: Now that there's a paved road to Orotina and the Pacific Coast, Puriscal residents are about an hour's drive to the Pacific beaches. Instead of three hours!

ALAJUELA

Near the country's major airport, Alajuela is one of the less expensive yet pleasant places for foreigners to live. Situated on the western edge of San José, this small city is convenient to the airport and a twenty-minute bus ride from downtown San José. Clean, modern buses run every few minutes during the day, stopping at the airport on the way to and from San José. (If you have a small amount of luggage, this is an inexpensive way to get downtown from the airport.)

Your first approach to Alajuela can give a misleading impression. The highway comes in on a higher level than the town, providing an unfortunate panorama of tin roofs in every direction—some new, some rusted, some painted red to resemble tile, but actually of corrugated iron, plastic, or aluminum. Of course, in the United States a tin roof usually implies cheap construction, basically used for structures such as storage sheds or temporary buildings. But as explained in chapter 2, this is earthquake country; those picturesque tile roofs can be deadly when they collapse. You may see genuine tile roofs, but you can be fairly sure that underneath all that pretty tile is a heavily reinforced substructure. Since the temperature never gets hot or cold, the insulation value of a heavy tile roof is beside the point.

Alajuela's focal point is a large park in the center of town (called the Parque Central, of course), a pleasant place shaded by tall trees, with chessboards built into some of the cement benches that surround the park. If you would like to meet North American retirees to ask for information about Alajuela, this is the place to come; sometimes it seems that there is as much English spoken here as Spanish. This is the place to find out about housing rentals, who is leaving for the States, who has a car for sale, and who can recommend a gardener or a maid. In the evenings a mixture of classical and pop music can be heard from the park's bandstand, where professional musicians entertain a couple of times a week.

Alajuela was the home of Juan Santamaría, the young hero of the final battle against the American buccaneers under Gen. William Walker. Every year on April 11, the town celebrates Juan Santamaría Day with a jubilant parade through town, a public fiesta, and dancing in and around the Parque Central. On one corner of the square, a museum dedicated to the hero is located in what used to be a jail. About two blocks west of the park is the Public Market, the perfect place to find the freshest veggies and choicest cuts of meat.

A good way to become acquainted with the expatriate scene in Alajuela is to visit restaurants and cafes in and around Alajuela center that are frequented by *gringos,* who drop in for an afternoon snack or a cold drink. If you spend enough time drinking coffee in one of Alajuela's more popular cafes, or sunning yourself on a park bench, you'll likely meet every *gringo* in Alajuela.

Alajuela is an excellent example of moderate housing costs, for both sales and rentals, in the Central Valley region. Prices are neither as elevated as they can be in upscale areas of Rohrmoser or Escazú, nor are they depressed as in poorer working-class neighborhoods. Neighborhoods here are middle class: Newcomers will feel comfortable, and neighbors can tell you exactly who lives in which house on the street. The expatriate community is scattered throughout the better sections of Alajuela and not very concentrated in any one location. The same is true of Heredia.

HEREDIA

When we first visited Costa Rica, Heredia was a small provincial capital of about 10,000 persons. Today the population is reported to be over 40,000. Heredia has expanded to meet Alajuela's growing sprawl until they've essentially joined into one large town, with nothing but a city-limits sign to indicate where one ends and the other begins. Situated northwest of San José on the sloping hills of the Barva and Poás Volcanoes (extinct, of course), Heredia's higher elevation provides a cooler climate and more rainfall, which keeps things looking green and fresh throughout the dry season. Rural areas farther up the sloping hills toward Barva are renowned for quality coffee production. Small- and medium-size coffee farms are scattered here and there, a few owned by foreign residents. Others own homes with orchards of citrus, avocados, and tropical fruit instead of coffee. Most places enjoy breathtaking views of the valley below.

The center of Heredia, like Alajuela, features a large, friendly Parque Central complete with weekly band concerts. This park is shaded by stands of enormous mango trees and has the usual park benches for informal meetings and gossiping. Like the Parque Central in Alajuela, Heredia's park has a large church at one end—a cathedral, actually—that has watched over the square for more than 200 years.

The center of town is somewhat congested, but that doesn't stop expatriates from meeting at their special restaurant on or near the square, browsing an English-language bookstore, or taking care of banking and other errands near the plaza. One resident points out that "Heredia isn't exactly a 'culinary mecca,' yet you can find some nice restaurants nearby in addition to the McDonald's, Taco Bell, and Kentucky Fried Chicken that cluster around the plaza."

La Universidad Nacional, the country's second-largest university, is located not far from the plaza. A private school, Universidad Interamericana, and several language schools teach Spanish to North Americans here. Many exchange students from the United States and Canada take classes here and become part of the expatriate scene in Heredia.

Heredia's famous market is large, featuring quality meats and exceptionally fresh vegetables, fruits, and greens of all descriptions. Much of the market's exotic produce is grown by local residents in their backyards. Saturday is market day, and selections are bountiful as well as fresh-picked. People from all over the valley come here for their weekend shopping. The market is near the Parque Central and dates back more than one hundred years. Like most other cities on the Central Valley, Heredia homes don't have street numbers. But instead of saying "150 meters north," it's customary to say "150 meters *arriba* [uphill]" because the town slopes uphill toward the north. "Two hundred meters *abajo*" would, of course, mean 200 meters to the south, downhill.

Continuing *arriba* is the town of Barva, location of Costa Rica's largest coffee producer, Café Brit, where many tourists visit for a tour of a coffee plantation. Up the slope toward the extinct Barva Volcano, many lovely homes are tucked away among the tropical vegetation that crowds the side of the narrow highways.

From Heredia's northern edge, hills and mountains rise steadily toward the Poás Volcano. All along these foothills, winding roads travel past beautifully maintained homes, alternating with evergreen forests, small farms, and verdant pastures. This is one of our favorite parts of the Central Valley (we almost bought a coffee farm here a few years ago). As roads climb higher into the mountains, temperatures become progressively cooler, allowing prospective home buyers and renters to make precise adjustments to their environment by buying farther uphill or downhill.

An interesting place to check out is nearby San Isidro, a small village to the east of Heredia. A number of foreigners have made their homes here. They point out that the village is small enough that they can interact with villagers and get to know everyone in town. They enjoy the rustic, rural ambience—a place where oxcarts are often used for everyday farm chores.

Incidentally, those foreigners who own rural parcels and who spend half the year in Costa Rica and the rest of their time in their home country are sometimes willing to rent their property in their absence to ensure that someone will keep an eye on their place and protect it from vandalism. Some attractive rental deals can be worked out in these instances.

OTHER TOWNS AND VILLAGES

To the south of Heredia and Alajuela, several smaller towns and open countryside sprinkled with small farms and beautiful homes draw *ticos* and foreigners alike who want to escape the city's crush. The road from Heredia to Turrucares is particularly striking, with lovely, high-quality homes interspersed with small, neatly kept farms and residences. Our taxi driver, who was renting his cab and services by the day, drove us there and pointed out some of the prettier homes along the way. "I was born in this area," he said proudly. And then, with a hint of sadness in his voice, he added, "Of course, it is too expensive for me to live here now."

Grecia

The picturesque town of Grecia is often described as one of the cleanest places in Costa Rica. Grecia, by the way, is Spanish for *Greece*. Interesting, because a nearby town, also popular with retirees is Atenas (Spanish for *Athens*). Positioned southwest of San José, Grecia is situated along the edge the Central Valley with beautiful mountain landscapes in the background.

It is in the continual process of being "discovered" by a growing number of expatriates. Conveniently located about thirty minutes from the airport, Grecia's turnoff from the Inter-American Highway is marked by a monument that tries to resemble the ruins of an ancient Greek temple. The town center is reached via a picturesque road that traverses sugarcane fields, high-quality coffee plantations, and small farms. The views are spectacular, overlooking deep valleys and lofty mountains in the distance. Grecia is noted for wide streets and prosperous-looking middle-class neighborhoods. The population is in excess of 15,000.

The center of Grecia features a lovely square in front of one of the country's most interesting old churches. Called the Cathedral de la Mercedes, the deep-red Gothic-style church was assembled from metal pieces imported from Belgium back in the 1890s. Imagine, if you will: Every piece of wrought iron used to construct the church was hauled over the mountains by oxcart from the Caribbean port of Limón, a tedious two-week journey!

A favorite place to meet local expats is the central square located in front of the church. You'll usually find some of them there most weekday mornings, sitting on benches or having coffee in the cafe across the street. Near the plaza is a large central market that, in addition to the usual collection of veggie and meat vendors, has a wonderful *tico* restaurant serving some of the best *comida típica* we've ever tasted.

English-speaking residents here vow that this is one of the friendliest and safest places in the country, and I tend to believe it. As I've driven the roads in the area, I've noticed a surprising exception to the rule of bars on windows; many homes, especially those up in the hills overlooking Grecia, do not have bars. There doesn't appear to be any one particular enclave where *gringos* live; they seem to be dispersed about the landscape, sometimes on small plots of land near town or in Grecia itself. Some prefer one of the nearby villages such as San Rafael, San Roque, Tacares, or any number of similar locations.

Atenas and La Garita

More to the west of Grecia and only ten minutes farther from the airport, Atenas and La Garita are charming little towns with rural settings and neat town centers with wide streets. These towns sit along the alternate highway that winds down through Orotina, toward the Pacific beaches not far away. Both towns are clean and prosperous looking, with luxury properties interspersed with modest-priced, livable homes. There are adequate community services, including a health center, ambulances, schools, banks, boutiques, and supermarkets. The expatriate population here is estimated to be around 600 residents.

Atenas and La Garita are gaining popularity with those who want pleasant weather but want to avoid the Central Valley traffic congestion. Residents here are famous for claiming to have the "best climate in the world." They point to an article in *National Geographic* as evidence. Of course, "best climate" is a matter of personal opinion, but there's no question that it is a bit cooler and fresher here than in the Central Valley. Some properties farther up the hill, where the highway crests for its downward, twisty run to the ocean, offer some spectacular views of the Central Valley. A few locations not only overlook the San José city complex to the east, but to the west they have a view of the Pacific Ocean.

The recent completion of the new highway past Ciudad Colón to the Pacific has dramatically reduced the traffic through the towns of Atenas and La Garita. This promises to increase their desirability as communities for retirement. The area is somewhat more affordable than some other desirable neighborhoods. You can find moderately-priced homes on good-size parcels of land with wonderful views. Atenas is thirty minutes from Jacó, only ten minutes from the International Airport, and twenty minutes from San Jose.

San Ramón

An often overlooked possibility for relocation, San Ramón has just as much going for it as most other Central Valley locations. A pleasant and well-maintained city of about 30,000 inhabitants, San Ramón sits almost halfway between San José and the port city of Puntarenas. The exit is just off the Inter-American Highway that joins San José with the Pacific Coast, twenty-two miles (thirty-five kilometers) from the airport and thirty miles (forty-eight kilometers) from San José. The altitude here is a bit higher than nearby Grecia and Atenas and therefore slightly cooler. Hot, sweltering days are almost nonexistent.

Local residents like to call San Ramón "the city of presidents and poets" because several of Costa Rica's famous political and literary figures were born or were longtime residents here. These include three former presidents, the most famous being José Figueres Ferrer—a champion of democratic reform who abolished the military—and several celebrated poets and novelists. In keeping with San Ramón's cultural past, there is a campus of the University of Costa Rica here, as well as a regional hospital.

This is a place where you can experience the genuine, low-key Costa Rica that you'll not find in busy, tourist-oriented towns. The pace here is slow. The central market seems to be the heartbeat of the city. There is also a huge weekly market. San Ramón is a place where neighbors stop to gossip on the street or meet in the central park around the old church. There is no hurry. At the present time, there is only a small contingent of expatriates living in the city of San Ramón. Most prefer to buy property in the picturesque rural areas within a few kilometers of the city center.

When I asked one resident about the cultural advantages of living in or near San Ramón, he replied: "Well, let's see . . . San Ramón is an hour closer to the Guanacaste beaches. Also, there's a three-screen movie theater, plus a Longhorn Tavern (Casona del Cerdo) featuring great BBQ ribs, cut-with-a-fork *Lomito,* and real corn on the cob, yellow and sweet!" (All of that, plus two kinds of homemade draft beers—what more could anyone ask?)

The North American population here is not overwhelming, by any means. One resident estimated less than one hundred expats in and around San Ramón. "Not nearly as gringoized as Grecia and Atenas, where they have regular gatherings at the park and such," he added. The opening of a store/office/club in downtown San Ramón has created a gathering place. It's called the Solo Bueno, or in English, "Only the Best." It offers an Internet cafe, used English-language books, mailboxes, and a real estate office. The owner says: "Seems like whenever *gringos* come to town, they drop by to see what's happening, have a cup of coffee, check e-mail, or pick up a paperback."

Cartago

Costa Rica's first capital city, Cartago is famous for its rich history. Colonial buildings and ruins dating back to the sixteenth century are reminiscent of an era when Cartago was the center of the country's breadbasket. Nearby rural villages with ancient adobe buildings and colorful wooden houses provide glimpses of the region's vibrant past. Sitting at the base of majestic Irazú Volcano, the town of Cartago has an elevation of almost 5,000 feet (1,524 meters) above sea level. This provides a much cooler environment than the rest of the Central Valley. Cartago's population is more than 26,000.

Cartago used to be a major stopping place on the now-defunct San José–Limón railroad line. While waiting for the train to resume its slow crawl to the coast, we used to stroll around the nearby market and feast on steaming empanadas while listening for the train's whistle to announce the continuance of its journey. We liked the town at that time, wondering why it wasn't being "discovered" by *gringos* looking for an "authentic" Costa Rican relocation haven.

Costa Rica guidebooks seldom mention Cartago except to note the ruins of an ancient cathedral dating back to the sixteenth century and the slightly newer cathedral that houses Costa Rica's religious icon, the Black Virgin. Also of interest is the fact that Cartago was Costa Rica's first capital city. Cartago is one of the obligatory places to take visitors—close enough to San José's suburbs for an afternoon's visit to the historic monuments, a lunch at a *tico* restaurant, and then home before nightfall. But that's where tourist interest in Cartago ends.

I feel that things are starting to change. Bearing out my observation that North Americans feel at home almost anywhere in Costa Rica, the city of Cartago and surrounding communities are attracting a few newcomers. This idea isn't exactly new: Some expat residents have lived here for more than twenty-five years. Only ten or so expatriates live in Cartago itself, while at least fifty live in or around the nearby suburb of Paraiso. There you'll find one of those Mega Supers, as well as a shopping mall.

An expat resident from Ohio who lives with his wife in Taras (at the beginning of the road to Irazú Volcano) said, "I was surprised that so many expats say that they live here mainly because of the climate. I always considered it to be cool, and my *tica* wife says it's cold. Also, the rainy season here is probably a little wetter than in San José."

Cartago doesn't seem to have a "hangout" where *gringos* go for morning coffee like some other towns do. For the most part you run into them in the various shopping centers or on the downtown streets. They will tell you that they enjoy the quality of life in Cartago and that the people really do accept expats and make you feel good about where you live.

ALSO IN THE TEMPERATE ZONE

The following locations do not exactly lie within the Central Valley, but they do have similar climates. These are places for those who don't care to put up with the heat and insects of the jungle, yet they are close enough to salt water that you can usually drive down to the beach for the day and return to sleep under a blanket that same night. Temperatures here are wide ranging, with places like Arenal being very cool and San Isidro del General being rather balmy.

San Isidro del General

At first glance, this town would seem to be a rather unusual place for North Americans to choose as a place for residence or retirement. There is nothing spectacular about San Isidro del General; it is an ordinary, medium-size Costa Rican city. It's neat and orderly, with the ubiquitous mountain views common to most other parts of the country. Few vacationers visit San Isidro, and those who have passed through the town may get it mixed up with one of the half dozen other San Isidros in the mountains. But, those North Americans who have discovered San Isidro's secrets love living here. The climate is considerably warmer than that of San José, which suits some folks just fine, and the pace far slower. San Isidro's population is almost 35,000.

Located on a wide ridge, not far from the high peak of Cerro Chirripó, the town enjoys a continuous breeze that keeps the air clear and aromatic with flower-blossom perfume. Daytime temperatures are pleasantly warm for my taste (maybe hot for some folks), and evenings are tempered by cool air flowing down from Chirripó Peak. Although San Isidro is not as serene and idyllic as some other Costa Rican towns, once you are away from the main square—and the inevitable cars, motorcycles, and trucks circling in search of a parking space—the pace slackens to a very peaceful stride.

Like most older Costa Rican towns, San Isidro features a main square in its center, the usual well-kept park. Since the park is the social gathering place for local residents, it isn't surprising that members of the North American community use it as their social focal point as well. The open-air restaurant of Hotel Chirripó faces the park, and at any given time you can count on at least some of the tables being occupied by English-speaking patrons.

Real estate and rentals are exceptionally inexpensive here. Since it is off the ordinary tourist routes, with no beaches and lacking in discos and other flashy attractions, San Isidro is likely to remain inexpensive. On one visit I talked with an American who had just completed building a small, two-bedroom home and was eager to find a tenant. He was offering to rent it for almost nothing just to have someone to take care of it while he returned home.

Several North Americans have taken advantage of the climate and low-cost real estate, living on small farms on the outskirts of town or along the highway toward the beach at Dominical. The views along this road are absolutely spectacular, with neat, prosperous-looking farms and pictur-esque homes in the mountain valleys below resembling toy buildings from a model train set.

Lake Arenal District

The northern portion of the Cordillera mountain chain, until recently ignored by North Americans, has one of the better potentials for expatriate population growth in the northern regions of Costa Rica. Certainly that's my opinion and one shared by other North Americans who are buying property around Lake Arenal as quickly (and quietly) as they can. Those who know about Lake Arenal would love to keep it a secret, but truth will out! The character of this region is so different from that of other parts of Costa Rica that it's difficult to believe you are in the same country.

The Lake Arenal district is in the upper end of the same mountain chain, but that's as far as the similarity with other highland areas goes. As I understand it, the mountains dip lower at this position in the chain to form a low break or window in the Cordillera. This interruption in the mountain ridges permits a reversal of wind patterns, allowing strong easterly winds to bring moist air off the Caribbean with an abundance of rain. There is no such thing as a dry season in the Arenal area; it's a year-round wonderland of greenness and lush vegetation. When I asked one longtime resident how much it rained, she replied, "On average, about fourteen months out of the year."

Before the government started building the dam that created the won-derfully scenic lake, the region was lightly populated. Still, about 2,500 people had to be relocated to make room for the seventy-two-square-mile lake. The project required several thousand workers and support people

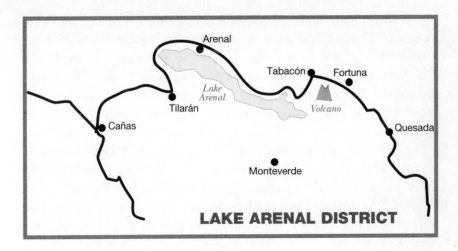

and took sixteen years to complete. Roads were cut into the area, opening it up to Costa Rican settlers who started farms and small villages. After the lake was created, many workers elected to stay on in the company housing that was built during the construction stages. The population here seems to be growing daily, including numerous foreigners who have "discovered" the Lake Arenal region.

To get here via paved road, the quickest way is by turning off the Inter-American Highway at Cañas, in the center of a flat and tallgrass area often referred to as "cowboy country," because of the cattle ranches found around here. Take the road to the north. A half-hour drive up a winding road toward Tilarán, and the air conditioner can be shut off, and the car windows rolled down to take advantage of the delightful fresh air.

Tilarán

By the time you reach the little town of Tilarán, only sixteen miles (twenty-five kilometers) from Cañas, a sweater might feel comfortable when the sky happens to be overcast. The population here is about 7,500. The country-side changes from pool-table-flat to steep-sided hills; colors change from dusty dry to emerald green. The road climbs gently now, as vegetation seems to become fresher with every curve, past fat cattle grazing fetlock-deep in richly grassed pastures and, where land hasn't been cleared for cattle or agriculture, some astonishingly heavy stands of tropical forest.

A surprisingly nontropical-looking town—with wide streets, neatly maintained homes, and prosperous businesses—Tilarán has become the home base of a number of expatriates. The climate is temperate and spring-like due to a continuous eastern wind that drops moisture on Tilarán even during the dry season. Local residents publish their own newspaper, in English and Spanish, which promotes ecology and recycling projects for the nation.

A few kilometers east of Tilarán, the view of Lake Arenal bursts upon you, one of the prettiest lakes in the world. The fact that it is artificial fades in importance when the overall effect is considered. Sailboarders claim this is the second-best place in all the world to enjoy their sport. What the first place is I don't know, but it surely can't be any more beautiful than Lake Arenal.

Almost all residents in this area live on or near the drive that skirts Lake Arenal. The paved portion of the road has a scattering of European-type homes, chalets, and an occasional commercial unit such as a *pulpería*, those community store–tavern combinations so common in rural Costa Rica. Many homes were obviously constructed more recently, evidence of a developing region.

Several charming little villages and occasional inns or small hotels are spaced along the highway between Tilarán and Arenal. The road is paved and is usually in pretty good condition. A short drive east of the town of Nuevo Arenal, the road turns into graded clay and occasional stretches of blacktop. The condition of the road is never predictable. At the beginning of the dry season, after bulldozers scrape the road into a smooth surface, fill in the gigantic potholes, and sometimes cover it with a bit of gravel, the route feels like a superhighway to drive.

When the road is okay, the distance from Nuevo Arenal to Arenal Volcano seems like nothing, with a wonderful view of the lake and thick tropical vegetation lining the road. Other times the road is an absolute nightmare. Entire sections can be missing. Water and mud can bury a four-wheel drive up to its windshield and other horrors. I believe the problem is that the steep mountain slopes along the north side of the route come down from rain forests above, bringing water and mud sluicing down onto the road. What doesn't get washed away gets covered with mud. The lesson here is to make inquiries about taking a shortcut from Fortuna to Tilarán. When the road is good, it is very good; when it is bad, it is horrid.

Nuevo Arenal

The town on the lake is called Nuevo Arenal or, more often, simply Arenal. This is a surprisingly prosperous-looking place, with neat little houses interspersed with expensive-looking ones. The town sits high on the sloping bank of Lake Arenal, and most homes and businesses are situated to take advantage of the lake view. Streets are well paved, though parts of town have an oddly unfinished look, as newly paved streets and vacant lots mix with an occasional house. The center of town has the inevitable soccer field with spectator benches curiously pointed toward the street, away from the field, as if the soccer team is so bad that locals would rather watch the traffic, scarce as it is.

Arenal obviously was a development planned by the government during the dam's construction phase. Many of the current homes here are left over from that era. Unlike the traditional Latin American residential style—built close together and against the sidewalk to allocate space for interior patios—some Arenal homes have real lawns, reminiscent of small-town USA. This adds to Arenal's strange, non–Latin American look.

Because of the area's beauty, the temperate-tropical combination climate, and the low cost of real estate, the Lake Arenal region is undergoing a buying frenzy. Buyers from Canada, the United States, and Europe are furtively looking at property and investing. Germans, Swiss, and Italians appear to be the biggest sharks, biting off chunks of the land as quickly as they can. They try not to appear eager as they snap up bargains, and they do their best to keep this place a secret, lest hordes of other foreigners descend upon paradise and ruin their plans of being the only ones here.

It's not surprising that prices are going up on property around Arenal. It's a very desirable area. Still, it's hard to conceive that inflation could be anything like that along the Pacific beaches. Another favorable circumstance: Since this is lakefront property, it doesn't fall under the complicated and restrictive laws that regulate ownership and construction on beachfront parcels. Here waterfront property is owned outright instead of being leased from the municipality. However, be aware that the water level in the lake fluctuates from dry season to wet season as water is drawn off for irrigation and hydroelectric power. Your waterfront lot could end up with a broad frontage of dry land in the dry season.

Library in Tilarán

In 2006, when Edward and Leslie Woods arrived in the town of Tilarán, they were very disappointed by the lack of bookstores or other sources of English-language books. Then they realized that neither were there outlets for books in Spanish.

Ed said, "Everything we had read on Costa Rica lauded the education system and near universal literacy. What we found was quite different. Maybe Costa Rica has the best educational system in Central America, but it still leaves a lot to be desired. Students are faced with severe shortages of books in the schools and no options for obtaining books outside of school.

"We wanted to start a library for the local children but had no idea how to go about the start-up or where to source the books. Many *gringos* told us we were wasting our time because '*ticos* do not read.' We were pretty sure the reason they did not read was because they didn't have books. So we persevered.

"On one of our visa renewal trips to Nicaragua, we met the wonderful Jane Mirandette, who has founded a network of libraries throughout Central America. With Jane's help and a starter kit she calls 'Library in a Box,' we began our adventure. We met with the local officials and told them of our plans. The supervisor for the Ministry of Education donated an unused building. The local women's organization, called Ladies of the Lake, held a fund-raiser that provided the seed money to buy the Library in a Box starter kit. Members of the group and spouses volunteered many hours and funded supplies to rehabilitate, paint, and furnish the donated space. We opened our library in May of 2007."

The facility is now open four days a week with a young Costa Rican lady acting as librarian. They learned early on that volunteers can burn out very quickly, so they hired a permanent librarian. Leslie said, "We felt it important for the community to see that we are connected to them and providing opportunity for *ticos*. We had a very successful 'name the library contest,' receiving 1,200 entries from the local students. The name selected was El Camino del Saber ('The Road to Knowledge'). We had a big celebration of our opening, covered on local radio and with local government officials attending."

As soon as the library opened in Tilarán, the volunteers began to plan a second branch for the town of Nuevo Arenal. They were given space by Kendall Sanborn, a local businessman. This branch opened on February 11, 2008, with the same four-day-a-week schedule and a paid *tica* librarian.

Their biggest issue, of course, is fund-raising. It costs over $400 per month for librarian salaries, and additional funds are needed to expand their collection of books. The library currently has 2,000 books in Tilarán (all in Spanish) and about 400 in Nuevo Arenal (as of one month after opening). They receive requests regularly for additional titles and want to begin procuring copies of all the school texts for students to use.

Most of the fund-raising was done by Sarah Benson, who divides her year between Nuevo Arenal and Key West, Florida. Donations of money or books in Spanish would be greatly appreciated. The library's website is www.discoverypress.com/TilaranLibrary.

La Fortuna

No trip to Costa Rica can be considered complete until you've visited the Arenal Volcano, about ten minutes from the town of La Fortuna. Active continuously over several centuries, the volcano's northern slope suddenly exploded almost fifty years ago, destroying a village and killing more than sixty people. (A geologist had tried to warn them of an impending eruption, but nobody believed him.) The nearest and best place to observe the activity is in the hot pools of Tabacón, a resort wedged into a steaming-hot river canyon at the volcano's base. You can sit on underwater stools at the bar and sip piña coladas while every twenty minutes or so, a jarring explosion shakes the swimming pool, accompanied by puffs of smoke and red-hot boulders tumbling down the volcano's steep side. (That's time to order another piña colada.)

The volcano has done marvels for tourism hereabouts. The nearby town of La Fortuna has become prosperous serving the needs of the hordes of volcano visitors. New hotels, restaurants, and stores are appearing each season. La Fortuna is an exceptionally neat and pleasant community, one that could well make a good place for retirement. With a relatively new road going through San Ramón, San José is only a two-and-a-half-hour drive away.

A small town with a friendly atmosphere, spic-and-span streets, a population of less than 6,000, and a great climate, La Fortuna has my prediction of a place that could someday have a sizable expat community. Sitting at approximately 1,312 feet (400 meters) above sea level, La Fortuna is too high to be tropical, yet it's low enough to avoid chilly winds. A short distance from the entrance to Arenal Volcano National Park, La Fortuna serves as an ideal base for tourists visiting the volcano, popular Tabacón Hot Springs, and Lake Arenal. As it's not far from Caño Negro Reserve and such outdoor sports as sailboarding, fishing, and whitewater rafting, it's almost obligatory to stay at or pass through La Fortuna to enjoy these activities. The tourism potential will do nothing but grow over time, and this will bring more North American residents. The town and vicinity have an expanding number of hotels, *cabinas*, restaurants, and travel/tour agencies. On the road leaving La Fortuna toward Tabacón and Lake Arenal, several new tourist facilities with terrific views of the volcano are always under construction.

A small group of foreigners are now settling into the Fortuna area. Of course, everybody knows everyone here, but to date they haven't formed any residents' club or formal organization. That will come later, when a critical mass of expatriates forms around La Fortuna. In the meantime, as one resident says, "Most of us come here to enjoy living with our *tico* neighbors and being independent."

San Carlos

When people talk about "San Carlos," they could be referring to the northern region of Costa Rica, from below Ciudad Quesada on up to the Nicaraguan border at the San Juan River. They could also mean the small city known as San Carlos, located in the more southern portion of the San Carlos region. To add to the confusion, you won't find the city of San Carlos on the map, because officially it is called "Ciudad Quesada." However, for some reason unknown to me, *ticos* always refer to Ciudad Quesada as San Carlos.

San Carlos offers another example of Costa Rica's microclimates. With a lower elevation than the Central Valley, the region is warmer than the San José area and receives more rain during the dry season. Yet it doesn't have the heavy rainfall of the nearby Lake Arenal area. Agriculture is a year-round activity, with citrus, macadamia, and other orchard crops as well as numerous *fincas* (ranches) with horses and cattle tended by expatriates.

These lands were once tropical forests, which during the past decades have been transformed into cattle pastures and fruit plantations. The exceptionally rich farmland here has attracted a number of *gringo* farmers and would-be agriculturists. San Carlos's agricultural zone devotes almost 70 percent of the land to raising cattle. The area produces first-quality milk, beef cattle, and agricultural products. Expatriates have set up on small to moderately large spreads; some experiment with reforestation. Some people have been planting teak, even though some experts claim that teak needs definite dry seasons alternating with wet periods to force the tree to produce oil and densely grained wood. Time will tell, because it takes many years before teak is ready to harvest.

Ciudad Quesada, or San Carlos, or whatever, is the main center of services and commerce for the Northern Zone. This prosperous-looking city-town was settled in 1840 when the Quesada family moved here from San Ramón and founded a village. As is the custom, the center of town holds a central park and the ubiquitous Catholic church. Nearby is the customary central market full of colorful stalls selling fruit, vegetables, herbs, and locally made leather products and crafts.

Acosta

A few years ago, the Ministry of Tourism came up with the idea of promoting "rural tourism" as an economic-development project for communities with limited tourist attractions and no hotels or other tourist facilities. The idea is to attract certain types of tourists, those who aren't looking for golf courses, beaches, discos, and the traditional tourist glitz that draws many foreigners to Costa Rica. This special kind of tourist will be curious about the everyday life of the *ticos*: who they are, what it would be like living in a "typical" Costa Rican village. Since these isolated communities rarely have hotels suitable for tourists, local residents organize to turn their homes into bed-and-breakfasts and welcome visitors. Since the community goes all out to make visitors welcome, it occurs to me that retirees might be received even more warmly as permanent economic benefits to the area.

Finding this idea intriguing, I decided to investigate by making a trip to one of the designated rural tourism areas, an area known as Acosta, the general name given to a half dozen villages in the mountains south of San José, about an hour's ride by bus from the center of the city. An excellent road snakes its way upward, winding through small villages and past some very interesting homes. The drive is spectacular, with deep valleys and ravines, lush vegetation, and spectacular views of San José and the Central Valley way down below.

The largest village is San Ignacio de Acosta. It's difficult to know the population, because none of the people I met there could make an estimate that agreed with anybody else's. There's a lovely church and a large, landscaped park. The surprising thing is the high quality of the housing. It was explained to me that at one time the *tico* government was making low-interest loans for quality housing, and many people took advantage of this and upgraded their homes. The setting is overwhelmingly beautiful. San Ignacio de Acosta is perched on the top of a rounded mountain, with an astonishing view of other villages so far below that the houses look like toys. San Luis de Acosta is about five minutes away, looking down the other side of the mountain into other valleys. Coffee farms are interspersed with forested land and small farm homesteads. Except for the main roads and some town streets, all roads are graded gravel, some in excellent condition, others not so great. The climate is superb, one of the best in the country, at least for those who like year-round springlike weather. The temperatures are seldom over 75 degrees or below 65 degrees. Air-conditioning and heating are unknown here.

I was welcomed enthusiastically as a visitor and was given a room in a private home, where I was treated as one of the family. I joined with the family in the local fiesta celebration and was very impressed. In my opinion, a place such as Acosta is a retirement option for certain types of North Americans: those who speak at least some Spanish or those who are willing to learn. Acosta would be appropriate for those who do not require a large circle of English-speaking friends. The local *ticos* are exceptionally friendly and open. I feel that before long, a retired couple could easily be involved with the *tico* society, with friends and volunteer activities keeping them very busy.

7

Costa Rica's Pacific Coast

The western side of the country is characterized by wet summers, dry winters, regular surf from the open ocean, and a much larger population of foreigners. Although most come from North America, a considerable number of Europeans are moving into the area. Many come from Germany, Switzerland, and Italy. Some expatriates operate successful hotels, restaurants, and other tourist-oriented ventures that the business-friendly Costa Rican government makes possible.

Costa Rica's Pacific Coast can be divided into three basic geographic sections: the Nicaragua border to the end of the Nicoya Peninsula area, the beaches from Jacó to Uvita in the center, and the Golfo Dulce–Osa Peninsula area to the south. Each area has its boosters who will assure you that there is no place in all of Central America as nice as their favorite location. I've seen them all, and I can say that making a choice among them would be difficult indeed.

A nice feature of most of these tropical beach areas is that they are easily accessible from the Central Valley—within a few hours' drive by bus or automobile, almost no time at all by airplane. Some locations require longer driving times than others, but as pavement replaces gravel roads, travel times will decrease.

Eastward from the ocean's surf, rolling hills of forest and farmland spread inland and up the mountain slopes, becoming steeper and more picturesque with each kilometer. Much of this land is wilderness, traversed by occasional dirt roads that become quagmires in the rainy season. Despite isolation and transportation difficulties, foreigners find these rustic sections exceptionally desirable places to live. As the government gradually paves the roads along the coast and into the interior, more and more settlers are swelling the ranks of North Americans and Europeans who live here and operate businesses. With easy access, property values ought to increase dramatically.

Panama
Playa Hermosa
Potrero
Flamingo • Liberia
Brasilito
Conchal
Playa Grande
Tamarindo
Junquillal
Playas del Coco
San Juanillo
Ostional   Nicoya •
Nosara
Playas de Nosara
Carmona •   • Puntarenas
Sámara
Carrillo   Naranjo •
Paquera •
Tambor
Montezuma
Malpaís •
Cabo Blanco

Lake Arenal

NICOYA PENINSULA

GUANACASTE REGION

A number of important beach locations on the north coast attract Costa Ricans and foreigners alike for vacation, retirement, or business opportunities. These beaches are easily reached from San José in three to five hours by car. The main highway is paved and in generally good condition but can be agonizingly slow when you are stacked up behind a string of slow trucks on their way to or from the Pacific docks. Slow as this ten-mile (sixteen-kilometer) stretch may be, you will be glad you have to go slow, because there are some shoulder drop-offs that could be dangerous if you drive carelessly. The secret to driving this section of the highway is not to be in a hurry. Relax and go with the flow. Enjoy the spectacular and ever-changing scenery of the Inter-American Highway.

Rainfall amounts are lower here than anywhere else in the country. Unlike most of Costa Rica, here the dry season is truly dry, with almost no rain falling from January to May. This is similar to much of California, but in reverse. That is, in California it almost never rains between May and October. In Guanacaste's dry season grass turns parched and yellow and many trees lose their leaves, often replaced with a gorgeous display of colorful blossoms. Around homes or along inhabited beaches, however, you'll see more evergreen trees and broadleaf plants because they've been deliberately planted and cared for.

PLAYAS DEL COCO AREA

A quickly developing complex of *playas* (beaches) begins at Playa Hermosa and Playa Panamá, stretching south through Playas del Coco and ending at Playa Ocotal. A nice beach in this complex and one with development potential is Playa Hermosa. *Hermosa* means "beautiful" in Spanish, and Playa Hermosa lives up to its name. This is a lovely place, with a curving shoreline of clean sand and a peninsula that shields it from the open ocean and dangerous riptides.

Playas del Coco, however, is the most commercially developed of all these beach communities. Since the pavement ends in the center of El Coco, tourists tend to stay here rather than braving annoying stretches of washboard gravel roads to get to nearby beaches. Coco's scenery consists of the horseshoe-shaped Coco Bay, with islands in the distance and steep hills and cliffs on either side.

This is probably not the place in which you'd want settle down, not if you are looking for a "typical sleepy fishing village" (as I've seen it described in a recent tourist publication). Actually, I don't believe Coco ever sleeps—it offers some of the wildest nightlife in the country. The town boasts over two-dozen bars, discos, and nightclubs that rock all night, every night. There are also two casinos.

There can be no question about Coco's potential for business, retirement, or long-term living. Several very successful American-owned enterprises operate here, and more are probably on the way. But if I don't sound particularly enthusiastic about the place, it's probably because this is where I locked my keys in my rental car and struggled for two hours in the hot sun before figuring out a way to get inside without breaking a window. A good car thief could have done it in less than twenty seconds.

A few kilometers to the south, Playa Ocotal manages to maintain a village atmosphere despite also hosting a deluxe tourist resort. The accommodations are tasteful, blending in with the natural surroundings. The village is on the shore of Bahía Pez Vela (Sailfish Bay), and the fishing is said to live up to the name. Each time we visit, we see a noticeable increase in housing, making it another viable retirement option.

FLAMINGO BEACH

The next beach complex to the north is just a few kilometers away and is probably the most popular residential complex on this part of the Pacific Coast. New paved roads have opened the area to increased settlement. This array of beaches starts with Playa Pan de Azucar and continues south to Playa Tamarindo, including the beaches of La Penca, Potrero, Flamingo, Brasilito, Conchal, Playa Grande, Tamarindo, and Langosta.

By far the prettiest beach is Playa Flamingo. A wide, curving stretch of white sand with startling blue waves that turn to white-capped rollers before crashing loudly against the shore creates one of the loveliest scenes imaginable. Hotels here cater to affluent tourists who can afford to fly in from San José and spend $150 a night for rooms. Tourists on ordinary budgets will find few (if any) reasonably priced rooms, but ongoing building activity may change all this.

As you might imagine, foreigners have taken over this beach and have built some very spiffy places. At one time, I considered Flamingo the "Cadillac" of Costa Rican beach communities, but several other locations along the coast have surpassed Flamingo, at least in price. The hillsides display sumptuous homes, set in tropical landscaping and overlooking a gorgeous beach view. The scene is reminiscent of Acapulco many years ago when it was the playground of the Hollywood and European jet set. Needless to say, Flamingo is not the place to look for inexpensive ocean-view lots.

The beach adjacent to Flamingo is Brasilito. Instead of having a tourist-resort atmosphere, the village of Brasilito is more like a typical Costa Rican pueblo, complete with a soccer field, small bars, and restaurants. This is a bedroom community for workers employed by affluent residents and businesses in Flamingo. It's also an inexpensive place for *ticos* and foreign residents on a budget to find a *cabina* or room and enjoy the beach. The beach isn't bad at all; I'm surprised there isn't more commercial development and foreign settlers. For a beach community, property here is reasonably priced.

The next village is at Playa Conchal. The Spanish word *conchal* refers to the shells on the beach. In fact, the entire beach is composed of tiny, water-worn shells instead of sand. This area has attracted numerous expatriates in the past several years. This is another place with a large resort spread over 2,400 acres of lush land, including a golf course and 350 rooms. Several really nice housing developments are also found here, including gated communities, all near the beach.

Just north of Flamingo, the tiny fishing village of Potrero is attracting a growing number of foreign residents. They're building along the beach toward Flamingo, eventually to become an integral part of one community. The village itself is much more laid-back and relaxed than Flamingo, with some residents' homes built on the hillside overlooking Potrero's exceptionally gentle beach. This is a place where you can hire a local fisherman to take you out in his *panga* to fish for dorado or parga.

REGIONAL DEVELOPMENT

The entire west coast of the Nicoya Peninsula is slated for eventual tourism development by the government's tourism ministry (ICT). Of particular interest, with short-term plans in the works, the stretch from Sámara north to Tamarindo is drawing a great deal of attention. Two circumstances account for this recent flurry of building activity. The first is the newer bridge over the Tempisque River, which cuts at least an hour's driving time from the trip from San José. The second is the possible paving of the road from Sámara north to Tamarindo. Construction is rumored to start "soon." (We're not holding our breath.) This plan sets out certain areas as high-density tourism centers, suitable for large hotels, intensive usage of beachfront, and full-service tourist facilities. Sámara and Garza are so designated. Other places are planned for residential and low-intensity tourism.

Nosara was supposed to fall into the latter category, much to the delight of local foreign residents. This is precisely what they wanted: protection of the beach and forest, yet development of low-impact tourism to boost prosperity for the natives. Unfortunately, the desire of local residents has little effect on the determination of tourists to enjoy the Nosara beaches, not to mention the determination of developers to accommodate tourists and new residents. The region is booming, with more facilities and homes being built every year.

TURTLE BEACHES

An excellent example of how tourism and conservation can work hand in hand is found from Playa Grande south along the peninsula beach communities. One noteworthy turtle conservation project is at Playa Grande, just north of Tamarindo, a broad, sandy beach area famous as nesting grounds for endangered leatherback turtles. It used to be that local residents awaited the arrival of these huge, prehistoric survivors, collected the eggs in buckets as they were being deposited, and sold the harvest to bars and restaurants all over the country.

Alarmed by the possibility of the turtles' extinction, the Costa Rican government instituted a model conservation program. Local people are enlisted to help protect the nesting grounds; guarding the beaches and guiding tourists through the nesting grounds put local people to work. Hotels and restaurants have opened to accommodate the ever-increasing number of tourists; jobs are created for even more local residents. This boom has only begun, and future ecotourism development seems inevitable.

Conservationists have expressed mixed feelings about this program. While they praise the protection of the nesting grounds, they point out that the extra tourist foot traffic causes damage when visitors inadvertently step on the hatchlings. On the other hand, the number of baby turtles killed in this manner is nothing when compared with the unborn ones that used to end up as tasty *bocas* in San José bars.

Playa Grande

Turtles need a wide, sandy beach with ample portions not touched by normal high tides, and Playa Grande fills these requirements admirably. It used to be relatively unpopulated, with few human footprints to disturb the solitude. Until a few years ago, only a handful of homes and one or two tiny motels were to be found near the beach's access roads. Today development is under way. However, as part of the Tamarindo Refuge, the beach area will always be somewhat restricted in tourist development, even though the region's natural beauty and wildness are bound to attract even more people in the future.

One place I looked at was a large, tastefully constructed home with a neatly manicured lawn ending at a beach wall marking the fifty-meter boundary. The owner half-apologized for the home's isolation and lack of anything to do, adding, "The hope of this little community is that things won't change. What we offer here is location, nothing else." He indicated the broad expanse of beach visible through a stand of coconut palms and said, "The whole idea here is to fit into the ecology without disturbing things, particularly not the nesting turtles and their life cycle." The house's window frames were made of wood instead of the more practical aluminum "because metal frames reflect moonlight and confuse the hatchling leatherbacks. We don't allow any lights from our homes to escape at night. For bright lights and nightlife, you have to go to Tamarindo." Since my writing of these lines, a number of bars and restaurants have opened near Playa Grande, and several housing developments are under way.

Local turtle-watchers report some good news: The number of turtles visiting the beaches to lay eggs grows each year, with new turtles joining the flock (or should it be covey? Band? Could it be a herd of turtles?). The numbers still remain below what they were in the 1980s, but locals are hoping this will become a trend.

Playa Tamarindo

Playa Tamarindo begins where Playa Grande ends; a picturesque estuary separates the two. Tamarindo is where leatherback-turtle-watchers find hotels. Launches begin ferrying passengers across the estuary around midnight. Visitors tiptoe quietly along the beach and pause to observe the huge turtles as they awkwardly pull themselves up on the beach to bury their eggs six feet deep in the sand. This is an unforgettable sight; some of these turtles are said to grow to more than twelve feet across and weigh up to 1,500 pounds! The one I watched laying eggs may have been a pygmy; she was barely six feet wide. Our guide claimed that during the peak of the season, as many as 350 turtles can be on the beach in a single night. What an amazing sight!

Because of excellent surfing beaches and nearby Playa Grande turtle beaches, Tamarindo has always been a magnet for tourists of all ages. The coastal region here is easily accessible by pavement rather than gravel and dirt roads. This ensures a steady stream of visitors as well as new residents who often become part of the business community. The new international airport in nearby Liberia has also accelerated development. Arriving passengers no longer have to stay overnight in San José, with a long drive to the coast the next day. An hour or so in a rental car or taxi, and you're on the beach the same day.

Tamarindo's popularity with tourists and expatriate residents has transformed the sleepy village of a few years ago into a busy, highly commercial entity. The town is a textbook example of foreign development of a Costa Rican beach community: totally developed, and with a cosmopolitan mix of nationalities. Almost all businesses—restaurants, hotels, shops, bars, and so forth—are owned by foreigners: North Americans, Italians, Germans, and French, with several other European nations also represented.

Some residents and longtime visitors lament these changes, while others appreciate the presence of upscale restaurants and quality retail and food shopping options, including a supermarket and conveniences that a mere village would lack. While some yearn for the "good old days," Rob Gibson, a Tamarindo homeowner, says: "The surroundings are still spectacular, and the relative success in protecting Playa Grande and the estuary behind it from unbridled development has been key to maintaining its attractions."

A few years ago, a Tamarindo *tico* complained to me: "We keep selling our land and moving farther back into the hills. Now we are working for foreigners on land we once owned. Before long we won't be able to afford to live in our own village!" That prediction has come true; the price of real estate makes property ownership impossible for local families, and hotels are priced out of range for vacationing *tico* families. However, Rob—who speaks Spanish with local working people—observes no general sense of resentment. "Most *ticos* say that tourists and part-time residents are good because they bring money and create jobs in the area. I love the practicality and lack of xenophobia among *Costarriquenses,* and if we *gringos* behave decently, perhaps we can keep it that way." Rob also points out that there are definite advantages to living in an expatriates' enclave. "I don't know how much my *gringo* neighbors would help me in a crisis, but it is nice to have so many of them around."

For those with school-age children, this is the only region outside the Central Valley with an international K–12 college-prep school. Country Day School Guanacaste is a private facility located between Tamarindo and Flamingo. It isn't inexpensive, but as one parent said, "The school is small enough for the teachers to have a one-on-one relationship with their students." There's also a bilingual elementary school, Niños del Mundo, with classes for students from pre-kindergarten to fourth grade.

Playa Junquillal

South of Tamarindo, the coast is lightly populated by foreigners or *ticos*. This is partially due to the seasonal condition of the dirt roads along the coast. Most residents believe that a paved road will be built not too far in the future and that beaches along this coast might have potential for development. A series of beaches front the Pacific along this coast, some with tiny villages, others almost unpopulated. Among the beach villages are: Playa Avellana, Playa Negra, Playa Junquillal, and Playa Lagarto. These beaches are graced by large waves rolling in from the open Pacific and are very picturesque. Since I'm not an expert swimmer and know little about ocean currents, undertow, and riptides, I can't vouch for the safety of these beaches. You'll need to consult local authorities on the subject. This is a sensible practice anywhere in the country.

A place that's attracted our attention is Junquillal, a growing village positioned on one of the longest beaches on the Nicoya Peninsula. The region is known for exceptional surfing waves in the Playa Negra and Junquillal areas. Endangered leatherback and green turtles come ashore to lay their eggs in the sand. Most businesses in the area are owned by Americans, Canadians, Italians, and Germans who are trying to develop more tourism in the area. Meanwhile, residents are hoping that Junquillal doesn't develop to the same extent as the more popular beach towns. One Canadian expatriate said, "We like progress, but we'd prefer to keep the area as a serene place to come for relaxation and the natural beauty."

One small hotel right on the beach is owned by several California couples who take turns managing the establishment as their excuse for a working vacation (presumably tax-deductible). One partner said, "It's a very small operation. We consider a month successful when we don't have to dig into our pockets to make the payroll." A few kilometers from the village center, an elaborate residential development is being purchased exclusively by Canadians and Americans. Construction quality is tops, with all amenities. Since Junquillal has a small population, major shopping and other services are available about forty-five minutes away. There is, however, a mini-supermarket that provides most basic supplies.

BEACHES OF NOSARA

We "discovered" Beaches of Nosara (Playas de Nosara) more than twenty years ago, while researching Guanacaste beach communities on the Nicoya Peninsula. Driving north from Sámara over a dirt road that parallels the ocean beaches, we stumbled on an almost isolated community inhabited exclusively by North Americans and a few Europeans. Because the road was not paved, and several rivers needed to be forded, few tourists bothered to investigate the heavily forested and lightly populated community. Over the years, we've been privileged to see many profound changes to Beaches of Nosara.

Starting at the Nosara River, three lovely beaches and a wildlife reserve extend south along Playa Nosara and Playa Pelada to Playa Guiones. Nosara started as an experiment in a different concept of foreign development. The emphasis was on private homes and pristine beaches rather than tourism and commercial enterprise. Along more than five miles (eight kilometers) of oceanfront, to this day only two small restaurants are located on the beach. As you stroll the ocean's sandy shores, you'll see no discos, fast-food restaurants, miniature golf courses, or other evidence of higher culture. Just beach and jungle. At least for the first 200 meters—after that, all bets are off. There's a possibility that in the future the government could relent and allow building closer to the beach, but residents are hopeful this will never happen.

A major problem has always been that newcomers aren't as ecologically aware as the original owners. Residents and old-timers continually try to educate newcomers about the importance of not cutting down the trees or destroying the animals' habitat. Howler monkeys need regular "trails" through the treetops that they use daily to go from one feeding area to another. Since it is set in the forest, a great deal of the Nosara project was zoned as greenbelt, forever to be public parklands, never to be developed or built upon. Until recently parklands have been sacrosanct, with development verboten. Longtime residents are determined that their parklands remain protected from development. This is their insurance that their unique forest won't be replaced by lawns, T-shirt shops, and condos.

When this book first described Nosara, development was still in its infancy. Services were limited and property prices were very modest, probably one-half to one-third of more accessible beach locations such as

Tamarindo or Flamingo. Then, at the turn of the new century, change began accelerating. New residents began arriving in a steadily increasing stream, looking for homes to buy or construction lots. An astounding amount of commercial construction seems to be going on everywhere. Many original residents shake their heads in disbelief at these radical changes. Others are happy, convinced that this growth will force the government to pave the road. At the present time, it takes an hour to drive the dirt road to the nearest pavement. That doesn't stop newcomers.

SÁMARA AND CARRILLO

A welcome development for those traveling to the Pacific Coast from San José and points inland is the "Friendship Bridge" constructed by the Taiwanese government. This bridge replaced the cumbersome ferry across the Tempisque River. In the time it would take the ferry to cross the wide stretch of water, carrying a limited number of vehicles, a thousand cars and trucks can zip across the bridge. Travel time to the peninsula has been shortened by about an hour. This access is having a profound impact on the development of the entire coast, with Sámara and Carrillo being affected the most.

Much of this area is already developed, particularly in and around Sámara. New hotels and condos are going in, and more expats are building homes south of town, extending toward Carrillo. However, this is only the beginning. As we noted earlier, the Tourism Institute has targeted the Sámara-Carrillo area for high-intensity tourist use. We expect to see some large hotels and probably a resort going in before long. Smaller hotels, restaurants, and shops will naturally follow. If Sámara develops as did Tamarindo, we can expect a large percentage of new businesses to be owned by North Americans. It seems to be working out that way.

Sámara and Carrillo share opposite ends of the same bay, one of the most beautiful imaginable in a country of beautiful beaches. Several long stretches of beach are flanked by a wide road fringed with coconut palms, making the beaches freely accessible to all. At the northern portion of the bay, Sámara attracts more *tico* tourism from the Central Valley area at the moment (on weekends and holidays they arrive by the busloads). Toward Carrillo, more hotels cater to foreigners and are higher priced. This is where the airstrip is, which makes it handy for visitors.

All along this part of the coast, some low mountains sit back about a kilometer from the shore, and here is where many expats make their homes. The views of the bay are magnificent up here, whereas homes built at sea level have views of nothing but trees or the nearby hotel.

An item of interest about Carrillo: A short distance south of the airstrip there is a bridge over a small river where two large crocodiles lurk. Local residents regularly feed them by throwing frozen chicken carcasses tied with nylon line into the river. They then troll the tasty morsels toward the bridge to lure the monsters from their hiding places. Although the river isn't posted against swimming or wading, I would strongly recommend that you refrain from this activity. Naturally, the crocodiles strongly disagree with this advice.

LOWER NICOYA PENINSULA

On the southern tip of the Nicoya Peninsula, a string of beaches with tremendous potential are undergoing development. The beaches run from Naranjo on the Gulf of Nicoya side to Cabo Blanco at the very tip of the peninsula, and then up along the coast via impassable roads, toward Carrillo. Most investors agree that the economic growth between Cabo Velas and Cabo Blanco could be among the best in the country. It all depends upon when (and if) the roads will be made passable.

Getting to this area from the northern part of the peninsula has always been a problem. The paved highway ends abruptly at the little town of Carmona, presenting about a nineteen-mile (thirty-kilometer) stretch of dirt road to the coast. The road paralleling the Pacific Coast dwindles to a trail from time to time, and you have to ford several good-size streams. Even rugged four-wheel drives avoid the coastal route. An easier way is to take a ferry from Puntarenas to Playa Naranjo or Paquera, which shortens the drive considerably. It's possible that the road is currently in much better condition. Make inquiries first.

Playa Tambor

The setting of Tambor is an extraordinarily calm horseshoe bay called Bahía Ballena (Whale Bay). Two long projections of forested and rocky coastline protect beaches from ocean swells. A major tourist attraction used to be the migration of whales into the bay's protected waters during the summer season to give birth. Nowadays, probably because of the increased boating and fishing activity, whales stay further offshore. Bahía Ballena's beaches of dark volcanic sand and shallow water offer perfect swimming for even the most timid of bathers. It's not good for surfing, but it's great for snorkeling and diving. The nearby Curu Wildlife Reserve is known as a place for viewing wildlife and lush vegetation.

This is also the location of a controversial hotel-resort by the Barceló chain. I say controversial because a few years ago the construction caused a maelstrom of controversy, with ecologists accusing the hotel chain of doing damage to the environment. Oddly enough, the huge Playa Tambor resort doesn't seem to affect the atmosphere of the village of Tambor. It's the same laid-back, friendly place as before—ever popular with retired foreigners, who appreciate the conveniences that Tambor offers. You'll find golf, tennis, and a small airport with daily twenty-five-minute flights to San José.

The reason tourism at the expensive resort hasn't affected the town could be the fact that the hotel and grounds are self-contained and guests seldom venture elsewhere. Interesting to note: The hotel enjoys a nice white-sand beach (ecologists complain the sand was imported from elsewhere). The little surf that Tambor beach gets is rather gentle, always peppered with little *tico* children splashing and laughing.

Several gated communities are in place set back on the hillsides, and others presumably are on the drawing boards. A little farther west, the gated community of Tango Mar provides an elegant contrast to funky Playa Tambor. Tango Mar is basically a private (and expensive) resort with deluxe accommodations; it is also a retirement community featuring a small golf course, tennis courts, and a lovely beach.

Montezuma

Located about nineteen miles (thirty kilometers) down the road from Playa Tambor, the village of Montezuma is the entry point to a beautiful string of beaches. A description of "laid-back" or "tranquil" would hardly describe this picturesque little village. It is widely known for its bohemian flair and reputation as a party town. Although many tourists you meet are younger, many residents are older, reliving the continuous party scene of the 1970s. Along Montezuma's main street, you'll see a continuous parade of characters, such as aging hippies, tattooed surfers, and Rastafarians, plus some occasional visitors who seem overwhelmed by it all.

Just a few steps from the hustle and bustle of the town center, you find yourself on Playa Grande, a great place for a walk to secluded coves, tide pools, and sunbathing. The village itself is sheltered by vertical cliffs overgrown with vines and green tropical foliage. Several streams flow down from the hills, creating scenic waterfalls and natural swimming pools. Monkeys, parrots, and other wildlife are frequent visitors.

Montezuma is not only a mecca for backpackers and surfers but also a special retirement place for more mature counterculture people. (Maybe I fall into the latter category, because I've always felt right at home in Montezuma with kindred spirits my age blending into the scene.) It's not for the early-to-bed set, needless to say. *Gringos* who love the Montezuma scene enjoy a lively and active social life; those who covet peace and quiet will probably want to look elsewhere. Residents and businesspeople are very ecology-minded and maintain a continual campaign for clean beaches. The last few miles of road to Montezuma are usually bad during the rainy season.

Malpaís

Malpaís is Spanish for "badlands." The region certainly lives up to its name, with rugged, twisted, and bizarre rock formations breaking the surf as ocean waves crash into spray and foam. Malpaís is said to be one of the better surf destinations in Costa Rica—actually it's at nearby Santa Teresa. The settlements here are located about as far as you can drive around the tip of the peninsula. The road up the other side of the peninsula is just about nonexistent. I've heard people claim they've driven four-wheel drives up the western edge, all the way up the coast to Sámara, but that seems reckless to me.

Along with most of the Nicoya Peninsula's tourist areas, the Malpaís area is continually growing and attracting more retirees and businesses. I can see a promising future for the region if the road is ever paved. The government is eager to develop places such as this and will surely devote whatever resources are available for roads and infrastructure.

Unlike Montezuma, the village of Malpaís can truly be described as tranquil. The area is sparsely settled, with not much in the way of a village commercial center. Rather it's a long collection of houses, restaurants, and small hotels scattered along a gravel road parallel to the ocean. Cabo Blanco Nature Preserve is to the south. Despite the small population, a surprising number of expats live here in houses dotting the beaches, some more cliffs than beach. The area seems to be peaceful and quiet, probably as quiet as Montezuma is noisy. The last time we visited, there were a number of development sites being laid out in anticipation of new expatriate settlers.

MID-PACIFIC COAST

If there is any place in Costa Rica that's bound to bloom with foreign investors and retirees, it would have to be that stretch of beachfront from Jacó to Dominical and, with the recently paved road, south toward Palmar Norte.

Although pretty beaches line the entire Pacific Coast, the Mid-Pacific beaches are the most readily accessible for residents of the populous Central Valley. A short drive or bus ride makes this coast practical for overnight sojourns. A weekend home here is convenient and usable by family and friends, whereas one that requires a five-hour drive over horrible roads might sit vacant most of the year. When the coastal highway has been totally paved and time-saving shortcuts completed, a drive from Escazú or other suburbs will take as little as an hour to Jacó or two hours to Dominical. Today, add an extra hour to allow for the dirt road south of Quepos to Dominical.

Playa Jacó

Very popular with residents of the San José region, Playa Jacó and other nearby beaches offer the most convenient opportunity to enjoy the Pacific Ocean. From the residential resort at Punta Leona to communities south of Jacó, a string of beaches attracts thousands of weekenders for surfing, swimming, and partying. Since Jacó is about a two-hour drive from San José, it's entirely possible to drive here in the morning, enjoy the surf, and be home in time for supper. No surprise that many Central Valley residents have weekend homes here. Several hundred North Americans and many Europeans make their permanent homes here, either seasonally or year-round.

Jacó is the largest and most developed town along this portion of the coast, with about 10,000 year-round inhabitants, with almost double this number during the peak tourist months. The town has everything you need, from good medical care to discos and casinos. The main street is

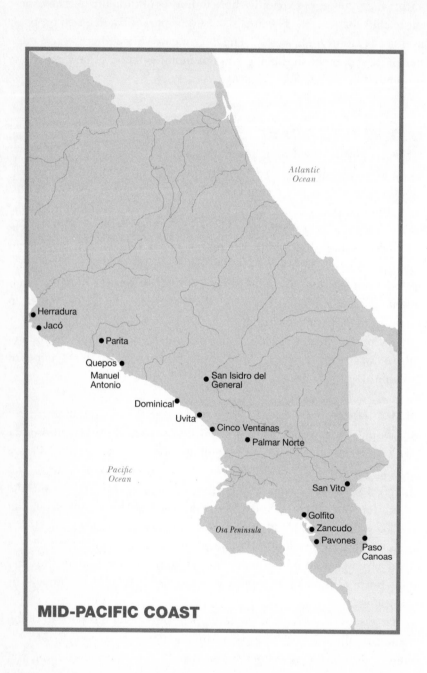

Atlantic
Ocean

Herradura
Jacó
Parita
Quepos
Manuel
Antonio
San Isidro del
General
Dominical
Uvita
Cinco Ventanas
Palmar Norte
Pacific
Ocean
San Vito
Golfito
Osa Peninsula
Zancudo
Pavones
Paso
Canoas

MID-PACIFIC COAST

sprinkled with open-air restaurants where members of the foreign community can be seen socializing, day or evening. Discos, nightclubs, casinos, and salsa bars make Jacó come alive every night. This is especially attractive to the younger crowd, although it may turn off some of the more sedate residents.

Since Jacó is one place where beach property can be owned rather than leased, it's possible to find a home right on the ocean, with beach and surf for your front yard. Jacó's two miles (three kilometers) of beach are fairly pedestrian and uninspiring when compared with beaches such as Manuel Antonio. Instead of white sand, as you might expect in the tropics, the beach here is dark gray, probably of volcanic origin. However, the surf is more than adequate for those more interested in waves than scenery. There have been a few complaints of pollution from a river that empties into the ocean here, but at last report, the municipality is working on a solution.

Many if not most tourist businesses here are owned by *gringos* and Europeans. Some do quite well because the area's many tourist attractions bring streams of visitors in search of adventure. Every surf and nature sport, from surfing to crocodile safaris, ensures plenty of tourist business. Two eighteen-hole golf courses are open to public play here, one at Marriott's Los Sueños resort, a short distance north of Jacó, and another to the south at Quebrada Amarilla, the Tulin Resort.

Playa Herradura

Playa Herradura is smaller than Jacó, enjoys gentler surf, and has more shade trees. At the moment Herradura offers economical tourist hotels and weekend homes for highland residents, both *ticos* and *gringos*. But the town extends a promise of better things to come. For a beachfront community, Playa Herradura boasts property that is reasonable—at least compared with prices at Jacó or Manuel Antonio. Many building lots can be found within walking distance of the beach, and construction is booming. An upscale development known as Los Sueños overlooks Playa Herradura. With its large-scale marina, luxury homes, and condos, Los Sueños raises the general tone of Herradura and brings in more development. An eighteen-hole championship golf course is located in the Los Sueños complex.

About a five-minute drive north of Herradura, Punta Leona has an attractive private club (with day admission for nonmembers) with a complex of condos and cottages owned by retirees and weekenders from the Central Valley. Like Los Sueños in Herradura, there is a very safe feeling about these gated communities, but prices reflect the additional costs of privacy and luxury.

Manuel Antonio

It was the middle of February, and we were sitting with a group of friends in a restaurant overlooking the Pacific. A long, palm-fringed beach stretched out into the distance as far as we could see. Behind us loomed mountains covered with rain forest, sweeping down to accent the beach, with its azure blue water and sparkling surf. The sun was at its zenith, beating directly down with dazzling strength. Two members of our group were complaining about the heat. We consulted a thermometer and found that the temperature was eighty-five degrees. Suddenly they broke into laughter as they realized that Baltimore, their hometown, was dealing with four inches of sleet and snow. Two weeks of Costa Rica's idyllic weather had turned them into indignant complainers over an ordinary day at the beach! We all ordered cold beer served over ice cubes (a Costa Rican tradition) and looked out over the panorama with renewed appreciation for where we were: Costa Rica's famous Playa Manuel Antonio.

Manuel Antonio? What kind of name is that for a beach? According to legend, a husband, worried about his pregnant wife, placed her in a dugout canoe and headed north toward Puntarenas, hoping to find a doctor to deliver the baby. But before they could go very far, the wife went into labor, and they paddled ashore to camp in the shelter of a gentle beach cove. His wife gave birth to a healthy child, whom they named Manuel Antonio; the beach has been called that ever since. Travelers who have visited beaches all over the world swear that Manuel Antonio is the most beautiful of all.

The coastline north of Manuel Antonio is a long shore of golden sand that catches the full force of the Pacific's waves as they roll in from China. Then, at Manuel Antonio Park, a narrow peninsula juts out into the ocean, curving to form two protected coves on either side of the land. Here the waves suddenly become gentle, a place where you can float on your back for an hour without worrying about getting surf in your face. You'll often find a sailboat or two anchored here, gently swaying, resting on the way to the Panama Canal or the big voyage north to Acapulco.

Originally United Fruit Company banana property, the area was made into a national park in 1972 with almost 1,730 acres (700 hectares) of land, partially expropriated, partially donated. The park contains three beaches, each with its own character. The first is Playa Espadilla Norte, which sees occasional riptides, although many people swim here anyway. Next is Playa Espadilla Sur, and then Playa Manuel Antonio, both quite safe for swimming and snorkeling. From the beginning the emphasis has been on preserving the natural beauty and protecting wildlife. Whiteface capuchin monkeys frolic in the trees, competing with arboreal iguanas for food. A tropical storm in 1993 ripped up some of the trees, causing the sloth population to go elsewhere, but other than that the damage was minimal.

Since Manuel Antonio's fame makes it an almost obligatory part of a tourist's itinerary, a bed-and-breakfast or room rentals can be a viable business. Rooms are likely to be rented solidly through the Costa Rican "summer" (December, January, and February) and to have low vacancy rates during the rest of the year. On a past trip we rented an apartment from a woman who came from Florida several years ago to build a small house for herself. She added a couple of rooms for extra income during the tourist season. As the volume of tourism during the off-season increased, she added more rooms until she had a pleasant ten-room hotel, plus two apartments across the road, all with a splendid view of the ocean. "I hadn't considered becoming a hotel owner when I came here," she explained. "It just happened to work out that way."

Over the thirty-plus years that I've been visiting Manuel Antonio, I've seen the most profound changes of anywhere in the country. It has gone from a very rustic, low-density tourist destination to a full-tilt, full-service community. The road from Quepos to Manuel Antonio Park is jam-packed with hotels, restaurants, and other tourist accommodations. Scarcely a square meter of land remains undeveloped. Oddly enough, this doesn't seem to detract one iota from the region's beauty and charm.

Dominical

South of Quepos and Manuel Antonio, along the twenty-eight-mile (forty-five-kilometer) stretch of gravel road to Dominical, you'll find country that is for the most part either palm-oil plantations or flat farming land. This part of the Pacific Coast Highway is a surprise because of the terrible condition it was once in. Until recently it took a full two hours of slow driving and bouncing to navigate the road. However, the road crews have done an impressive job of smoothing roadbed and replacing old, one-way bridges, preparing for pavement. Now the driving time to Dominical is closer to one hour.

Before long the Pacific Coast Highway will be paved all the way to Panama, joining the Inter-American Highway at Palmar Norte. This route will take considerable pressure off the present Inter-American Highway as well as open the region to tourism and development.

As paved roads replace the almost impassable stretches of rock-and-mud obstacle courses, ever-increasing traffic streams along the coast—tourists looking for rooms and retirees buying property. Dominical and its surrounding communities can't help but flourish. As you might guess, many foreign residents prefer things the way they are; they dread the thought of developments and tourists destroying the peace and tranquility that have been theirs for so long. As one man said, "It is funny to think that in a few years we'll be looking back fondly to the time when there were no traffic lights in Dominical."

If you want to drive on pavement, instead of gravel and rock, all the way to Dominical, travel south on the Inter-American Highway and turn toward the Pacific at San Isidro del General, then just follow the signs through town. Because of San Isidro's system of one-way streets, you may have to ask directions by pointing in whichever direction you are going and asking, "Dominical?" Someone will steer you in the right direction.

In its own way, this road is one of the more scenic in all of Costa Rica. The narrow pavement traverses rich farming country, up somewhat steep grades, running along ridges with breathtaking views on both sides of the road, looking into deep valleys where the farmhouses are so distant that they seem like toys. Even during the dry season, the countryside is lushly green, plants heavy with foliage and banana trees shading the roadside. Although the drive is less than twenty-five miles (forty kilometers), it takes about forty-five minutes. That's the way it should be, because the scenery is so spectacular that you might miss something if you could whiz along at top legal speed. Also, the pavement has a way of disappearing from time to time, turning into stretches of gravel road where construction crews are still at work. The problem is not serious; just slow down and relax.

The paved highway ends at the recently paved coastal road at the Barú River, a picturesque mountain stream that empties into a lagoon at this point. A turn to the left, over the river's cement bridge, and you find Dominical. Take the first right turn past the bridge. This is another place I've watched develop over the years, from a sleepy village to an awakening, cosmopolitan community. It is my impression that this region is one of the fastest growing along the coast—at least as far as residential development is concerned. Excellent restaurants and other retail businesses seem to be popping up in response to the growing number of expatriates in the Dominical area.

Dominical's main street follows the river past several rental cabins, motels, restaurants, and businesses. It ends at the beach, where another road follows the shore down to Punta Banda, also known as Roque Azul. Camping beneath a grove of shade trees is free on the edge of the broad, sandy beach of Playa Dominical. Restrooms and showers are strategically spaced along the beach. For the most part, campers are *tico* families and backpackers, but all are welcome. As with anywhere in Costa Rica, be careful of leaving valuables in a tent while you are surfing or dining in a restaurant.

Open ocean surf here is spectacular, booming across the beach, occasionally making swimming hazardous when riptides harass those not used to handling them. "You usually don't realize what is happening," said a longtime resident here. "It seems as though you are staying still in the water, yet the beach is moving away from you. We lose a couple of tourists every year to these tides, and it isn't necessary. Instead of trying to swim against the current, the best thing to do is relax and leisurely swim parallel to the beach, until the shore stops moving away. The current is only a few feet wide. Then work your way back to shore, pausing to float on your back and rest. The water is so warm and salty that you can float all day long and never get tired. There is no reason for anyone to drown in a riptide."

The road from Dominical south to Palmar Norte (where it joins the highway going to the Panamanian border) is brand-new and a marvel compared with the old rock-and-mud nightmare trail of a few years ago. South along this coast, numerous beaches face the open ocean, some with houses or tiny farms, places that will someday become villages. One of the prettiest on this part of the coast is called Punta Dominical. A high point juts out into the ocean, with cliffs and surf reminiscent of California's Big Sur or Spain's Costa Brava. Below a small hotel, cliffs and rocks catch the full force of the ocean's strength as waves crash and send cascades of white foam flying high in the air.

Uvita and Ojochal

Playa Uvita, according to tourist publications, is one of the top six most beautiful beaches in Costa Rica. Long described as a sleepy little village, the town of Uvita has been awakened by the new paved road from Dominical to the Inter-American Highway at Palmar Sur. Rapid development is under way as much prime land is now available for development. According to one report, Uvita now boasts two banks, a new supermarket that offers a wide range of formerly hard-to-get products, a large new furniture store, and a new appliance store. Residents of Uvita and nearby Ojochal no longer have to drive to Palmar Sur for shopping. Newcomers seem to be buying property almost weekly.

A longtime resident named Lillian said, "We looked all over Costa Rica before settling on Uvita. We found a ten-hectare [twenty-five-acre] plot up on the mountainside. Not only do we have a gorgeous view, but there are also six beautiful waterfalls on the property. For me it's like having my own national park." She added, "We are holding it in trust for our two grand-daughters, as a future for them."

Nearby Ojochal, a short drive south of Uvita, is about halfway between Dominical and Palmar Norte. The first time I made the drive from Dominical to Ojochal, in 1993, the trip took two hours of hard driving. Today, with the smoothly paved highway it's just a matter of twenty minutes or so. The road zips on down the coast past areas that not too long ago were seen only by four-wheel-drive daredevils. This growing little paradise village consists of a variety of hotels, restaurants, bars, and various businesses. Ojochal offers many amenities, including a doctor's and a dentist's office, hardware store, supermarket, beauty salon–barbershop, and more. According to locals, the village is growing and attracting newcomers from the United States and Canada. A new hospital is located in Ojo de Agua, just to the south of Ojochal. This is in addition to the hospital in Palmar Norte.

One very interesting place we encountered on a trip to the Osa Peninsula is called Cinco Ventanas, a little north of the village of Ojochal. Even though development here is rather new, there are already 1,400 properties owned by foreigners (only a few live here full-time). A fourteen-unit shopping center, including a small supermarket, gasoline station, and restaurant, serves the area. The majority of the foreign property owners are French-Canadian, but other North Americans are discovering the area and will be moving in as well.

The developer explained why there are so many French-speaking residents: When she and her husband started their project here, they advertised heavily in the Quebec area as an experiment. They sold building lots by mail, with the buyers being assured that if they didn't like the property when they arrived, they could either have their money back or choose another lot. Before long, most of the lots they had were gone, bought by French-speakers. "They just love it here," she said, "and since French is similar to Spanish, they have no problems with language."

Just east of Ojochal and Cinco Ventanas, the mountains quickly rise to more than 3,000 feet (900 meters), probably providing the same kind of "air-conditioning" as in Dominical, with cool breezes coming inland during the hot part of the day and flowing down the mountains at night. By the way, the name Cinco Ventanas (Five Windows) refers to some natural caverns in the cliffs by the water's edge. Residents in this area have exclusive rights to cross the private land between the highway to Playa Ventanas, a small bay with a wide beach and bordered on both sides by rocky cliffs ranging in height from 60 to 200 feet (18 to 61 meters), making this one of the few "private" beaches in the country.

SOUTHERN COSTA RICA

For years I had heard people speak of Golfito and the Osa Peninsula. The area sounded like a place of adventure—panning for gold in forest streams, fishing for trophy sailfish, or hiking rain-forest trails. In order to complete research for this book, I resolved to spend some time around Golfito to collect information. But when I asked folks around San José who either owned property or regularly visited here, I found their answers short and vague, always skirting the subject as if trying to draw my attention elsewhere. When I spoke with a man who owned property on Zancudo Beach, his face burned angrily as he said, "Zancudo is my special place, and I don't want any damned travel writers drawing attention to it! It would destroy things for all of us!"

Obviously, our interview was over, but now I knew I had to go! I jumped in a car and was soon on my way to Golfito, the jumping-off place for the

Pavones–Zancudo Beach area. The drive south on the Inter-American Highway is gorgeous. One unbelievable view after another invites a pause wherever the car can be parked safely off the pavement. Ordinarily the trip takes six hours, but by the time I stopped several times to sample pork *chicharrones,* marvel over the views, and take a nap in the shade of a banana tree, the trip stretched into an eight-hour day.

Golfito

Golfito is the jumping-off place for nearby and regional expatriate communities. This is an often-neglected part of Costa Rica, with scanty information provided by most tourist guides. The town of Golfito began its existence as a banana port for United Fruit Company but was abandoned when a disease damaged the banana crops and the company decided that the operation had become unprofitable. When it was a banana port, there was no incentive to develop it as a tourist attraction, although today the area is trying hard to do so.

The town itself can hardly be described as anything but picturesque. It looks like a cliché movie set of a banana-shipping port. Just a few blocks wide, the town follows the water's edge, with some houses actually standing over the water on stilts and others clinging to the cliffs and hanging out into empty space. A couple of excellent hotels accommodate the growing number of curious tourists, but many lodgings are rather ordinary to downright rustic. They are often full with Costa Rican shoppers who take advantage of the port's duty-free warehouse. From the slope of a low mountainside overlooking the town, a rain forest serves as a wildlife preserve and watershed, ensuring Golfito a pure water supply.

Golfito's main commercial street, looking delightfully ramshackle and picturesque, climbs a hill that parallels the highway and waterfront. Foreign residents patronize a couple of open-air restaurants here, as well as hardware stores, shops selling tackle and boating supplies, and several red-light bars. A surprising number of North Americans live in or around Golfito. A few actually live in town, but most have places scattered along the shores of Golfo Dulce and commute via motorboat. Ferries commute between Puerto Jiménez and to Zancudo. You'll often see expats hanging out in the restaurants in the commercial area or along the waterfront. Ask around to find out which are the favorite haunts of the day.

The government is working hard to bolster the economy in this region, trying to attract new businesses to fill the void left when United Fruit abandoned ship. One popular program that brings hoards of residents into Golfito: duty-free warehouses. Anybody, resident or tourist with a passport, can obtain a permit to enter these warehouses and purchase a wide variety of goods duty-free. To make sure that Golfito tourist facilities gain from this, buyers must register the day before—thus ensuring that they will spend money on meals and accommodations. You are allowed $500 per person tax-free every six months.

Another project that helps local commerce is a Free Trade Zone, a special place for manufacturing and exporting by Costa Rican and foreign businesses. Those operating within the zone's coverage are exempt from some taxes and customs on importation of raw materials, components, and parts. This should attract investors who would like to take advantage of the tax breaks and the availability of good local workers.

Zancudo Beach

Although Golfito is the central focus of the area, many North Americans prefer to live nearby rather than in the town. Their homes and business interests are in nearby villages or on isolated bays around the Golfo Dulce. Playa Zancudo is one of the secluded communities that attracts expatriates. It's a relatively small village stretching along one sandy street with a handful of restaurants, cabin rentals, and a small hotel or two. The black-sand beach is backed by homes not far from the water's edge but concealed from the view of swimmers and surfers by the usual coconut and strangler fig trees. Zancudo is a popular place for local *ticos* to come to swim on weekends. Unlike Pavones, the famous surfing beach to the south, Zancudo's beach is very swimmable, with gentle surf.

Several bars and restaurants serve as social centers, with occasional weekend dances. A stop at any of the local open-air restaurants will usually find a table or two of North Americans or Europeans discussing local news and making plans for the development of their properties. Paving the road is a common topic. Those who own homes along the beach shudder in horror at the image of the throngs of tourists, property buyers, and developers a paved highway will surely bring. They feel that since they have discovered this part of Costa Rica, it is rightly theirs, and it would be downright rude for others to crowd in. (I'm exaggerating, of course. Residents of Zancudo are as gracious as you will find anywhere.) Actually, those who have businesses, who depend on tourists and new residents to make their enterprises grow, eagerly look forward to the road and the increased prosperity popularity brings. Property owners are delighted to see values of their holdings increasing.

We spoke with several folks who routinely come here for three months or longer every year. A house or a cabin with a small kitchen, right on the beach, can usually be found at reasonable rents during the off-season. By all means, stay for a couple of months before deciding to invest or build, get to know the other expatriates, and know whether you will find enough compatible friends. This will also give you the opportunity to talk with local residents and get the latest on land values and who has properties for sale.

A local resident remarked, "Everyone wants to come here in the winter months [referring to winter and summer in the North American sense]. People seem to think that summer is a total monsoon. But the weather is wonderful then. It's actually a little cooler during June, July, and August. Every morning is sunny, and at least part of the afternoon is usually rain-free. Often it doesn't rain at all." The hottest month of the year is March, according to local residents, just before the rainy season gets started.

Buses and stake-bed trucks bring families from nearby towns on weekends, loaded with children eager to enjoy the beach. The waves are gentle, the water's warm, and the kids are in danger of nothing worse than sunburn. An easier way to get here is by water taxi from Golfito. Schedules vary with the tides.

The shortest way to the beach is a two-hour drive over a gravel and sometimes-rocky trail. This same road splits off and goes to Zancudo's sister beach to the south, Pavones. During the rainy season this route requires a four-wheel-drive vehicle, and it's not all that great in the summer. Maps don't help much in finding either Zancudo or Pavones. I have three different maps; for all practical purposes they might as well have been of three different countries, because each has a different version of the road system, none approaching reality. It's best to stop often and make inquiries.

San Vito

Shortly after World War II, Luigi Sansonetti and his three sons, from Italy, decided to investigate Costa Rica as a place for a new beginning, away from the chaos of postwar Europe. They fell in love with a beautiful valley surrounded by mountains and rain forests. Their discovery was in the canton of Coto Brus, just north of the Panamanian border, in one of the coastal mountain ranges of the southern region. At 3,200 feet (975 meters) above sea level, with cool mountain breezes and ample rainfall, this seemed to be the perfect place to grow coffee and begin life anew.

They notified friends and relatives back in Italy of their discovery and invited them to relocate here. Before long, Italian immigrants were settling the town of San Vito de Coto Brus and planting coffee on the hillsides. It wasn't easy. The pioneers suffered hardships as they established their colony: hand-sawing huge trees for lumber and cutting them into boards to build houses; no electricity; little food; having to wait for three years for coffee to be ready for harvesting. Partly by courage but mostly by stubborn determination, they survived.

Fortunately, in the early 1950s the world market for quality Costa Rican coffee was at an all-time high. Coffee plantations could not help but prosper. Their economic success is reflected in San Vito's infrastructure today and in the quality of homes and farms surrounding the town. You'll find banks, supermarkets, Internet centers, great restaurants and bakeries, and taxi service, as well as a hospital and nearby airport. A charming plaza in the town center makes a pleasant place for young people to congregate and residents to relax.

San Vito's population today is around 10,000, and the town still displays prosperity, even though the coffee market tanked several years ago. Many of the original families have moved on, but they've left their mark on today's population. Around the square and in outdoor cafes, you'll see beautiful young people with faintly olive-colored skin and strikingly beautiful gray-blue eyes characteristic of regions in Italy. You'll often hear Italian spoken. You might hear *ciao* instead of *adios* when someone says goodbye.

San Vito's best restaurants are Italian, as you might expect. One is the dining room of the popular Hotel Ceibo, where lasagna, scaloppini, and other traditional dishes are served. The owner, Antonio Papili, was one of the original settlers; he was five years old when his family emigrated from Italy. He is proud of his heritage, and it doesn't take much encouragement for Antonio and his wife, Carmen, to talk about the old days.

I have to admit that I had reservations about including San Vito in this book. Why? Because I made friends with some of the North Americans who've relocated here, and because some worried that publicity might cause a land rush, bringing hordes of new residents, along with some unde-sirables. I gained their grudging support when I pointed out two things: First, adding a few new residents would only increase their support group of English-speaking neighbors, and second, the undesirables they have in mind are the types who prefer the action of beachfront discos and all-night reggae or rap music. All of which are extremely rare in San Vito.

I am convinced that it will be some time before we'll see surfboards and party animals elbowing aside the two-dozen or so expatriates in res-idence in San Vito. The most exciting things to do here are: gazing at breathtaking vistas of the mountainous Amistad International Park and the volcano across the Panama border; visiting the nearby, world-famous Wilson Botanical Gardens; and having cocktails at homes of other San Vito expatriates.

8

The Caribbean Coast

The same mountain chain that creates the delightful temperate weather in Costa Rica's highlands separates the country into eastern and western tropical zones. Because of this separation, the Caribbean and the Pacific zones have dissimilar personalities. Not only will you find differences in weather patterns and varieties of animal, plant, and marine life, but distinctive cultural differences as well. The Caribbean is Jamaican/African; the Pacific is Latin/European.

The word "tropics" implies long stretches of deserted beaches with thick jungle hovering at the edge of the sand. It means monkeys jostling branches in the strangler fig trees while parrots, macaws, and a thousand other birds screech, twitter, and sing lyrically in the sunset. Costa Rica's Caribbean Coast has all of the above and much more.

Often referred to as the Talamanca Coast, it consists of two distinct regions. The northern half is almost uninhabited, visited mostly by fishing fanatics, tourists, and ecology students. (Incidentally, Costa Ricans usually refer to this entire coast as the "Atlantic" rather than the "Caribbean.") The southern coast is populated with a mixture of Jamaican culture and black, white, and Indian races, creating a distinct type of *tico* personality.

The northern inland lagoons and waterways are famous for world-class fishing of all kinds. Record-size tarpon and snook are routinely hooked in these scenic jungle rivers and inlets. The best snook angling is usually from the shore, around river mouths, with twenty- to thirty-pounders not uncommon. Anglers also bring in jacks, mackerel, barracuda, snapper, and other species when fishing the Caribbean Coast. While waiting for exciting action, you are treated to the sight of monkeys frolicking in the trees, an occasional parrot or toucan darting among the branches, and sometimes a crocodile lurking along the shoreline. The Tortuguero area is known as an important nesting place of the endangered green sea turtle.

THE CARIBBEAN COAST

No passable roads enter this northern region; the only way to get here is by airplane or motor launch. My belief is that the area is far too isolated and the climate too humid for development other than ecotourism projects.

SOUTHERN CARIBBEAN

The southern Caribbean Coast attracts surfers, snorkelers, and reggae enthusiasts, as well as ordinary tourists and ecology buffs who want to savor the unique tropical environment. Weather patterns here are unpredictable, with no sharp distinction between winter and summer. Rain can fall at any time and usually does. Winds often blow down from the north, sometimes causing the Caribbean Coast to replicate Miami's weather. The plus side of the Caribbean weather is that things stay green and lush year-round, unlike the Pacific Coast, where it seldom rains between December and May. The downside is that this weather is always more humid, and insects tend to grow healthy and robust on this edge of the continent.

There is a tendency among North American expatriates to view this region with suspicion due to crime and drug use. There have been a couple news stories of crimes that did severe damage to the tourist image. However, those who live here paint an entirely different picture. They point out that these incidents can happen anywhere, and just by chance they occurred in their region.

Our experience with this area is limited to short stays and visits with friends, never staying more than a few weeks at a time. Therefore I felt it would be best to get opinions from folks who actually live here before making recommendations for relocation. We've interviewed several expatriates who live on the Caribbean Coast for their views and recommendations. One person—who prefers to be called "Expat Hatch"—lives near Puerto Viejo and had the following to say about the eastern coast of Costa Rica:

"The Talamanca Coast (not Limón city, but from Hone Creek to Puerto Viejo, then down to Manzanillo) to me represents what *pura vida* is all about: the jungle, the beach, the environment, and the people. It's a unique mix that you either love or you hate. I happen to love it.

"Yes, there is the Caribbean drug corridor, but the serious things that go down remain largely invisible—just don't get involved. And yes, you may find yourself feeling even more laid-back after breathing the ganja-laden collective cloud coming from backpacker and surfer hangouts and wafting over the area from Playa Negro to Playa Cocles. But if crime were truly serious here, you wouldn't see the elderly *gringo* ladies who live here riding their bikes up and down the road with smiles on their faces.

"I personally believe that most of the negative hype about the Caribbean side boils down to culture shock. Things are definitely not clean and tidy there. Limón is a third-world city populated by Caribbean descendants of Jamaica, Panama, and Nicaragua. If that's not what you want to experience, then don't go there, because it's not been prettied up for tourism at this point.

"But as you go from Limón down the Talamanca coast, you will meet a broad mix of people: *ticos,* indigenous Indians, Jamaicans, Panamanians, Nicaraguans, and Europeans such as German, French, Polish, and Italian. It truly becomes a rainbow soup of humanity, which I personally think makes it that much more interesting.

"But *pura vida* does have a price here—forget making a list of twenty things to do in the day. Because you'll only get two of them done if you're lucky. Things are more primitive here. I just smile, say *"¡Pura vida!"* to myself and chalk it up to the universe forcing me to slow down after working seventy-hour weeks in the US rat race for so many years. The bottom line for me is that I can sit in a hammock, writing on my laptop, with the beach in front of me, the jungle behind me, and howler monkeys making awesome sounds while they meander through the trees in my backyard. That's why I moved to Costa Rica—not for conveniences."

Limón

The city of Limón, a two-and-a-half-hour drive from San José, is probably where Columbus sighted the American mainland for the first time back in 1502. Since nothing of value was found, the explorers moved on, leaving this coast to the native Indians. Later, scattered villages cropped up where bananas were grown for export. Until a railroad was constructed from San José to Limón, the area was mostly ignored by those living in the highlands. Many of the settlers were English-speaking Jamaicans of African descent. They came to work on the banana plantations and later to build the railroad.

At best, the city of Limón has always been a ramshackle affair—a tropical banana port, too large to have the charm of a small town, yet too small to offer the amenities of a real city. The population is predominately black, and the major business here is related to shipping. Not many expatriates will care to relocate here, in my opinion.

Having exposed my bias toward Limón, I must point out that there are those who disagree with me. A number of North Americans who reside in the community testify to the charm and friendliness of their African/ Jamaican neighbors. Racial tensions, resentment, and animosity that are so common in some US cities are virtually unknown here. The social atmosphere here is relaxed, friendly, and neighborly. In fact, Costa Rican race relations and attitudes toward citizens of color are very different from those in many other parts of the world. Because many people in Limón speak perfect Spanish as well as English (with a British-Jamaican accent), those with education are much in demand in the business world since they can communicate with London, New York, or Geneva (English being the lingua franca of business today) and deal with North Americans and Europeans who speak very little Spanish.

The number of foreigners living in Limón is difficult to ascertain. I asked a friend who lives in Limón to make an estimate, and he replied, "I can't put a solid number on the expats here, but we just celebrated Thanksgiving with about twenty-five of them. We had a great dinner with turkey and all the trimmings—a full-blown Turkey Day, including watching football. I've met teachers in the Caribbean School [English-Spanish], Peace Corps people, semi-retirees, evangelical missionaries, and ship's chandlers [people who are commissioned to buy or supply provisions for all the freighters that come into port]. We have also run into a few retired people who have been here for many years and still haven't learned any Spanish."

Cahuita

More than 150 years ago, the beaches of Cahuita and Puerto Viejo were uninhabited except for the seasonal campsites of Miskito Indians who followed the migration of green and hawksbill turtles. ("Miskitos" are a mixture of native Indians and escaped African slaves who fled Jamaica and Cuba to settle the coasts of Nicaragua and Panama.) The newcomers named their camp *Cahuita*, which means "Point of blood trees" in Miskito dialect, because of the large number of blood trees growing on the promontory now known as Cahuita Point.

The region remained uninhabited until the late 1800s, when William Smith, an English-speaking Afro-Caribbean who came from Panama every year to fish and hunt turtles, decided to build a permanent home on Cahuita's beach. He was joined by a group of Jamaicans who originally came as construction workers on the railway from Limón to San José. In addition to working on the United Fruit Company's banana plantations, the settlers worked at subsistence farming, hunting, fishing, and small-scale cultivation of cocoa. Settlers here were pretty much self-sufficient, having had little contact with the rest of Costa Rica. (In fact, for many years the central government prevented people from the coast from traveling to the highlands for fear of spreading yellow fever and malaria.) The first road to Cahuita didn't connect with the outside world until 1976. This isolation enabled people here to preserve their African-Jamaican-Caribbean heritage and bring it intact into the twenty-first century.

Because English is the area's first language (usually spoken with a delightful Jamaican patois), the spot is favored by tourists and visitors who don't want to bother learning another language during their stay. The genuine lack of racial tension here is refreshing for those of us who have been used to the self-imposed social barriers and chasms of hostility that separate black from white in some areas of the United States. I personally feel welcome here and enjoy basking in the warmth of genuine hospitality.

The village of Cahuita is a three-hour scenic drive from San José. It's about four hours by bus. The village's Afro-Caribbean setting has a picture-book quality. Many houses stand on stilts to discourage insects, as is the custom in African and Caribbean villages. These buildings tend to be painted with bright, contrasting pigments similar to flamboyant island styles. Slender, colorfully dressed women and girls carry bundles on their heads with grace and enviable posture. It's easy to imagine you are in an African seashore village.

The main road follows the shore, past black-sand beaches and coral reefs to the north and past more coral and beaches of yellow sand to the south. Along the yellow-sand beach is Cahuita National Park, a long stretch of jungle complete with howler monkeys (which the Costa Ricans call *congos*), feisty parrots, and wildlife of all descriptions. A foot trail parallels the beach through a thick tangle of tropical trees, vines, and orchids. Butterflies, orange and purple land crabs, and iguanas keep you company on the hike.

Many North Americans and Europeans live here year-round, some operating successful businesses. Others regularly arrive in November and head home by May. I had the good fortune to meet a young Californian couple that invited me to visit their winter quarters in Cahuita. They lived in a picturesque, thatch-roofed cabin perched next to a coral reef and shaded by graceful coconut trees. Their house was very rustic, with minimal furniture, but they enjoyed their winter home immensely. Surf washed over rocks in front of the home, spilling into a small depression of smooth black coral where their children played in their own private saltwater swimming pool.

Puerto Viejo

The village of Puerto Viejo is a ten-minute drive south of Cahuita by road and somewhat less by the beach trail. To make matters a bit confusing, there are two Costa Rican places called Puerto Viejo. The one here is formally called Puerto Viejo de Limón, and the other is a small river town in the northeast, near La Selva Reserve: Puerto Viejo de Sarapiquí.

This Puerto Viejo, on the southern Caribbean Coast, used to be much sleepier than its sister village of Cahuita. Things have changed, with surfers, Rastafarians, and tourists of all descriptions now thronging through the town. Puerto Viejo has the reputation of being one of the hippest spots in Costa Rica. When discos are going full tilt, especially on weekends, you might find it impossible to find a room. Young visitors and adventure seekers, mostly from North America and Europe, crowd the streets in the evening, visiting bars and restaurants throbbing with reggae music.

Yet, intermingled with the under-twenty-five crowd, an older generation of expatriates has its own parallel scene. Dozens of retirees, residents, business owners, and seasonal visitors age fifty and way above live here, many of their homes just steps from the main street action. They blend in with the younger generation as smoothly as cream and coffee liquor.

There's no question that the beaches here are much nicer than Cahuita, as is the case down the coast, toward the Panamanian border. Not only that, the businesses, bars, restaurants, and so forth are just steps from the beach, often visible through palm trees from the bar stool where you are sitting. An additional attraction is that homes can be built anywhere within 328 feet (100 meters) of the surf, a happy condition of which many local people take full advantage. However, in 2012 the government threatened to dismantle the houses and businesses located within the prohibited zone. Of course, everyone raised a ruckus. Their point was that these houses and businesses were built before the laws prohibiting construction in the zones were passed. The destruction was postponed, and hopefully a resolution to the problem will be forthcoming.

WHY THE CARIBBEAN COAST?

People who love Cahuita and Puerto Viejo will tell you that the rest of Costa Rica is too tame for them. They prefer this movie-set tropical ambience: romantic, picturesque, and inexpensive. One bar in the very center of Cahuita features on its front porch extraordinarily powerful loudspeakers blaring Jamaican rock music day and night. The volume was such that it rattled windows a block away and peeled the paint off passing automobiles. I love to visit here, but for long-term living in the tropics, my personal preference would be the Pacific Coast. It's my age, I suppose.

Others have a completely different take of lifestyles on the Caribbean. To get yet another viewpoint and perspective, I took advantage of my friendship with a couple who make their home in Puerto Viejo by asking how they made their decision. The couple had moved here from Arizona a few years ago and said that numerous other people had e-mailed similar questions about living on Costa Rica's east coast. They wanted to know the "whys" of choosing the Caribbean side rather than other, more popular, sections of the country. Here's what the husband (Doug) had to say about living here:

"We made our decision from the position of someone who wants to live on or very near a beautiful, tropical beach. We realize we're in the minority, since many more people prefer the Pacific beaches. Our viewpoint is sort of a Caribbean versus Pacific comparison, so here it is:

"We honestly believe that the southern Caribbean Coast is the best-kept secret in this entire country. The half-hour drive from Cahuita down through Puerto Viejo and Manzanillo and to the Panamanian border takes you past some of the most beautiful beaches we've ever seen, with white sand and palm trees, where the jungle comes right down to the shoreline. For the most part, the beaches are almost deserted. You can have a whole cove all to yourself if you want.

"On the last short stretch of this section, south of Manzanillo to the border, there's hardly even a road! You can walk along an easy trail right on the beach, and you see nobody. Beaches here are spectacular, clean, unspoiled—if you feel like skinny-dipping in crystal-clear, warm water, knock yourself out!

"Weather is another important factor: seventy degrees early in the morning and then about eighty-five degrees in the afternoon—that's all twelve months of the year! We don't keep blankets on the bed, just a couple of sheets. The downside is that there is no defined dry season. It can rain anytime, but the showers are usually short, and the rain is always warm.

"Another reason for choosing this area is the price of land. It's much cheaper than just about any place the Pacific side. Our house is 100 meters (the legal limit) from the beach, sitting back in the jungle. When we relax on our veranda, we can hear the ocean, but we can't see it. On all four sides of the house, trees grow very high and lush with vegetation—all you can see is green. In the front yard we frequently see three-toed sloths, iguanas, parrots, gorgeous blue morphus butterflies, and more. I'm the first to admit that this is not paradise, but it is damn close to it.

"We had the house built a few years ago: two bedrooms, one bath, a little more than 1,300 square feet, with a huge veranda out front, a covered carport, and gorgeous hardwood floors (we sort of splurged on that). Total cost of land and building was about $45,000. Try doing that over in Tamarindo, with just a minute's walk to the beach!

"Another reason we love it here: Small villages are cool places where everyone knows everyone else. When we go into the grocery store, the hardware store, or the bank, they call us by name. That's a touch you just don't find anymore. Yes, I've read about how crime is so bad on this side of the country, but I really have no idea where all that comes from! Sure, petty theft is 'alive and well' over here (as it is everywhere); we've had hiking boots and other items taken from our porch when we were foolish enough to leave them out at night. But neither our house nor our car has ever been broken into. (By the way, we do not have bars on any of our doors or windows. I refuse to live in a prison.) We feel perfectly safe strolling through the village at night or walking along the beach at any hour. We do it all the time; we just use common sense.

"Maybe the main reasons we chose this coast are the attitude of the people and the laid-back lifestyle. There's a very strong Jamaican 'yeah, Mon' sort of thing here; it's unlike anywhere else in Costa Rica. You almost get the feeling that time stood still on this coast. They say it looks pretty much the way it did forty years ago. On the other hand, you'll find places on the Pacific side where, if you didn't know better, you'd think you were in San Diego or Hawaii. Thank God, the big resorts and commercial developers haven't discovered this place yet.

"I will be the first to agree that this coast is not for everyone: no shopping centers, no movie theaters, no golf courses. But that is exactly why we live here! If we had wanted all of that other stuff, we would have stayed in the States! To sum it up in terms of my sixties generation: 'If you were a yuppie, you belong on the Pacific side. If you were a hippie, come on over here!'"

9

A Healthy Country

Costa Rica is a healthy place to live. The United Nations noted that Costa Rica is in first place in Latin America for the development of preventive and curative medicine, ranking with the United States and Canada among the twenty best in the world. Infant mortality is lower in Costa Rica than in the United States, and the average life expectancy is longer than in the United States. This is not happenstance: The Costa Rican government spends a great deal of money on health care.

For example, in many developing countries, you play a game of Russian roulette every time you choose a restaurant. A dining room can look wonderful, with white tablecloths, gleaming silverware, and tuxedo-attired waiters, but the kitchen can be a virtual cesspool. Not so in Costa Rica. If a restaurant looks good, then its kitchen will probably be just as nice. I've found very few places where I would hesitate to eat, and I've never been served spoiled food. This is due in some measure to the high quality of the underground water supply but also to the *ticos'* natural inclination toward neatness and order. The level of cleanliness of Costa Rican restaurants is remarkable. This is reinforced by frequent visits by health inspectors to make sure that the normal *tico* cleanliness is maintained.

Another factor in restaurant safety is the relative scarcity of houseflies in most parts of Costa Rica. Since this is the tropics, you might expect to see more insects than you would in the temperate zones of North America, and you do, but in balance. For some reason you'll see remarkably few houseflies, true villains in spreading intestinal disease. In San José and other towns on the Central Plateau, you can eat outside at a sidewalk cafe without sharing your lunch with flies. This seems strange to visitors from North America's Midwest, where the fly population blooms in the summer to a plague. Yes, an occasional fly might drift past, curious as to what you are having for lunch and hoping to join you, but nothing like you expect back home in the summer.

The same thing goes for mosquitoes: In the dry season they are as scarce as houseflies. In many areas of Costa Rica, people don't use window screens. (I wouldn't advise this, because you never know what kind of critter might be attracted to house lights in the evening.) However, when in an area where dengue fever is known, mosquito repellent is essential. Mosquitoes can carry this flulike illness, which has also appeared in the southeastern United States. So far it's affected only a few parts of Costa Rica, around Puntarenas and Cañas. A continuing campaign to wipe out the particular mosquito that carries the virus is under way.

One health condition that never fails to impress visitors: You can drink the water. Unlike most Mexican and Central American cities, safe drinking water is the rule rather than the exception. Most small towns have excellent-quality water, as do most hotels, where drinking water comes from safe wells. As part of its commitment to serving the public, the Costa Rican government spends large sums of money on water and sewage treatment. All water systems, even private ones used by only a handful of people, are strictly monitored. Every two months, at a minimum, tests are made for purity and submitted to the government agency overseeing water control.

COSTA RICAN MEDICAL CARE

The US health-care system, with its exclusion of more than forty million citizens from the ranks of the medically insured, is a major reason some folks think favorably about living in a country where health care is not only available but affordable. In a typical US hospital, for example, patients with Medicare coverage usually pay more for the deductible share of an operation than the total surgical and hospital bill might cost in Costa Rica.

Should you visit an emergency room in the United States, you have to provide proof of a hospitalization plan or a personal credit card. If you have neither, you could be told to get lost. If you have Medicare, you will find a growing number of doctors who won't accept you as a patient. When someone goes to an emergency room in any government hospital in Costa Rica, there is no mandatory charge for resident, visitor, or even someone in the country illegally. If you can pay, they appreciate it, but you will never be turned away. This affordable medical system is another of the benefits

Costa Rica enjoys because there is no military or defense industry to absorb resources. Statistics show that the general level of care is equal or superior to that in the United States—and it's available to all citizens, not just those who can afford premiums.

Obviously, the level of health care and facilities cannot be the same in rural and isolated communities as in the metropolitan area of San José. Yet the government tries. To ensure that most villages have medical backup, a system of mandatory medical service sends newly graduated doctors to remote or rural settings for a one-year period. These new doctors have to work for minimum wages for this time as a way of repaying the country for the education received in state universities.

Why is quality health care inexpensive in Costa Rica? A prominent physician (in private practice in San José) explained it this way: "Here, our government considers medical care a public service and obligation, just as it considers education and highways a public responsibility. The government builds hospitals and trains medical specialists to serve the people, not as a business. But in the United States, medical care is a profit-making industry, a big business where profits are maximized to the highest point people can pay. Here, a doctor working for a government clinic earns between $2,000 and $4,000 a month. In the USA, where doctors work for profit, $20,000 a month is more common."

The doctor went on to say, "Where there is no competition, medical specialists can charge what they like. But here in Costa Rica, we have competition between our free public hospitals and private clinics staffed with private doctors such as mine. We private doctors must keep our fees in line or we lose our patients to free clinics."

MEDICAL BILLS

In San José a routine visit to a private physician's office costs between $35 and $70. Specialists tend to charge toward the upper end of the scale. A day in a first-class private hospital can cost less than $300. Hospital food is excellent, by the way, not the skimpy, tasteless food we're used to in US hospitals, but delicious food and usually more than you can eat. That $300 rate is at one of the country's better hospitals—for a private room, a private bath, and a color television, plus an extra bed and meals for an *acompañate* (a companion). It's customary for a family member or friend to spend the night in your room after an operation or when you are in serious condition, at no extra charge.

If you are willing to put up with sharing a bath with the room next door and can do without your own private phone, the daily room cost can drop to almost half. Think about it: A day in a first-class hospital in Costa Rica costs the same as an ordinary hotel room in New York City! Compare these prices with those in your community. In the United States, if you can get out of a hospital for less than $2,000 a day just for the room, consider yourself lucky.

MEDICAL INSURANCE

An appreciable number of folks decide on Costa Rica residency because of the country's excellent and affordable health-care system. This applies particularly to those quitting their jobs and retiring before the magic age of sixty-five, when Medicare kicks in. With no health-care benefits coming from the workplace, early retirees join the forty-million-plus US citizens who face total disaster should a life-threatening illness or an accident strike.

There are two systems of medical insurance available in Costa Rica for residents: the government's INS insurance monopoly coverage and the government's Social Security system. Some people choose to belong to both plans, for reasons that will be explained later. Understand, Medicare is not valid outside of the United States.

The government insurance plan costs around $50 a month for men under age fifty-nine, and around $85 a month for men between the ages of sixty and seventy-five. The plan covers 70 percent of examinations, doctor visits, prescription drugs, hospitalization, and 100 percent of surgeons' and anesthetists' fees, up to a limit of $17,500. You can choose your own doctor, which is important. Over age seventy-five, you cannot apply for coverage. Dependants under nineteen years old pay about $22 per month; women between ages nineteen and fifty-nine pay about $75 a month, and women sixty to seventy-four pay about $110 monthly. Therefore, a couple in their early sixties would be paying under $200 a month for excellent coverage, impossible to match in the United States. (All of the quoted payments were valid at time of writing. They are subject to change over time, and depending on individual status.)

Several clubs and organizations offer insurance with a group discount (usually 10 percent). Among these are the Association of Residents of Costa Rica (ARCR), the American Legion, and the Canadian Club; sometimes a property owners' association can obtain the discount. Most plans allow you access to any doctor, hospital, clinic, lab, pharmacy, or provider of medical goods and services of your choice. Under other policy plans, you are given a list of affiliated providers.

Foreign residents can also "buy into" the Social Security system (*Caja*, as it's called in Costa Rica) by paying as little as $37 per month for a family where the principal insured person is over fifty-five years of age, and $60 per month where the principal insured is under the age of fifty-five. It may sound odd that younger policy holders pay more than older ones, but this is because if you're younger than fifty-five, your premium includes a compulsory pension fund payment. Presumably, at some time you will receive this back.

However, since Costa Rica's Social Security medical care is almost free, it isn't surprising to find the public system well used and crowded. When people don't feel quite up to snuff, they traipse off to the hospital to see a doctor. This means long waits. For emergency treatment there is no problem—you are seen immediately—but for an ordinary office visit with a government doctor, you could find yourself standing in line or sitting in the waiting room for a long while. And you don't have a choice of doctors. For elective surgery, you can expect a wait of several months for your turn.

However, there is a better way. By joining both systems, you can use your personal family doctor who is in both public and private practice. That way you can see your private doctor by making an appointment whenever you have a minor problem and paying for an office visit. But if something expensive comes up, such as a major operation, your doctor will check you into the government hospital for free treatment—and you will be treated by your personal doctor.

Even if you don't choose to have medical insurance, costs are ridiculously low compared with those in the United States. For example, in San José the typical bill for a gallbladder operation is $2,500, and for an appendectomy, $1,200 to $1,800. Again, for those with Medicare, be aware that you're not covered outside the United States. If something really serious comes up, you can always fly back to the States and use your Medicare benefits.

All expatriates we interviewed swear by the quality of Costa Rican medical care. A friend told me: "I've had good and bad experiences with the *Caja*. I had an emergency appendectomy, got great treatment, speedy, all good, that would have been a whopping $300 out of pocket if I had not had the *Caja* (at Hospital Mexico)."

Another says, "My son has had excellent care since birth for his hyperthyroid condition, and an operation he had for frozen head plates came out fine. Hospital de Niños is first-rate. But my cancer situation was different. I had a couple of small operations, then went out of the system for a third, because I felt I was not getting the kind of care I needed. My out-of-pocket for massive surgery (radical neck dissection), six hours in the O.R. at Clinica Biblica, whole thing, O.R., surgeon (US residency at U Michigan and U Miami, head and neck ontological surgery specialty), anesthesiologist, two nights at the hospital, excellent service, food, care, etc., was $6,000, and subsequent radiation at a state-of-the-art outpatient center was $3,000."

DUAL SYSTEM FOR DOCTORS

After graduating from medical school, many Costa Rican doctors go to universities in the United States for further study and to do residencies. This is particularly true for specialists. Since Costa Rica is such a small country, there aren't enough patients with the same problem to give a doctor the opportunity to see the wide variety of patients needed to get experience in his or her specialty.

I asked a physician from the United States who had retired to Costa Rica some years ago, "Why would a Costa Rican doctor who does a residency in the United States or Canada return here to work for Costa Rican medical earnings?"

"You have to understand," he replied, "that most doctors only work half-time for the government. The rest of the time, they work for themselves. Take the case of a cardiologist who charges $50 an office visit. If this doctor sees five patients a day, that's $250 a day, or about $50,000 a year, plus his salary from the government. Many doctors in the United States have to pay two or three times that amount just for malpractice insurance. When you consider that income taxes and the cost of living are far less here, and that high malpractice premiums aren't necessary, a large percentage of the doctor's earnings are available for savings or investment. Even though Costa Rican doctors earn a fraction of what US doctors do, they live here just as well or better. And the best part is, they get to live in Escazú instead of Kalamazoo!"

SAN JOSÉ HOSPITALS

Three large Social Security–system hospitals provide San José with round-the-clock emergency care, with regular hours for laboratories, X-rays, pharmacies, and doctors' appointments. These are the Calderón Guardia, San Juan de Díos, and Mexico. Some private hospitals are the Clinica Santa Rita, the Clinica Biblica, and the Clinica Católica, all excellent hospitals.

Next to the Clinica Biblica is the Clinica Americana, an office complex with a group of English-speaking doctors, most of whom did residency in prestigious US university hospitals. The KOP Medical Clinic in Escazú specializes in treating foreigners, with a staff that speaks English, French, Spanish, and Japanese. They offer a wide range of services, including obstetrics, gynecology, pediatrics, and dermatology.

Some emergency rooms specialize; for example, Hospital Mexico specializes in heart problems, and San Juan de Díos has a burn center. All towns of any size will have a hospital, and those that are too tiny often still have a doctor or paramedic and emergency equipment.

The latest and most impressive addition to Costa Rica's medical care system is Hospital CIMA San José, which is located in Escazú. This is one of the largest, most modern facilities in Central America, offering complete clinical laboratory services, radiology (including the only open MRI in Central America), and a full range of medical and surgical specialties. The hospital is affiliated with Baylor University in Dallas, Texas.

BLUE ZONE LIFE EXPECTANCY

Blue Zone is a concept used to identify a demographic or geographic area of the world where people live measurably longer life spans. This describes Costa Rica, especially the Nicoya Peninsula, where an extraordinary number of people routinely live well into their nineties and hundreds. For example, mortality at age ninety in Costa Rica is at least 14 percent lower than in at least thirteen higher-income countries. This phenomenon is not necessarily due to the level of medical care or use of preventative medications. As a matter of fact, most of the extreme winners in Costa Rica's longevity race come from families living in rural, often subsistence, farming communities. The old-timers are too poor to afford medical care other than that provided free at local clinics, and only then when folk remedies don't work.

Some attribute these statistics to the Nicoya Peninsula's water supply, which has the country's highest calcium content. Some studies show calcium to be effective in controlling heart disease, as well as leading to stronger bones and fewer hip fractures. Another explanation is that, being poor all of their lives, the survivors seldom or never depended on automobiles for transportation. Instead, they continually exercised by walking, traveling by horse, or peddling a bicycle. To this day, you'll occasionally see elderly people trudging along the road, heading for the village grocery store, which could be an hour away.

Don't misunderstand; Costa Rica's longevity is not confined to rural communities on the Nicoya Peninsula. The entire country ranks relatively high among nations for longevity. In fact, Costa Rica ranked thirtieth, eight nations *above* the United States (just below Cuba). According to these statistics, male life expectancy in the United States is 75.6 years, whereas in Costa Rica the life expectancy is 76.5 years. It's true that this is only a hundred days difference, yet with the high-technology medical care available in the US it is bewildering. Once, I asked a Costa Rican doctor friend if she prescribes statin drugs or other high-tech medications, as doctors in the States do. Her reply was: "Impossible. The average monthly dosage prescribed in the United States costs as much as my typical patient *earns* in a month!"

Thus, despite spending $3,000 to $4,000 a year for the latest pharmaceuticals and despite the availability of the ultimate in high-tech medical treatment, the average American's life expectancy is about the same as the average Costa Rican farmworker who cannot afford prescription drugs. Go figure.

To see the longevity statistics chart, go online: http://tiny.cc/pt4wdw.

ASSISTED LIVING

Retirement in Costa Rica has always been popular, but it began in earnest in the mid-1980s. In those days, folks didn't retire at an early age, as they often do today. They typically held on to their jobs to age sixty-five, or retired at sixty-two at the youngest, not like today, when retiring at the earliest possible moment is in vogue. If my math is correct, those who retired in the late 1980s are now in their eighties or nineties. As much as we hate to admit it, the time comes when all of us must evaluate our options in advanced-age living accommodations. Many decide to give up Costa Rica and return to their hometowns, where they have family and friends to rely on for help in case of need. When everyday living becomes difficult, they can always move into a modern assisted-living facility where their children and grandchildren can visit frequently.

However, suppose you hate your hometown and have no close ties there? Suppose your children and grandchildren are scattered to the four winds? Furthermore, can you afford the $5,000- to $7,000-a-month fee to live in a modern assisted-living facility? What about a cut-rate old-folks home where conditions are basic, but the monthly cost is only $3,000 a month? Suppose your Social Security check is only $1,500 a month; will you have enough assets for a long stay? What are your alternatives should you choose to tough it out in Costa Rica?

A few years ago, there were few alternatives. I only knew of a couple of assisted-living facilities in the country. Actually, this is a rather new concept, because *tico* families traditionally take care of their elders at home. However, in the past couple of years, at least a half-dozen assisted-living centers have appeared on the scene, some that specialize in English-speaking expats. At least one of these facilities offers specialized care for Alzheimer's patients: Golden Valley Hacienda in Alajuela. Another place I've heard of is also in Alajuela: the Villa Comfort Geriatric Hotel, which specializes in folks who are not bedridden but who need care in everyday living. A facility in Los Yoses, the Hogar Retiro San Pedro, was given high praise by an American woman there for the care.

Understand, this is by no means a complete list, and I haven't investigated any of the facilities mentioned here, so I cannot make recommendations. If you are not fluent in Spanish, my recommendation is to personally check out the facility and speak to the employees to see if indeed they can communicate in English. Management can exaggerate the facility's English-speaking ability in order to gain new patients. Not being able to communicate your needs can be very frustrating. I have a friend who was in a recovery facility that he had been assured was bilingual. Once he had a terrible pain in his back and called for some medication. Instead, the confused aides couldn't understand what he wanted. They brought him a washcloth, then a glass of water, and finally some cigarettes (he didn't smoke).

At the time of this writing, several retirement facilities owned and managed by North Americans or Europeans were either open or under development. Estimated costs range from about $1,500 to $2,500 a month. For those who are fluent in Spanish, there are places that are much less expensive, reputedly around $1,000 a month. Again, I cannot make recommendations without having personally investigated these facilities.

However, the aforementioned facilities' costs are for "assisted living," which implies that the patient gets around okay but needs "assistance": getting bathed and dressed, taking medications, having meals cooked, and so forth. But what about someone who requires round-the-clock care? Someone with Alzheimer's, or too weak to even feed himself? According to the Alzheimer's Association, the average lifetime cost of Alzheimer's care in the United States for an individual is $170,000. Even in Costa Rica, care will be expensive, but never as costly as in North American facilities.

Let me give an example of how friends of ours handled this problem. Our friend's father—in his late eighties—wasn't totally incapacitated, more or less lucid, but nevertheless required supervision twenty-four hours a day. They investigated a dozen facilities in their home state of New Jersey and found none of them acceptable, much less affordable. The father's only income was $1,500 a month in Social Security. Although he had modest savings and investments, paying the $6,000-plus a month required by a so-so New Jersey nursing home would have soon bankrupted the entire family.

Retiring in Costa Rica was what my friends had planned on for years. They had built a beautiful home with a view of the Pacific Ocean, but they couldn't just leave the father alone in New Jersey. After much thought, the group solution was: take Dad with us! They found an inexpensive, two-bedroom house in the center of the village, near a twenty-four-hour doctor's office. Three village women were hired to be with the father around the clock, and a young man with paramedic experience was hired to oversee everything. The total cost came to $1,800 a month, which included salaries for the caregivers, food, and miscellaneous expenses. They were able to visit their father at least once every day, since his home was only a fifteen-minute drive from theirs. About twice a week, the couple would take the father to dinner at a local restaurant. There, he would absolutely beam with smiles.

We felt this to be an exceptionally heartwarming story. The father spent the last three years of his life happy in Costa Rica, rather than dying lonely in New Jersey.

COSTA RICAN DENTISTS

The University of Costa Rica trains medical specialists of all kinds, including highly skilled dentists, periodontists, and orthodontic surgeons. Like medical expenses, dental expenses in Costa Rica are affordable. I go to an English-speaking dentist in Pavas who has a very modern clinic. After he received his degree in Costa Rica, my dentist did postgraduate work in the United States.

When asked about Costa Rican dental prices compared with those in the United States, the dentist replied, "Depending upon where you live in the United States, dental care there can be three to six times as expensive. For example, in Costa Rica the standard price for a porcelain cap is $135. In Los Angeles the same work costs from $600 to $700. A bridge typically costs $375 here, but a similar job in Los Angeles would cost at least $1,800. I've had patients who fly here, pay for their hotel, food, and airfare, and still save money."

What about quality? "Dental work in Costa Rica is equal to that done in the USA," he replied. "There is absolutely no difference in the competency of the dentists. However, the quality of dental laboratory work is usually better here in Costa Rica. Don't misunderstand, the USA also has excellent dental labs, but because they can get the work done cheaper in the Philippines, many dentists routinely send bridgework and dental caps overseas to low-cost laboratories. The quality just isn't up to the standards of Costa Rican or American labs. If I were to have caps or bridgework done in the USA, I'd certainly insist that my dentist use an American dental laboratory."

Charges for dental work vary widely, depending on the part of the country in which you live and on the financial status of the dentist's clientele. You'll pay more in the more affluent suburbs of San José and less in small cities in the provinces. Many smaller towns and few villages have no dental services other than visiting dentists who are sent in by the government to take care of schoolchildren's teeth.

Along with cosmetic surgery, cosmetic/restorative dentistry is becoming a big business here, with huge savings over the cost in the United States or Canada. People have reported savings of $6,000 to $18,000 over prices quoted in the United States and Europe. They've also reported satisfaction with the treatment and quality of the dentists.

PLASTIC SURGERY

Costa Rica has gained worldwide recognition for another of its medical services: reconstructive surgery, commonly known as plastic surgery. San José is becoming known as "Beverly Hills South" because of the number of people coming here for body renewal. Several excellent surgeons specialize in face-lifts, liposuction, breast reconstruction, and other corrections of nature's imperfections. Not only are Costa Rican plastic surgeons ranked among the best in the world, but their fees are based on Costa Rican medical standards: in a word, inexpensive.

Why would Costa Rica be so popular with those wanting to rid themselves of wrinkles? Besides affordable costs and quality surgery, it turns out that San José is a perfect place to slip away to have an operation because of its climate—never hot, never cold—which makes recuperation faster, safer, and more comfortable. Since the healing process takes three or four weeks, many patients find this a great time to learn Spanish in one of the many "total immersion" schools around the city. These schools provide for homestays with Costa Rican families and have small classes or even individual instruction if you prefer.

Another attractive thing about Costa Rica as a base for cosmetic surgery is that many folks feel embarrassed about having their friends and family know they are going to have it done. Therefore, a growing number of them vacation in Costa Rica, where they are unlikely to run into acquaintances; they have the operation; and they return home a month later, when all traces of the surgeon's handiwork have disappeared.

What does all this cost? Happily, the cost of a face-lift, a breast job, a tummy tuck with liposuction, or a body-lift, including surgery, postoperative care, and hospital stay, is a fraction of what one might pay for a similar procedure in the United States. For example, a complete face-lift costs from $2,000 to $4,000, plus $2,000 to $3,000 for the operating room and two recovery days in the hospital. The same operation in New York or Los Angeles would be $25,000, plus much, much more for the hospital.

San José's leading plastic surgeon is Dr. Arnoldo Fournier, who did his fellowship in reconstructive surgery at New York's Columbia University and who has the oldest established plastic surgery practice in Costa Rica. Dr. Fournier charges $800 to $1,500 for an eyelid operation when done separately. Nose surgery or liposuction to abdomen and thighs costs about $1,500 to $5,000, compared with US rates of about $15,000 for the same procedures.

How safe is it? Costa Rican hospitals are excellent, with all modern equipment. Personnel are highly trained. Dr. Fournier points out, "Most of my surgery is done under local anesthetic and sedation. The patient is given some pills a couple of hours prior to the operation, and intravenous medication is given by an anesthesiologist during surgery. This is much safer than using a general anesthetic. Some patients just stay one night in the hospital and then check into a bed-and-breakfast for a few days. Others prefer to stay a while, since hospital rooms don't cost much more than a first-class hotel." For information about plastic surgery, go to www .drfournier.com.

10

The Real Estate Game

A common mistake newcomers make is rushing to buy a home. You really should rent for a while to get an idea of where you want to live. Communities and neighborhoods vary greatly in quality of shopping, access to transportation, compatibility of neighbors, and, of course, price. There are some areas where you definitely wouldn't want to live—you can usually detect "bad vibes" quickly—and there are other areas that may look great at first, but later you could be sorry you didn't know about another, more interesting neighborhood. Take your time when looking for a place to live, and ask many questions of fellow expatriates.

To get an idea of what you might have to pay to rent a house or an apartment, check the *Tico Times* classifieds for a wide range of rents. The last time I looked, houses and apartments were offered at rents ranging from $350 to $2,500 a month (and even higher). While the $2,500 place should be spacious and luxurious, chances are the $350-a-month place could be perfectly livable and just as nice as places back home that rent for several times that amount. Don't rent on price alone, however; check out the neighborhood closely.

For many Costa Rican families, the idea of paying even $350 a month is prohibitive. (Remember, $350 is considered a nice monthly salary for many *ticos*.) So if you are looking for the rock bottom in rents, check the classifieds in the Spanish-language newspaper *La Nación*. The ads in that paper are read by local people who do not have the ability to pay higher rents. Better yet, when you find a neighborhood you like, don't hesitate to ask at stores and businesses if they know of rentals, or even ask people walking along the street.

When trying out Costa Rica for livability, most people don't enter into long-term rentals or sign leases until they are certain they want to settle in for a long time. An ideal way to savor living in the country, particularly in the Central Valley, is to rent an apartment by the month or the week. Short-term rentals are particularly useful when determining which neighborhood you'd like to settle in. San José has several *apartotels,* small furnished apartments complete with cable TV, telephone, and cooking utensils—in short, everything you need for a trial of Costa Rican living.

Another excellent way to discover whether you like a neighborhood or a city is to rent a room in a Costa Rican home. Because of pressure on hotels for tourist rooms a few years back, many private families converted spare bedrooms into rentals for the busy seasons. They're delighted to host North Americans on their visits, to take them into their homes and treat them as part of the family. Another possibility is a bed-and-breakfast located in the neighborhood you want to investigate. The owners can provide invaluable information about the area.

The standard recommendation to visitors is to wait at least six months before buying property. However, many catch real estate fever within the first few days of their initial visit and end up buying something anyway. For a while, the buying spree in Costa Rica increased in volume, with people from all over the world plunking down money to buy something—anything—before it was all gone. At the present time, the dollar is weakening against foreign currencies, down more than 25 percent under the European euro. This makes Costa Rican properties, which are traditionally priced in dollars, very attractive to Europeans who desire to move to Costa Rica.

Some people are surprised when researching home prices on the Internet in general or by looking at ads in the *Tico Times.* Prices are sometimes higher than expected. There are plenty of properties to be found at bargain prices, but you must realize that there are several levels of real estate, from the very cheap to the ultraexpensive. If you're looking for something at the lower end of the scale, the Internet and English-language newspapers aren't the best places to find them. When property is a real bargain, it won't be on the Internet and the *Tico Times* website. The more affordable properties are usually bought and sold by *ticos,* who read *La Nación* or *La Republica,* and who don't have access to the Internet. When the price is much over $80,000, most *ticos* and those *gringos* with ordinary budgets can't buy. The advertisement for these properties goes into places where well-to-do buyers will see it, like on the Internet. The same goes for rents. A house or apartment that rents for $500 a month doesn't need to be advertised in a newspaper or posted on the Internet; word of mouth takes care of it. But a luxury place that rents for $3,000 or sells for $500,000 needs to be exposed to a different market.

For more than twenty years armchair experts have been saying that Costa Rican real estate is overpriced, that the market has peaked and is sure to tumble. Overpriced compared to where? Clearly, you can buy a home in Nicaragua, El Salvador, or Honduras for a fraction of the price in Costa Rica. (If you want to live in Honduras, be my guest.) Yet prices kept going up, despite the fact that you could buy cheap property in places like Oklahoma, Nebraska, or Kentucky. The reason Costa Rican real estate is priced higher than Nicaraguan properties is a basic principle called "supply and demand." When a surplus of buyers feel they'd rather live in Costa Rica than Nicaragua, prices will be higher in Costa Rica.

The real estate market in the United States is still stagnating at the time of this writing (late 2012). Inflated prices, shaky mortgages, and foreclosures have plagued the market, forcing asking prices downward by shocking percentages in some parts of the country. It stands to reason that property here in Costa Rica will be affected by conditions in the United States. However, since most properties in Costa Rica are sold on a cash basis, mortgages and foreclosures do not enter the picture. Folks with paid-for Costa Rican properties aren't forced to sell for a loss, so if they can't get their price, they tend to hold on until the demand for property resumes. This has happened several times in the recent past. My guess is that the real estate boom will stall for a time, then resume when the next sellers' market appears on the horizon.

Having pointed out that bank-financed property in Costa Rica has been the exception rather than the rule, I must say there has been a slight trend toward US-style financing. A few private banks have started granting mortgages. Previously, this was unheard of. Sales had to be handled by cold cash up front. Of course, the loan will be in dollars, and interest rates are somewhat higher than you'd pay up north. (A friend is paying 8 percent variable on a fifteen-year loan.) If you're not a resident or a resident in progress, you'll probably pay a higher percentage of interest. I hope I'm not making this sound easy, because the few people I know that have received financing had to wade through complicated applications and provide letters from their home bank and/or employer. Obviously, banks are concerned that you can and will pay off the mortgage rather than walk away and leave them with a foreclosure.

PLAYING THE REAL ESTATE GAME

Many, if not most, countries in the world severely restrict the rights of foreigners to buy property. Some absolutely prohibit it. Not so in Costa Rica. This is one country where you needn't be a citizen, or even a legal resident, to own property. If you're financially capable of buying real estate, it's yours. However, too many newcomers fail to understand how the real estate game is played in Costa Rica. In this chapter we'll try to explain the rules of the game. In my opinion, this chapter is one of the most important in the book.

First of all, in North America, the vast majority of property sales are conducted through professional real estate offices. A real estate professional brings the buyer and seller together and helps negotiate the deal. But this is a North American concept that is foreign to Costa Rica. Almost all real estate offices in Costa Rica belong to foreigners. Costa Rican buyers and sellers simply do not use third-party negotiators. Traditionally, they sit down with family members to negotiate, with trusted lawyers sitting in. This is why you almost never see *tico* properties listed with an American real estate company. Also, you rarely see Costa Rican real estate offices.

How the Game Is Played

Newcomers with stars in their eyes do not realize how different these customs and the laws are. They take it for granted that the game rules are the same as back home. Let's look at the differences and see how they could affect your financial future in Costa Rica.

Back home: You visit a convenient real estate office and choose a salesperson you like. It really doesn't matter whom you choose because all real estate offices and real estate salespeople are pretty much the same. Brokers and agents have taken the same real estate classes, passed identical tests, and have basic experience in real estate before being granted a license. All sales practices are governed by specific laws.

In Costa Rica: There are neither training, tests, licenses, nor any laws regarding real estate sales. To become a broker or a salesperson, you simply announce that you are now available to sell property. Having printed business cards is all you need. (Even business cards aren't necessary.) Anyone, even tourists, can sell property and collect commissions without violating real estate laws.

Back home: You sit down with the real estate agent and go through the area's Multiple Listing Service (MLS). That is, descriptions of each and every home for sale in the community, in the price range you can afford. There's no need to go to another sales office if you can't find something you like, because all real estate offices have the exact same list of properties.

In Costa Rica: There is no such animal as MLS. Real estate offices and individual agents keep their listings to themselves and would be fools to share information with competitors. Therefore, you have no way of knowing what properties are for sale without going to each and every real estate sales office in your target area.

Back home: The salesperson conducts a tour of all available properties so you can narrow your choices.

In Costa Rica: You will never be given a tour of "all available properties." You'll see only those under contract to that particular salesperson or office. You have to go to *all* real estate offices! Even then, you won't see listings for properties for sale by owners. You'll have to ask around the community for available properties. Local *ticos* and *gringos* pretty much know what is for sale and how much the seller is actually asking.

Back home: You look at the list of comparable selling prices, which is a list of every home sold recently and the transaction price. By law, all selling prices are available to the public. You quickly determine which of your choices are overpriced and which are bargains.

In Costa Rica: There are no comparables. The actual sales price is a carefully guarded secret. Well, everyone knows how much is *asked* for a property, but not the final price. This is because property taxes and transfer fees are based on the reported selling price, so it is prudent to report as small a sales price as possible. To be blunt, many people fib about how much money they received or paid for a property to minimize taxes. This is routine behavior. In fact, in 2012 the country's *chief tax collector* and his assistant were discovered to have neglected or overlooked paying *their* property taxes!

Back home: You know more or less what the owner will settle for, so you make an offer a little below the asking price, assuming that the price has been boosted in order to have room for haggling. Eventually you reach a happy medium.

In Costa Rica: You haven't the vaguest idea of the price the seller wants for the property, because the real estate agent could be keeping the bottom line a secret. If so, the agent will likely refuse to give you a way to contact the seller so you can find out. Why? Too often, the property is being sold on a "net listing" contract. In most North American states or provinces, this type of contract is illegal.

A net listing works this way: The agent asks the seller, "How much do you want for your property?" Let's suppose the seller wants $100,000. The salesperson writes a contract guaranteeing the seller $100,000 less a 5 percent commission. Then the salesperson lists the property at $150,000, *not* $100,000! If there's a buyer, the seller receives $95,000 ($100,000 minus $5,000 commission). However, the salesperson's cut is $55,000, the commission plus the extra $50,000! If the home doesn't sell, the salesperson hasn't lost anything. Yet, the seller could have missed several potential sales because the asking price was too high, and would never know.

Since there are no laws or regulations in Costa Rica, this is perfectly legal. In the United States or Canada, the agent could go to jail for not properly representing his client. If the salesperson wants your listing, he or she will agree to a commission-only contract. If not, look for another salesperson.

Back home: When your offer has been accepted, you can safely assume that the deal is solid. You will soon have a home that will be livable, with no hidden problems. You can be confident that the seller actually owns the property, there are no major leaks in the roof, the title to the house is in order, the boundary lines of the property are exactly as represented, the house hasn't been condemned, there isn't an outstanding mortgage worth more than the house, or other routine problems. The law back home demands that these problems must be disclosed.

In Costa Rica: There is no obligation to disclose anything. It's up to the buyer's attorney to check out the legal aspects of the deal, and it's up to you to look carefully at the physical condition of the property. This is why a competent lawyer on your side is worth his or her weight in gold. A competent lawyer can see through every possible trick.

Game Rules

Although buying property in Costa Rica should be rather straightforward, it can be hazardous if not handled carefully. The following are some points to keep in mind.

The first rule: Under no circumstances should you use the same lawyer who represents the seller. Find a competent, English-speaking attorney to handle the deal for you. This can be a challenge in itself. Too many Costa Rican lawyers are part-timers and aren't truly familiar with the buying and selling of real estate. Inquire around the North American community for recommendations.

Why is this important? For one thing, your lawyer needs to make sure the person who is selling you the property actually owns it. It's up to your lawyer to make absolutely sure that no liens, mortgages, or second deeds are attached to the property. Your lawyer needs to examine the deal with a legal microscope, looking for bugs and hidden risks. The seller's attorney has no obligation to do all of this; it's up to your lawyer. Legally, an attorney can represent both sides of a transaction, but if the lawyer's first client is a crook, look out. The lawyer may well be part of the scam himself. It happens often since they aren't breaking any laws.

The second rule: Never count on a verbal contract. A handshake means nothing. You may think you have a deal, but when you return with the cash, someone else owns the place and is moving in furniture. Get everything in writing, in Spanish as well as English.

The third rule: Do not trust the seller or real estate agent just because he or she is a fellow North American! There's something about Costa Rica that seems to bring out latent tendencies toward larceny in some of our compatriots. An astounding number of confidence men come out of the closet the moment they arrive in Costa Rica. Most of the real estate agents who are just starting out are rank amateurs, but since they deal with people like you and me—also rank amateurs in business deals—even honest amateurs can cause serious damage.

The fourth rule: Do not be so overwhelmed by the beauty and tranquility of Costa Rica that you pay the first price asked. *Gringos* and *ticos* alike can display irrational streaks of optimism when valuing their properties. Foreigners, bloodthirsty for profit, can be the worst of all.

The fifth rule: If you're buying unimproved land, be absolutely positive you can bring electricity and year-round water to the property. (Some parts of Costa Rica suffer water shortages every dry season.) If there is no water connection possible, make sure that the local municipality will grant a permit to drill a well, and that a well will have water. Have the soil tested to be sure it's suitable for a septic system. If sewage can't be treated properly, it will sit around, back up, and make your new home smell like a cesspool. Some of these conditions could prevent you from getting a building permit, making your property virtually useless except for raising goats.

If you have to bring electric power to your place from the nearest source, it could mean paying a fortune to install power poles and electric lines. The last quote I heard was $15,000 a kilometer! The cost could be many times the price you paid for that lovely parcel in the mountains. Solar-power installations are not cheap, and they limit the appliances you can use. Don't believe assurances that telephone and high-speed Internet lines, or a paved highway, are on the way. They could be years away, or not even on the drawing board.

The sixth rule: When selling property, be wary of a listing agreement that doesn't pay you the full sales price less commission. As discussed earlier, these contracts are known as "net listings." I've seen net listing sales where the agent boosted the sales price of property by 100 percent over the price asked by the seller, keeping the balance, plus a commission. The agent can end up with more money than the property-owner client! If the salesperson wants your listing, he or she will agree to a commission-only deal. If not, look for another salesperson.

The seventh rule: When buying property, insist on talking with the owner. Ask him what his bottom-dollar price would be, and ask about any problems that the selling agent might not be aware of. If the real estate agent refuses to allow you to speak with the seller, you have every right to be suspicious.

NATIONAL REGISTRY

Since Costa Rica is so small, the government can keep all land records in one place, at a central title registry called the *Registro de la Propiedad*, or *Registro Nacional*. Most people just say "Registro." All valid liens and attachments against a property must be registered here, and the books are open to the public simply by going to the Registro's website. This makes it easy for your attorney to double-check the Registro before making an offer. You can check properties out yourself, although the final check needs to be done by your attorney.

If your lawyer finds no liens or mortgages registered against the piece of real estate, and has no questions about the legal standing of the owners, you can safely transfer the property to your name. (The use of a corporation is no longer permitted for home ownership. The property is registered as a deed, similar to what we are used to in the United States.) Any outstanding debts or obligations that didn't appear on the Registro records are none of your concern. But don't feel smug until you make sure that your lawyer actually registers your new property and the documents are stashed away in your safe-deposit box.

Incidentally, another valuable use of information provided by the Registro is checking the ownership of motor vehicles. You'll find the complete legal history of the automobile, motorcycle, or pickup you might want to buy. Before putting up the cash, you can see who actually holds the title to the car, whether there is a loan, and who the previous owners were.

TICOS ARE NOT NAIVE!

Newcomers to Costa Rica often have the mistaken notion that there are two prices for real estate: the "*gringo* price" and the "*tico* price." They sincerely believe that *ticos* are simple country folk who have no idea of the real value of their properties. The theory is that bargain real estate can be purchased simply by paying a Costa Rican to buy or negotiate for you.

First of all, it is more than a little arrogant for strangers to come to Costa Rica and assume that they know more about the real estate market than Costa Rican landowners. After all, *ticos* have lived here all their lives and are thoroughly familiar with the current market. To assume they might sell property at less than its value to another Costa Rican is actually naive on the part of the prospective buyer. When we are talking about desirable properties—those with ocean views or in pleasant neighborhoods with elegant homes—you must realize that virtually all of these properties are already owned, by wealthy *tico* families, North Americans, or Europeans—none of whom are ignorant of the value of their property.

Obviously, isolated land, up in the mountains, accessible by dirt road, will usually be owned by *ticos*. It's entirely possible that they have only a vague idea of the value of their properties. Yet, who *does* know? Certainly not a newcomer to the region. If that's the kind of land you want, having a *tico* bargain for you makes sense only because the landowners probably can't speak English. But it is a mistake to think that you can pick up land like this at a below-market price because these are "simple people."

DECIDING WHERE TO RELOCATE

Unlike in some foreign countries, expatriates in Costa Rica don't feel compelled to isolate themselves in gated or protected enclaves. Most North Americans feel at home in Costa Rica's city and suburban middle-class neighborhoods throughout the Central Valley. They don't feel the need to group together, living in compounds or sealed-off neighborhoods as expatriates do in other foreign countries. Because Costa Ricans and North Americans are similar in personality and worldviews, most expats feel right at home with their neighbors. Since juvenile delinquency isn't out of control in most middle-class residential areas, and because neighborhood kids are generally well behaved, Americans don't feel threatened as we might in some low-income areas back home. Granted, North Americans do tend to congregate in the more expensive areas with nice homes, condominiums, and plush housing developments. But not everyone can afford to live in these upscale neighborhoods, and not everyone wants to live in an English-speaking enclave. Therefore, you'll find foreigners scattered all over the Central Valley and, in fact, all around the country in small towns and villages.

One expatriate who has lived here for twenty years with his family of five said, "We live in a Costa Rican barrio with *ticos* who are typical of most Costa Ricans I know. They love their families, neighborhood, and country, and we all work together at watching out for one another. Our home has never been broken into, and we don't live in a fortress. We have no walls, pit bulls, Dobermans, or security systems. Five minutes and a crowbar could gain entry."

Not only are foreigners right at home in city and suburban areas of Costa Rica, but those who speak fairly good Spanish find that they are accepted without any fuss in rural settings and villages away from the Central Valley. This is something you'll definitely not find in the rest of Central America or even in Mexico. In other cultures, a *gringo* family living in a native community would stand out like pigs wearing miniskirts. Your neighbors would think of you as a little eccentric, and you would feel bewildered and lonely because the culture is so different. Not so in Costa Rica. I know many *gringos* who enjoy living in rather humble (and inexpensive) lodgings in picturesque villages, and their neighbors are proud that foreigners would like them so well that they'd want to be neighbors.

BEACHFRONT PROPERTY

Ocean real estate is wildly popular with Europeans and North Americans. Prices are somewhat erratic, in some areas having gone wild, while other places still have bargains available. The situation is somewhat murky, because some building lots right on the ocean will often have tough building and ownership restrictions that you might not be told about until you are denied a building permit. Property owners as well as lessees on most beaches are restricted as to how close to the water they can build. The most important point to bear in mind is that you usually *cannot* own beachfront property outright; it must be leased from the local municipality. Make sure you're comfortable with this concept before deciding on that wonderful stretch of coconut trees and sand.

Generally, the law goes like this: The first 200 meters ashore, starting halfway between low-tide and high-tide lines, is the "maritime zone," and it belongs to the municipality. It cannot be sold, but it can be leased. (This lease is called a "concession.") The first 50 meters from the beach is the "public zone," which belongs absolutely to the public and is off-limits to construction of any kind.

Construction between the 50- and 200-meter points must be approved by the municipality. Building permits are sometimes issued only for tourist-related projects. Remember, that $150,000 lot on the beach is not an outright purchase; you actually pay that money for the right to renew a lease every five years. It's yours provided you do everything right: make the lease payments, pay taxes on time, and obey all the rules.

Caution: A seller may claim that an existing building that falls within the first fifty-meter mark is legal because it's been "grandfathered." That's possible, but more likely someone in the past ignored the rules and the bureaucracy hasn't gotten around to enforcing the laws. The government could force you to dismantle the buildings and restore the property to its original state, when and if it chooses to do so. Check grandfather clauses with a skeptical eye—and a good attorney.

SQUATTER PROBLEMS

Anyone who has followed the battles between North Americans and squatters in the *Tico Times* is aware of hair-raising stories concerning squatters and legitimate property owners. The Costa Rican name for a squatter is *precaista.* If you're thinking of buying a piece of rural property, or any land that could possibly be farmed, you need to be aware of the squatter issues. (This only applies to agricultural land. Residential properties *cannot* be claimed as abandoned.)

We've all heard stories of North Americans who purchased lovely tracts of forested land with the intention of building a home someday, and when they returned a few years later, they were surprised to find the land cleared and a family living in a rustic home, raising cows. Squatters strike again!

If the property you are interested in buying has an extra house with a *tico* family living in it, beware! Don't let the seller glibly pass this off as the "caretaker's residence." It could be a squatter's home. "This family takes wonderful care of the place!" the seller might exclaim. "They never leave the property unattended." The seller should add, "They'll never leave, period!" Make sure you see documents proving that this is indeed a care-taker employee, not a squatter. In order to be an employed caretaker, the employee must receive the legal minimum wage rate, including Social Secu-rity, and all other legal benefits. The papers proving all this must be up to date. Insist that your lawyer examine the proof. If someone is paid to sim-ply look over the property on a regular basis, make sure there's a written receipt that he is being paid for this service and is not a squatter himself.

To most of us the idea of someone simply moving in on your property is outrageous. It's trespassing! It's theft! Can this really happen in a law-abiding country such as Costa Rica? Aren't property owners protected by the law? Isn't all of this illegal?

Well, it turns out that to a certain extent, it *is* legal. There are laws to the effect that unowned or abandoned property is open for homestead-ing, just as it was in the early days of the United States and may still be in some western states. These Costa Rican laws were intended to prevent a few wealthy people from hogging land they don't use and don't need. This is precisely what happened in some other Central American countries, where 2 or 3 percent of the people own 90 percent of the good land but don't use it. One reason Costa Rica is so much better off than its neighbors is that citizens have access to land. The laws are well intentioned and fair. The problem lies in how these laws are interpreted and who is doing the interpreting. Too often the bias is in favor of the squatter.

Just when is a piece of land abandoned? One law, which seems clear, states that after property goes unattended for ten years, whoever has been using the land in a "continuous, open, and peaceful manner" for those ten years may apply for a title. The intruder will be successful unless the original owner has a good lawyer and a valid excuse. Another principle of law is that the squatter must show that he had reason to believe the land was abandoned. This means that someone who was being paid to watch your land can be removed if he attempts to take it over for himself. (Remember, you need receipts and canceled paychecks.)

Typically, the scenario goes like this: A choice piece of unattended property becomes a tempting target for a *precaista*. He'll construct a cabin and plant a crop in the hope that he won't be discovered for a year. If the occupancy is less than a year, it's considered trespassing and is handled by the Ministry of Interior and the courts. If the trespass is less than ninety days, you call the local police, and they are obligated to evict the squatters and "present you" with a paper that confirms that you are the true owner of the property. (If the police fail to act, your lawyer can do something about that.)

But let the problem go a full year and the situation becomes a bit more serious. The owner usually has the option of paying the squatter for his expenses and "improvements" or else going to court. ("Improvements" could include cutting down all your beautiful trees to make a pasture.) When the bill is too high—you can be sure it will be padded—sometimes it's cheaper to walk away. Again, these problems seldom occur anywhere but on agricultural land. Land zoned or used as residential property does not fall under the category of this law.

The solution to this problem is a matter of prevention. While you are out of the country, have a friend or a management agent drop by the property at least once every three months. At this point, a simple complaint to the police is usually enough to boot someone off your land. Be sure to keep records of expenses and improvements to the property as proof that you haven't abandoned your land. Paying someone to clear brush once in a while is good enough. Be sure to keep a record of how many hours he worked and receipts for how much you paid him. Any place where there are a lot of foreign property owners, you'll find someone who watches property as a paid service. However, be absolutely sure you know who is taking care of your property, and keep records that he is being paid. My attorney advises, "Hire someone to check on the property, and then hire someone else to check on the person checking on your property." The last thing you want to do is hire a squatter to watch over your property!

Occasionally a problem arises when a foreign resident decides to return to the United States for an extended stay and has to lay off the maid, gardener, or other employees. If the property owner isn't familiar with the laws and neglects to pay workers' benefits such as severance pay, accrued vacation, and year-end bonuses, the employees could feel justified in taking over the land as compensation. Chapter 12 covers this in detail.

However repugnant the idea of squatting may be to you, it is important to operate within the law. After all, *precaistas* have rights, like it or not. One woman who had just purchased some property told me that she had been informed that "the only way to deal with squatters is to burn down their houses," and that's what she intended to do if she ever found any on her property. I was horrified to think of someone on a tourist visa, a guest in the country, taking the law into her own hands! This is the way problems start, and incidents of this nature have been known to escalate into gunfire. Sometimes squatters are well organized and have their own ways of striking back; the best advice is to leave this problem to the law. The law may work slowly, sometimes not at all, but this is better than killing or being killed for a piece of farmland. I have friends who had no problem kicking the rascals off their land and watched while the police burned the squatters' shacks.

If you are an absentee owner of undeveloped land and have reason to believe that your property is a target of squatters or property-theft scams, you should do the following: Make sure you are the legally registered owner; if you live out of the country, ask your attorney to conduct a title search from time to time to make sure you are still on the title, or at least check the Registro Nacional website yourself. Let the neighbors know who you are and that you own the property. Fence the property if possible, and post signs. Have a friend walk the property boundary lines every two or three months and file a complaint against any squatters encountered. If you hire a caretaker or agent to watch the property, make sure you have signed receipts showing that you've paid the caretaker for this purpose. Understand, these precautions are only for undeveloped property that is left untended by absentee owners for long periods. To summarize, the menace of squatters may be overblown and exaggerated, but it pays to be alert and aware of the potential problems.

BUILDING YOUR OWN HOME

Okay, you've made the big decision? You've done your on-location research? You've traveled Costa Rica to check out climates and expat communities? You know exactly where you and your spouse want to settle in?

Congratulations! Your next decision is: Do you rent, do you buy, or do you build?

Unless you have the capital to invest, the obvious decision is to rent. The downside is that you might have to accept whatever lifestyle and home designs are available instead of what you'd really like. Another problem is that many homes are used as vacation homes for the owners, so if you rent, you'll be limited as to when you can stay in the house. Being forced to move from one place to another is a frequent consequence of renting. Even with a long-term rental, there's no guarantee the house won't be sold out from under you.

Buying is the best and simplest solution for most people. You choose from among the best-designed homes on the market and simply move in. More often than not, the house will come completely furnished, including refrigerator, washer, and dryer. Often these are turnkey setups, including kitchen utensils, bedding, and garden tools, especially when the owners are returning to their homes back in the United States or Canada. It wouldn't make sense to drag furniture back home.

Building your home is the third option, the one my wife and I adopted, twice, but only after looking over the homes-for-sale market. We found features we loved in each of the homes we considered buying. Yet every home had at least one flaw we didn't care to live with. We decided to build instead of buying—that way we could incorporate all the nice features we'd seen and eliminate the problems.

First we needed a building site. We narrowed this down to two choices. The first choice: a lovely lot, high on the mountainside, with a gorgeous view of the beach. But the location was a ten-minute drive to the beach. We wanted walking distance. When friends and family visit, we didn't want to operate a taxi service back and forth to the beach. The second option was a lot, 200 yards from a beautiful beach cove, where we could hear but not see the surf, priced at a quarter of the cost of a distant ocean-view lot.

Next came the wonderful and exhilarating process of designing our dream home. We converted our dining-room table into a workspace, and we each began to make sketches of how we envisioned the layout should look: which features would be included; how bedrooms should be positioned; where stairs to the upstairs living quarters would go. At first, none of the drawings had any similarities. We debated and argued for our designs, making changes over and over. Finally, we arrived at a consensus. The design retained all of the good features and eliminated the bad. Or so we thought.

Our next step was consulting with our contractor. We handed him our final drawings and eagerly awaited his enthusiastic approval. Enthusiastic was not exactly his reaction. He pointed out several flaws in the design. One important flaw was that the stairway to the upstairs deck would end up in space, four feet beyond the house, rather than on the deck. Another error: We forgot to allow for a door into the downstairs bathroom. Back to the drawing board. The process continued with our altering designs and the contractor correcting them.

Finally we all agreed on the design. Next steps: finding an architect to approve the plans and getting building permits from the municipality and a construction engineer's report on the suitability of the building site and septic tank capability. Costa Rican architects have a strong lobby in the National Assembly; the law says you must use blueprints from a licensed architect, and the fee shall be a hefty 10 percent of construction cost. Actually, an architect here does much more than design: He or she is supposed to supervise all phases of the construction.

A drawback: Since the architect is paid a percentage of construction costs, he or she has no incentive to keep costs low. However, it turns out that there are many more architects in the country than building projects to keep them busy. Architects who work part-time at their profession are often willing to negotiate the fee, especially when the contractor is a friend or relative. This architect will look over the plans and recycle a similar blueprint for a negotiated price, resulting in significant savings for the client. Not all architects will do this, and those who have plenty of work will not do it this way. Again, it helps if your contractor and architect are friends or relatives. If you are building anything more than a basic, plain vanilla house, you probably don't want to take shortcuts. Hire a skilled, reputable architect, and have your lawyer help negotiate, to be absolutely sure you are aware of the contract agreements.

When estimating how long it would take to build our house, our contractor wisely said, "I might finish in three months. *No hay problema.* But since this is Costa Rica, I will promise *five* months. That way you will be delighted if I finish in only *four* months." Actually, he finished in four months to the exact day. He asked one of the workers to stop us that day, before we could get to the building site. The man took us to lunch and stalled for an hour while the crew installed the last of the windows. The contractor met us with a proud smile and took us through our new house.

When the day came to begin construction, the work crew set about cutting just enough trees to lay out the house. I watched over them to make sure they didn't cut too many. They thought this amusing. (Little did I know that trees here grow so fast they have to be continually trimmed and finally removed before they damage the roof and windows.)

I made friends with the workers by providing cold beer at lunchtime. They started calling me *"don John"* (a term of friendship and respect accorded to those older than you and who are well liked in the community). They still call me *don John*—twenty years after our first house was completed. As I drive to or from the village, someone is always waving at me and saying, *"¡Hola, don John!"*

Watching over the crew is a good idea, by the way—not because they will loaf, but because when you go away for a few weeks, contractors have a tendency to take their men and go work elsewhere. You can't blame them, because there is a labor shortage from time to time. They figure they can always get back to your house before you return. It does not always work that way.

During the early construction phase, I stayed at a nearby bed-and-breakfast and arose at dawn to hang around the building site and observe the wildlife that is so bountiful at daybreak. Monkeys, coatimundis, parrots, and other animals put on an early-morning show. Hanging around my building site at dawn brought surprises other than wildlife. I discovered something about the *ticos* who worked on my project: Not only did they arrive on time for work, they were there early—quite unlike the case in other Latino countries I've experienced. Starting time was 6:00 a.m., and at exactly 6:00 work commenced in earnest. They worked hard, with regularly scheduled breaks, until 3:30 p.m. (a nine-hour day). The famous *mañana* mentality wasn't apparent on this job. I'm not saying all *tico* workers are like this; I'm only relating my personal experience.

Don't misunderstand: Our building experience was not all peaches and cream—all expected problems raised their ugly heads, and a few creative problems joined in the fun. We quickly learned a Spanish lesson: the difference between *Hay un problemcito* ("There's a little problem") and *No hay problema* ("There's no problem"). Essentially, it's as follows: *Hay un problemcito* translates as "We have a problem here, amigo, and it's probably going to cost money." On the other hand, *No hay problema* usually translates as "We may or may not have a problem, but it's not my problem."

11

Business Opportunities

The first edition of *Choose Costa Rica* was published twenty years ago. How retirement strategies have changed! Back then, the US economy was growing by leaps and bounds. Those who wanted to, could stay with their employers until the traditional sixty-five age of retirement, and even older if they desired. Others, who couldn't wait until Medicare kicked in, looked upon Costa Rica's affordable medical system as a way to go into business or early retirement in Costa Rica. They were able to cash in on homes they had purchased some thirty years earlier for a fraction of the going rate of inflated home values. Quitting a job and starting a business didn't seem to be such a big deal. For some, Costa Rica became a target for a place to try out a business enterprise.

For many people today, retirement is no longer voluntarily. When jobs get shifted to India and China, paying what North Americans would consider starvation wages, retirement is often the only option. Also, age fifty is the age at which some employers like to trim the payroll, before pension benefits accumulate. Today there is no such thing as company loyalty or loyalty to employees. People are hired for whatever skills are needed at the moment—and are dropped the minute they're not needed. Other people are simply tired of working for someone else and recall the 1970s when "dropping out" was idealized. In the new millennium, "dropping out" becomes a goal as much as an option.

This all creates a restless population of not-yet-ready-for-retirement people who are itching to do something interesting with the rest of their lives. In fact, the word *retirement* isn't in their vocabulary. These are the youth-oriented activists (today known as baby boomers) who in the 1960s and 1970s used to say, "Don't trust anyone over thirty!" Determined not to get "old" in the way they perceived their parents to be, these youngsters are eager to get on with life. They have energy, talent, and workplace skills that they don't care to waste by playing bridge or swinging in a hammock. Since they can't find good-paying jobs in Costa Rica, the next option that comes to mind is going into business. And many of them do. Some popular tourist locales have more businesses owned by foreigners than by native *ticos*.

A FRIENDLY BUSINESS CLIMATE

Many countries severely restrict foreign business investment as a way of protecting their national businesses and industry. Special tax breaks are given to local commerce, and roadblocks are thrown in the way of foreign investors. There's some justification for this, because many foreign businesses only want to take advantage of cheap wages, then ship the products—and the profits—out of the country. But Costa Rica takes a positive attitude toward foreign investment. Outside money is encouraged as a way to spur development, yet labor laws and wage minimums are strictly enforced, giving the average *tico* worker enough income so that local stores, shops, and businesses flourish.

The end result is that Costa Rica is probably the most business-friendly country in Latin America. Foreign investment and foreign entrepreneurs are welcome. One obvious result has been the relocation of several high-tech corporations to take advantage of Costa Rica's educated and computer-literate workforce. This business-friendly climate has earned Costa Rica the reputation as Central America's "Silicon Valley." Companies such as Acer Computers, Microsoft, Abbot Laboratories, and General Electric have established sizable production facilities here. Intel Corporation's three production facilities produce one-third of Intel's computer processor chips, creating more than 3,000 good-paying jobs for *ticos*.

Any investment that promotes tourism, creates jobs, and doesn't harm the environment is considered welcome. Another plus: Many foreign investors *live* in Costa Rica, and spend their profits here. For expatriates, the whole point of going into business is to earn a living income while enjoying life in Costa Rica. They spend and reinvest profits in the country, further bolstering the economy.

To attract desirable businesses, Costa Rica offers generous incentives and tax breaks. Depending on the enterprise, there can be a twelve-year exemption from income taxes as well as waivers on import duties. When ecology is concerned—particularly projects involving reforestation—tax exemptions can be forever. Be aware, however, that continuing changes in tax laws may affect some of the tax breaks for tourist-oriented businesses.

GOING INTO BUSINESS

Before we delve into the subject of doing business in Costa Rica, you should ask yourself some important questions. Do you really want to move to a beautiful country and then spend your time working at a business? Ask yourself whether you'd be better off bird-watching, swimming, or tanning on the beach instead of doing bookkeeping, tending bar, or changing linens in your bed-and-breakfast. Do you feel up to the challenge of dealing with a quixotic, entangled bureaucracy, in a language you don't entirely understand? And finally, if it's so easy to start the business you have in mind—and make large sums of money from your idea—why hasn't somebody else already filled that niche?

Too often, dreamers feel confident that all that's necessary to become a successful businessperson in Costa Rica is to show up and dazzle the country with entrepreneurship. Well yes, this can happen, but mostly to those who know what they are doing, who employ skills and special knowledge gained from business experience in their home countries.

Since most businesses are registered in the name of a corporation or *sociadad anónima*—which translates to "anonymous corporation"—even a foreigner on a tourist visa can effectively control and manage a business enterprise. While it is against the law for noncitizens to *work* at an ordinary job without permission, it's perfectly okay to oversee your own business. Discretion is required here, since part of the scheme is to create jobs, and if a business owner is doing work that could be performed by a Costa Rican citizen, complaints could arise. This seldom happens, but it *can* happen.

Some North Americans have done exceptionally well in Costa Rican business ventures. They bring enthusiasm, expertise, and imagination, often re-creating successful enterprises they operated in their home country. One businessman from Illinois, who started a successful beach resort in Manuel Antonio about twenty years ago, said, "It's interesting to see who makes money here and who goes belly-up. Those who succeed are those who come here because of the attractive Costa Rican lifestyle and who go into business as a means of staying in Costa Rica. They usually make money despite themselves. Those who face one problem after another, and finally disaster, are those whose main interest is making a pile of money."

Foreigners often feel confident that they can be successful in tourist-oriented businesses because they understand the wants and needs of other foreigners who visit Costa Rica. That's often the case. Some restaurants and bars are popular with tourists because the owners know what tourists like. However, as in any business endeavor, you should know what you are doing, particularly in the restaurant or bar business, where the failure rate is unusually high.

Real estate development projects have created fabulous success stories as well as woeful tales of spectacular flops. Too many optimistic types start creating developments and resorts that look great on paper but never get past the fantasy stage. Be cautious about floating your investments on blue-sky dreams.

You needn't start your own business; numerous in-place enterprises are always available through ads in local newspapers placed by both *tico* and expat owners. Of course, just as is the case back home, you need to investigate *why* the business is for sale. Maybe the reason is too much work, not enough profit, illness, or perhaps the owner feels it's time to cash in the equity and stash the profit. Don't consider buying a business unless you're competent to handle it and understand exactly why the enterprise is up for sale. What makes you think you can make money at this if someone else failed?

Among the many businesses advertised in the *Tico Times* are bed-and-breakfasts, car-rental agencies, pharmacies, travel agencies, and plenty of bar-restaurants and discos. Also, apartment buildings, hotels, and beach resorts are always on the market.

A business consultant I once interviewed said: "Remember, it's just as easy to lose money in Costa Rica as it is back home. For a stranger in a foreign land, it's even easier. You must know what you are doing. My best advice is to come here for six months and look around. Study the existing businesses and find out why some are successful and why others fail. Above all, don't jump into a business just for the sake of being in business—particularly a business that you don't know much about."

BEWARE OF SCAMS

Because of Costa Rica's liberal attitude toward foreign business ventures and its sometimes lax enforcement of regulations, a surprising number of foreigners feel as though they have complete freedom to operate as they wish and that ordinary laws and ethics don't apply to them. This is probably why Costa Rica draws more than its share of swindlers, crooks, and con artists.

The Costa Rican government does what it can to keep on top of offenders, but it's impossible to do much more than prosecute crooks after the damage has been done. And prosecution rarely happens, because the swindler simply skips the country before the trial date. For this reason, look very carefully at any business deal presented to you. Make sure you have a good, English-speaking lawyer check with all the proper government agencies and verify the integrity of your deal before risking your hard-earned money.

Popular scams include phony mutual funds, nonexistent banks, so-called tax-shelter investments, gold mines, hotels and resorts that never leave the drawing board, and real estate that is sold to several people or that didn't belong to the seller in the first place. You'll be offered phantom teak, macadamia, and jojoba plantations—all the get-rich-quick schemes you can imagine.

After pointing out all the pitfalls of going into business, I have to admit that many people are having fun doing so. You can feel a dynamic sense of progress and excitement in Costa Rica. This is the country of the entrepreneur, of wide-open opportunity, inexpensive land, dependable labor, and a relatively honest government. Modern-day Costa Rica is reminiscent of the old frontier days of the United States and Canada, full of success stories about North Americans who've opted to "start all over again."

When interviewing entrepreneurs, I always ask: What is the best part of doing business in Costa Rica, and what is the worst part of doing business here? The replies are often: "The best part is that I can afford to live in Costa Rica. The worst part is I don't make enough money to live in the style I'd like."

Just be aware that there are as many tales of failure as there are of success.

EXAMPLES OF BUSINESS VENTURES

I had a discussion with an expat businessman about the high rate of business failure by Costa Rica newbies. He said, "If you take restaurants out of the equation, business success rates are probably not much different than in the United States. The problem with restaurants is that many start-ups are opened by people who have absolutely no experience. Yet a restaurant is usually their first choice."

What happens is that people fall in love with Costa Rica and decide to chuck everything back home and move to paradise. Too young to retire, they want either a job or a business. They've always loved to cook, and friends always praise their culinary skills. "Everybody always said I should open a restaurant when I retire." Good luck. One expat said to me, "It amazes me to see a new restaurant open up in our village, where there are already eight other restaurants. When one of these restaurants started to serve pizza, each of the other restaurants immediately bought pizza ovens and put pizza on their menus. Unless you have something extra-special to offer, how can you possibly succeed?"

Sometimes this works. A very successful Italian restaurant in our community was started by an Italian insurance executive from Naples and his wife, who was an accountant for a chain of hardware stores. They knew nothing of the restaurant business, but their location was wonderful, and there were no other Italian restaurants in the region at that time. To succeed, food didn't have to be more than just okay. Surprisingly, they eventually became gourmet cooks!

But all too often, novice restaurateurs have no clue as to what to do after making up a menu. Imaginative menus and good cooking are only part of the restaurant business. Without knowledge of buying, food spoilage, theft, and dealing with Spanish-speaking employees and suppliers, the new entrepreneurs are lost at sea.

Mexican Restaurant in Costa Rica!

The following story was related to us by Norman and Isabel Florez, who started a Mexican restaurant in the San José suburb of Alajuela. Longtime residents of New York City, Norman and Isabel made the move to Costa Rica as newlyweds, determined to create a new life for themselves. Norman says: "I was first told about Costa Rica back in 1999. My aunt Isabel had begun traveling to this paradise, and just could not stop raving about it. She would say: 'Norman, Costa Rica is just like the United States fifty years ago! You would love it! You just have to find your niche.'" After thoroughly researching the country, Norman and Isabel decided that moving here would become a dream worth looking forward to. While living in New York, Norman had been employed in restaurants since he was sixteen years old, and he knew the business well. Therefore, the idea of setting up a restaurant in Costa Rica became the goal long before any travel plans were in place.

"My wife and I arrived in Costa Rica in June 2003, as newlyweds, met by my aunt who knew her way around. She became our instant guide. We decided that Alajuela would be the chosen location for our venture (mainly because it was a place my aunt liked). We decided on a *Tex Mex* theme (although I prefer the term *Mexican American*). We figured that Mexican cuisine would be easier than anything else. We both enjoyed it so much, and there were no similar restaurants in the area.

"Being a die-hard pessimist, and having read about the bureaucracy involved in setting up shop, I told myself that it would become my own personal Costa Rican adventure. We found and rented a small place that used to be an office and turned it into a restaurant! Then we began the chore of dealing with Costa Rica's monster bureaucracy. From the beginning it was obvious that the local municipality's pace was not my own.

"Yet, actually it turned out not quite as bad I feared it would be! Two months later we were in business! *Jalapeños Central* was born! I was cooking, and my physical therapist wife was waiting on tables. It took a while, but before long, Isabel acquired the restaurant menu jargon perfectly. At first, if a customer were to ask anything not actually our menu, she would be dead in the water, speechless, and would simply yell, '*Norman!*'

"Dealing with suppliers was a true nightmare at first. This is when *tico time* and *mañana* came into the story. It was always '*later*' or '*I'll call you back.*' After the first year everything settled down, and there were no more mishaps."

Norman says: "It has been a great ride—easy to say, because it really has gone well for us. People have given us nonstop support, and along with the guidebooks and Internet, we—and our small stamp-size of a restaurant—are now considered a mini success. Our son Nico was born here, and along with our business accomplishments—another reason to feel right at home. Nine wonderful years later it feels like we've been here all our lives, without one single regret. I find myself encouraging people to do as we did. There are still lots of opportunities here. So, the more the merrier! All you really need is to keep your common sense with you at all times, remembering that this country, as beautiful as it may be, is still inhabited by humans. Some good and some bad!"

So, when you visit Alajuela, be sure to drop in and say hello to Norman and Isabella. You will find the Jalapeños Central in the downtown center of Alajuela. From behind the cathedral on the Parque Central (the park in the center of downtown), a block and a half north, following the flow of traffic.

Bed-and-Breakfast

When Charles Owens retired from the Civil Service in California, he and his wife, Jeanetta, tried returning to their home in Olympia, Washington, but soon discovered that wouldn't work out. Jeanetta says, "We found that it is really hard to go back. You change, the place you move back to changes, and nothing stays the same. What really woke us up was a group of seniors who met every morning in one of the local breakfast restaurants, their conversations on how many pills they took, what their health insurance covered, and what diseases they suffered from. We just knew living the normal USA lifestyle was not for us."

Having once done a tour of military duty in Panama, they decided that an investigation of Central America might zero in on a country suitable for retirement. Jeanetta's Internet search turned up a small apartment for rent in a large, lovely home near Grecia, not far from San José. They planned on staying just for three months, then moving on to Panama.

Jeanetta explains: "When we arrived in Grecia, we were delighted to find out the owner was an English-speaking American, yet we worried that she might possibly not like black people. Because you see, Charles and I both are truly black people. In Costa Rica, when someone sees black tourists, they naturally assume you're Costa Rican—from Limón or Cahuita—from anywhere but the USA. Fortunately, the lady who owned the place greeted us warmly and didn't care about our ethnic background and heritage."

They settled into the area and fell in love with the house and surroundings. Suddenly, the owner decided to leave the country for a while and offered to rent them the entire house. Charles and Jeanetta talked it over, and on impulse agreed to a year lease, provided that they could run it as a B&B.

They opened La Terraza Guest House in October 2002. At first they had one customer, who rented the apartment for three months. That paid for the furniture they needed to furnish the rooms. But they didn't worry, because they hadn't seriously considered this a real business. After all, they were both retired.

"We were surprised," Jeanetta said, "when a few months later, the owner contacted us to ask if we would like to purchase La Terraza! We agreed, even though we weren't yet turning a profit. Since Charles and I came here with a comfortable income to back us, that helped with our decision. Too many people move here with not quite enough money, overspend, and expect to have their business begin paying off right away. We've found doing things slowly and steadily has worked out well for us.

"Since we opened we've added three vacation rentals. We stay pretty full, but advertisement is the most difficult part of our business. Our repeat customers are the people who have kept us in business during slow times.

"Our experience as business owners in Costa Rica has been a good one. Establishing a presence has been easy, and we have been able to gain the respect of the people in our community. We've had the same maid and gardener for several years and currently have four full-time employees and one part-time employee. They have good employee benefits, and they are well respected by us.

"Our goal is to add something to the lives of people here in Costa Rica. We have gotten far more of a benefit from our business than just earning a profit. It feels good to see people have a great year and be able to change their lifestyles because they are working in your employ."

La Terraza Guest House maintains a website (www.laterrazab-b.com) with pictures of accommodations and landscaping, as well as retirement and relocation packages that include thirty-day accommodations and visits to popular retirement communities in the Central Valley.

(*Note:* Unfortunately, Charles passed away on January 2, 2009, but Jeanetta is determined to fulfill their dreams of retirement in Costa Rica.)

Private Social Club

Joe and Helena Wygal, from Cambridge, Massachusetts, decided to start one of the most unusual and innovative Costa Rican businesses imaginable.

They created an authentic European pub, complete with imported beers, rich wood paneling, custom brews from Costa Rica's draft beer producers, a dartboard, and even a small movie theater. That wouldn't be such an unusual enterprise if the pub were located in a city, but this setting is isolated, at least fifteen minutes from the nearest village. The Black Sheep Pub is situated on a mountainside, surrounded by a tropical forest, with a view of the Pacific in the distance. Howler monkeys and parrots provide background ambience not normally found in Europe or Britain.

Joe says: "My passion for pubs goes back twenty-five years to my first trip to Europe, which covered parts of England, Belgium, the German Rhineland, and the Netherlands. My interest in pubs moved to another level when Helena and I bought a home in Massachusetts, with a large basement that lent itself to becoming a pub. We became acquainted with beer brewers and enthusiasts from all over Europe and the United States, as well as local beer groups. Our parties became renowned throughout the area because we had beer on tap that was not available anywhere else. After a while I began to feel it was time to move our hobby to another level, perhaps a business, though I was not sure what that would be. We did sense that this would not be possible in the Boston area."

Joe and Helena had done considerable traveling in Costa Rica, until they finally decided on the Nosara area for their retirement. However, instead of buying the usual property in the village or Beaches of Nosara development, they decided on a building lot in a new development about a fifteen-minute drive from town. Joe says, "For a while I seriously considered locating the pub in the village of Nosara, but when construction on our home began, we reverted to the idea of having the Black Sheep Pub on our home property. We decided to operate it as a private club, with house rules and free membership."

Joe designed the exterior of the building in a traditional pub style with half-timbering, and the interior in European splendor. The business is actually two pubs, the first of which is a British pub room complete with an English-style bar. The second room is a continental European motif, with German-style long tables and paraphernalia from such countries as Germany, Belgium, and the Czech Republic. (My wife and I have visited there and can attest to the pub's authenticity.)

From the very beginning their target market was the American and European community in the Beaches of Nosara area. They gradually began to attract some of the surfer crowd as well as a group of young and lively *ticos* from San José. As special events were being celebrated, such as a New Year's Eve party, first anniversary bash, and a St. Patrick's Day celebration, the pub attracted more and more people.

Joe said, "From the beginning, I had wondered if a European pub would catch on in tropical Costa Rica, but when the special events became popular, when I could no longer see the bar due to the thirsty mob in the British room, I began to realize that my dream was coming true. A year later at our second New Year's Eve party, with over 200 people mulling around, with a long line forming outside the pub, with young girls wearing high heels and fashionable sexy outfits that would seem more appropriate at the Hotel Hilton, with all assortments of drinker types, with fireworks suddenly cascading over the pub, with the sound of different languages and accents ringing in my ears—I shook my head, shut my eyes, and thought, 'But it was only a hobby—what went wrong?'"

Reviving a Small Hotel

In 2004, Ed and Rita Reames, originally from Maryland, decided to take early retirement. Ed was formerly in telecommunications, and Rita worked as a teacher and an airline employee. Too young to qualify for Medicare, and not covered under any group medical plan, they moved to Costa Rica as "medical refugees" to take advantage of the affordable INS medical coverage.

At first, they tried living in Dominical, but they found the year-round summer weather to be a bit too much. So they moved to the San Antonio de Belen area, not too far from the Alajuela Airport. The weather there is year-round spring, much more to their liking. Still too young to adapt to a traditional retirement lifestyle, they began looking around for some kind of business, possibly a bed-and-breakfast—provided it was located in a cool climate. They have found that more opportunities exist in Costa Rica for people not yet ready to fully retire and those with limited capital to invest. In Costa Rica you can start over again, and age is not a deterrent.

They ended their search in Tilarán, renowned for its pleasantly cool and breezy weather. There, Ed and Rita discovered the small La Carreta Hotel and restaurant, which had been devastated and abandoned by its former managers after they unsuccessfully tried to turn it into a B&B.

Rita tells of their adventure: "We moved into the hotel during the rainy season. It was dark, dreary, and depressing. There were partially finished concrete walls, dust and filth that hadn't been cleaned in years, bathrooms that certainly gave you second thoughts about using them, boxes every-where, and, most of all, water. One morning we woke up to a flood. Our neighbor's *canoa* [large outside water gutter] had broken in the night. Our garage, which was full of unpacked boxes, was flooded. So was our kitchen. We were concerned that our appliances might be ruined by the water on the floors. We spent the day cleaning up and salvaging our belongings.

"It was not more than two weeks later when a second *canoa* broke. Another flood! This time it took about two weeks for the repairs. We began calling our new home/hotel 'water world.' As we were making our repairs and improvements, we came to know a terrific crew of local workers. They came to our rescue over and over. Now we are known all over the com-munity and have a great circle of friends and resources. Tilarán is a small community, and we have been drawn into its warmth. This experience has also done wonders for our Spanish!"

Today, the place is immaculate, with walls decorated with fresh and beautiful murals, new furniture, and many extensive (and expensive) changes. They opened for breakfast on November 20, 2007, and a Christ-mas brunch followed. They offer cozy standard rooms with queen-size bed, private bath, and cable TV, or deluxe rooms that include a queen-size bed and a twin bed, private bath, TV, and excellent balcony views of the garden and surrounding mountains. There is also a rooftop terrace with stunning views and a table and chairs for all to enjoy.

Those planning to visit Monteverde, Lake Arenal, or the volcano will find Hotel La Carreta a convenient base for their travels and adventures. This boutique hotel and art gallery is located in Tilarán between La Fortuna and Monteverde, within driving distance of primary forest and the dramatic Arenal Volcano and stunning Lake Arenal. The beaches on the Pacific Coast are a short drive. It's ideally located for one-day ecotours, mountain biking (rentals available), bird-watching, world-class sailboarding, hot springs, and freshwater fishing for tilapia. Their website is www.lacarretacr.net.

(*Note:* At the time of publishing this book, Ed and Rita notified us that they had returned to the US. The reason? They had reached the magic age of sixty-five and were now eligible for Medicare, so they no longer needed to rely on the Costa Rican health care system.)

AGRICULTURE AS INVESTMENT

Because of incredibly rich soil and year-round growing seasons, Costa Rica is an agricultural paradise. The country is checker-boarded with crops of all descriptions. Just about anything grows here, with bumper crops the rule rather than the exception. Therefore, agriculture would seem to be one of Costa Rica's best bets for investment. Actually, agriculture can also be one of the biggest investment disasters. Just because crops grow well doesn't guarantee you are going to make money. Furthermore, many native Costa Ricans are abandoning agriculture as a way to earn a living and going into less arduous occupations.

As an example: I have a *tica* friend from a large Costa Rican family— twelve children. Her father was a farmer, and so were all of his nine brothers. (Families of two generations ago were much larger than today.) Yet my friend points out that not a single one of the male descendants went into agriculture as a living. "They sold the land and went into some other occupation or business. Too much hard work for so little money," she explains.

One longtime agriculturist who has struggled to make a living in Costa Rica said, "Farming is a great way to go broke even if you are an experienced agriculturist. There are too many unknowns and too many marketing problems." He added wryly, "If I had invested the same amount in real estate as I spent trying to get an orange grove started, I would be a rich man by now."

Unusual or nontraditional crops that target overseas markets are sometimes a good idea, only if you personally are going to run the operation and you know marketing. You really have to know what you are doing and find a unique market niche. Expatriate farmers who succeed here specialize in crops destined for foreign markets or develop a demand overseas for their specialty.

An added incentive for abandoning traditional farming in Costa Rica is the upcoming CAFTA accord, in which North American "factory farms" will be allowed to export US-government-subsidized crops duty-free at prices Costa Rican farmers can't match. This is especially true for crops such as rice, corn, and citrus fruit. Personally, I believe this accord will spell disaster for *tico* agriculture.

Coffee Farm

In 1997, Janet Blakeley, her husband, and her daughter, Courtney (age six at the time), decided to make the move to Costa Rica. They found a gorgeous home in the hills above Grecia, with a sweeping view of the city and high mountains on the other side of the Central Valley. (I've visited their home and can attest to the breathtaking layout.)

They discovered that in addition to the house and landscaped grounds, the property included several hectares of coffee trees—the type that produced the highest-quality Arabica beans. Janet's curiosity led her to learn more about coffee, how it should be grown and processed, and how it could be gourmet-roasted on a small scale. She made friends with neighboring coffee growers and soon became fascinated with organic methods of coffee production. She bought processing equipment and began packaging her own brand of gourmet coffee, Tesoros Del Sol.

When her husband left the picture via a divorce, Janet needed to do something with the coffee to supplement her income. She had already been helping neighbors convert to organic coffee growing and looking for ways to help farmers get fair prices, stop losing their land, and to help the environment. Together the group organized a collective of coffee growers.

Janet says, "We are licensed as an organic project, which means my company of Tesoros Del Sol gets them all certified. We make no-interest or low-interest loans for approved fertilizers and such. We train and monitor farms monthly. We pay higher rates to help them during the three years of transition to organic, and much higher rates for their organic beans. We've cut out the middle man."

Farmers who participate in the program are also required to plant tree shade cover, which produces higher-quality coffee beans. They are urged to plant native trees, but planting alternate crop trees such as papaya, bananas, or citrus is also encouraged. Janet grows pineapples between the rows. Being certified organic enables her farmer associates to command a price commensurate with the cost of production.

Janet's marketing strategy: Package only top quality, hand-processed, pure Costa Rican beans (no blends), and market the product directly to consumers in the United States by way of the Internet. Coffee lovers there are delighted to pay a little more for 100 percent Costa Rican coffee that cannot be found elsewhere. It would have to be a low-volume business, Janet decided, but it could be done via the Internet. And it works!

Courtney thoroughly enjoyed her experience of growing up in Costa Rica and loves the *naturaleza* of their Grecia home. She is thoroughly bilingual and finds it easy to make friends with the neighbors. She says she finds them loyal and caring, and she feels as if they are extended family. Janet says, "I appreciate that I don't have to worry about drugs or violence, and that Courtney has grown up with 'people' values."

Janet maintains an exceptionally informative website (www.tesdelsol .com) that gives complete information about coffee production in Costa Rica, how it is grown and processed, and the differences between varieties of coffee. The site also provides ordering information for North American consumers who would like to try certified organic coffee.

Teak Plantations

These have been promoted in Costa Rica for years. According to promoters, raising teak trees is a surefire venture that will pay huge dividends. Forestry experts I've interviewed dismiss this as mostly hype. It is true that after an eight-year growth (trees will be from six to ten inches in diameter), they are typically cut into tongue-and-groove boards or into chips to make parquet floors. From what I understand, the profit from this first cutting sometimes just about covers the cost of planting and maintenance. Trees are thinned again every several years, with the last harvest at about twenty-five years, when they finally become high-value lumber. The *Tico Times* once ran an interesting series of investigative feature articles on teak as an investment. The controversy is ongoing, so before you invest, do some investigation on your own. You're likely to find some investors who feel they've made a mistake and others who are pleased.

Years ago, when the teak craze started, *tico* farmers throughout the country planted stands of teak on steep hills where ordinary crops wouldn't do well. It didn't cost much, and over the years, they ignored the trees. But since teak should be planted on flat areas and loses most of its value without early pruning, this teak is not bringing high prices. Today, when you buy tracts of forested land, chances are you'll find some rows of teak trees, some possibly ready for harvesting on a small scale.

I have an expatriate friend who discovered that by using a relatively inexpensive and easily portable sawmill, his workers can turn out stacks of teak tongue-and-groove boards—very much in demand for home building today. Instead of the traditional method of cutting trees, dragging them to a point where they can be loaded on trucks, and selling trees to lumber mills, these entrepreneurs bring the sawmill to the trees. Workers process them on the spot, turning low-value tree trunks into valuable lumber.

This system is much better for ecology, since it doesn't involve cutting roads through the forest or clear-cutting to get at the teak trees. My friend turns a nice profit and feels good about the sensible way the profits are generated.

Reforestation

The traditional way of marketing tree farms is to buy inexpensive, abandoned farms, then plant several thousand teak or pochote trees, then sell the land to investors. There are other ways of doing this: either sell shares in the project or sell trees to investors rather than land.

Fred Morgan, from western New York, found another approach. Instead of planting hectare after hectare of a single tree crop, his idea is to re-create the original rain forest by interspersing cash-crop trees with varied native and rare species of trees that were originally present before the rain forest or primary forest was destroyed to create pasture for cattle. Later, when tree crops are harvested, the rain-forest trees are left standing, with a good start for the future. The land will then be withdrawn from further planting, restoring the land to nature. Information about this project can be found at www.fincaleola.com.

When asked his advice for those thinking about going into the reforestation business in Costa Rica, Fred Morgan wrote the following:

"We from the first world perceive that successful business people are usually hard drivers. If you're that way in Costa Rica, you will find that, like walking chest deep in water, you will exhaust yourself by trying to run and not get anywhere much quicker. However, if you move at a reasonable pace (which is a little slower than you're used to), you will find that the water flows around you and even tends to support you when you stumble.

"Work with the characteristics of the culture: Here, community is considered more important than any particular business or enterprise. The labor laws reflect this way of life. You can fight against that for a while, but if your neighbors think it's against the good of the people, you can expect the current to start opposing you and to eventually wear you out. Our goals of re-creating rain forest and creating jobs are considered beneficial to the society, so not only do we rarely find ourselves fighting the culture, we also have been supported and carried by it at times.

"People buy trees from us with the understanding that after their trees are removed, the land will be maintained as perpetual rain forest. For people who want to help without owning trees, we have a program we call the Tree Avalanche that works by using donated trees to create a pioneer forest of valuable wood. Among these trees are also planted the 'succession trees' that will eventually make up the mature rain forest. When the pioneer cash-crop trees are removed, allowing the succession trees to form a forest, the money realized will be used to purchase more land and to plant more pioneer and succession trees.

"Since the money gained from the pioneer trees is more than it costs to plant, care for, and harvest them, the amount going into reforestation keeps multiplying. In the wake of this process, instead of leaving a path of destruction, the Tree Avalanche leaves a swath of new forest." (See the website for further details.)

REAL ESTATE DEVELOPMENT

The term "property development" usually stirs negative images in the minds of longtime Costa Rican residents. They picture a group of profit-hungry investors who have one goal: maximizing profits. If primary forest, mangrove wetlands, or wild animals get in their way, no problem. These kinds of developers show no conscience as their projects destroy the environment. The only thing of vital importance to them is getting the highest return for the lowest cost.

Those who live in Costa Rica for any length of time will understand what I'm saying. We've seen foreign companies—Spanish, German, North American—come in with bulldozers and chain saws to clear building sites and construct homes for wealthy foreigners, laying waste to the countryside and invading the beaches. The biggest offenders are those who have the most money and thus have *pata* (connections) with local authorities. Big developers can afford to hire plenty of workers to speed up the process of transferring pristine beaches into gated golf courses and luxury homes. Local authorities are sometimes intimidated by wealthy and powerful corporations and often are backed down when they try to control development.

Large-Scale Development

It doesn't have to be that way, and not all developers are that way. A notable exception is the Bosque Verde development on a low mountain near the

Pacific Coast village of Nosara. The developers, Julio and Barbara Batista, are originally from Phoenix, Arizona. Neither Julio nor Barbara had previous experience in land development or anything connected with real estate. Julio was an engineer working for Honeywell on the International Space Station, and Barbara was an educational consultant working with schools in Arizona.

This all changed when the Batistas first visited Costa Rica more than a decade ago (after reading an early edition of *Choose Costa Rica*). They fell in love with the Nosara region. They bought a lovely house with an ocean view and plenty of trees, where bands of howler monkeys, iguanas, and flocks of tropical birds compete for human attention.

By accident, they discovered a *tico* family interested in selling their family farm. It was perched on a low mountaintop with fantastic views of the Pacific Ocean and coastline. Julio and Barbara couldn't resist. Heavily forested and not farmed for many years, the 285-acre property had become a veritable wildlife refuge.

They planned to build a new home on the very summit of the property. When they began looking into the expense of installing electric power lines, digging wells, and building three pumping stations to bring water up to the building site, they realized that they were looking at several times more money than they paid for the land. A natural solution was to subdivide the property into building lots and amortize the cost of the infrastructure among those who bought building sites. Each lot had ocean views yet were out of sight of neighboring lots.

Most developers would, at this point, begin selling lots to buyers, giving flowery promises of future water and electricity—a fast way to raise money to begin development. Julio and Barbara didn't care to do this. They decided not to sell even one building lot until water and electricity were in place, ready to start construction. They didn't want to disappoint buyers in the event that they couldn't come through with the promised utilities. When laying out the building sites, they made sure that each home would have maximum privacy from other homes. Even though it's a gated community, they wanted residents to get the feeling they are the only inhabitants overlooking the Pacific.

They hired a Costa Rican forestry and tropical-plant expert and proceeded to plant thousands of trees, shrubs, and vines. Sixty percent of the land is dedicated as an ecological easement for residents to enjoy, thus protecting the natural ecosystems from further development.

Being an engineer, Julio used his expertise to oversee the construction of the roads, culverts, electrical distribution, and water systems. Finally, after drilling wells, designing and building water-pumping stations, and bringing water to every home site, Bosque Verde was ready to begin selling building sites. All of the above took eight years of intensive (and expensive) work, but it was finally completed in 2005. Julio says, "We feel very good about what we have achieved. We used our retirement money to create an ecologically friendly community where we can live with like-minded adventurers. It has been a creative journey."

Almost the moment the building sites were put on the market, one couple bought two of them—one for their home and one for future investment. An entry with lagoons and gardens for beauty and a gatehouse for security welcome visitors.

Contact information: Greg Smith or Susan Loudenslager, phone 8721-7372 or 8876-0919 within Costa Rica; or (615) 530-6365 from the United States. Website: www.bosqueverdereserve.com.

Small-Scale Development

Property development doesn't have to be done with unlimited funds and investment. A few years ago, José Pelleya, a Cuban American who lived in Florida most of his life, opened a very successful bed-and-breakfast, in Alajuela (the Vida Tropical). In 2002, he started looking around for another B&B to complement his business.

José says, "Unexpectedly I ran across a beautiful farm property, rolling hills and views to die for, on the outskirts of San Ramón, about forty-five minutes from the airport. It had a large seven-bedroom, two-bath home (in need of remodeling), sitting on an eight-acre parcel. I loved it and could immediately see possibilities for a unique country bed-and-breakfast."

Formerly an attorney specializing in Florida real estate, José used his skills to negotiate a lease with the option to buy, with seller financing for one year once he exercised the option. José points out that both lease-option and seller financing were practically unheard of in Costa Rica at that time.

So he set about remodeling and modernizing the building. This in itself was no minor project. *Tico* farmhouses are basic to say the least. The B&B opened in 2003, and Angel Valley Farm was an immediate success. Being a gregarious person, José realized it could be boring to live on all that property alone. "Why not invite others to share," he thought. So he asked for permission to subdivide the property into building lots and started planning.

"Six months later, I found my first buyer, so I exercised the option," he said. "Then I sold the lot, and away I went!" Divided into seven lots, four sold the first year. Incidentally, one of his clients, a lovely lady named Joanna, bought the last lot, built a house, and then married José. They still live there. José says, "At least she got a good deal on the lot!"

Things were looking good, so José purchased forty-seven acres adjoining his development and created twenty-eight more lots. All of those lots were sold in just two years, and at least a dozen homes have been constructed. This is creating an interesting community of expatriates, pooling their energy, resources, and creativity.

As if that weren't enough, José's latest project is a business in downtown San Ramón called *Solo Bueno,* "only the best." This is a combination Internet cafe, public mailboxes, used English-language bookstore, as well as a real estate exchange for rentals and sales in the San Ramón area. Whenever local expats go into town, they naturally drop by for a cup of coffee, check e-mail, pick up a paperback, and catch up on what is happening in the community.

José is now retired, and the only dirt he moves is when he tills his garden. He's busy trying to read all the books in his library, watching Netflix, surfing the web, hiking, cooking, and traveling back and forth to Florida (and Pennsylvania, to Joanna's old homestead) to visit family and friends.

12

Hiring Employees

During World War II the Costa Rican government passed a series of progressive labor laws that remain on the books and are strictly enforced. These laws seek to avoid conflicts between workers and employers by setting out concrete employment rules and a system of wages and benefits. In effect, these laws take the place of union contracts between worker and employer, guaranteeing individual workers benefits they probably couldn't negotiate on their own. If you look at the rules from the viewpoint of the worker, they are basically fair—and certainly not unreasonable from the standpoint of a considerate employer.

However, hiring a maid, a gardener, or an employee in your business involves more than an informal agreement about wages and hours of employment, as is the custom back home. Because we North Americans aren't used to such formal relations with employees, and because we are likely to be hiring workers, even if it's just domestic help around the house and garden, the rules need to be spelled out in some detail. Following the laws to the letter prevents unexpected and serious problems.

Briefly, here are some ground rules: Employers are responsible for making Social Security payments for an employee as well as deducting contributions from the employee's wages. All workers are entitled to paid vacations. After a thirty-day trial period of employment, an employee is entitled to severance pay as well as notice before being laid off. A Christmas bonus is neither a gift nor a nice gesture; it's an obligation mandated by law. The employer is required to give three months of maternity leave at half pay. All these rules are detailed below and should be studied carefully before hiring any help. One other piece of advice: Purchase an accident insurance policy for your employees, even if they are only part-time. Premiums are minimal, but your employees will appreciate the extra coverage. You'll also protect yourself should something horrendous happen to one of your workers.

GOOD LABOR RELATIONS

I once spoke with a woman who was visiting Costa Rica with the intention of starting some kind of business. "When hiring workers," she said, "I understand that the secret is to just hire them for eighty-nine days and then lay them off. That way you aren't responsible for benefits such as severance pay and vacations. Once they work ninety days, you are obligated; so you simply hire new workers every eighty-nine days!"

This upset me, and I told her so. Although her information was incorrect, that wasn't the point. Costa Ricans work very hard for a fraction of the wages employees receive in the United States or Canada, and the law guarantees them certain benefits. It's unfair to try to chisel them out of their rightful benefits. Attitudes like this can do nothing but tarnish the reputations of other North Americans. Those who have lived here for a long time generally realize the wisdom of paying their help more than the law requires. "I try to make it so my maid can't afford to quit," said one woman. "She is wonderful, and I couldn't stand to lose her."

Word quickly gets around the neighborhood if you are a good person to work for (or a difficult one). If you earn a poor reputation as an employer, your job applicants will be those who can't hold a job elsewhere. Then you'll wonder why your employees are lazy, don't show up half the time, or have a tendency to steal!

After I gave the newcomer a piece of my mind about her attitude, she explained that she had heard that if you lay workers off after they've worked more than ninety days, you must pay eight years' salary as severance pay. She heard wrong again. The facts are: For each year worked, an employee is entitled to severance pay of one month's salary—up to a maximum of eight months' pay. That is eight *months'* salary, not eight *years.*

From a worker's point of view, this is only fair. Let's suppose that after eight years of faithful service, it becomes necessary to let your housekeeper go. Does eight months' pay sound outrageous for eight years of loyalty and hard work? If it does, then maybe you deserve workers who are lazy, don't show up half the time, or have a tendency to steal.

The owner of a hotel and restaurant in Manuel Antonio told of his experience hiring Costa Rican workers. "It's important to gain their trust," he said. "When they begin working, they don't know anything about you or how you are going to treat them. At first I had trouble attracting the best workers. But I treated people fairly and tried to keep them busy during slack seasons so that I wouldn't have to lay them off. Before long I earned a good reputation. Now I have a waiting list of people who want to join my staff."

CONDITIONS OF EMPLOYMENT

1. **Length of employment.** The first thirty days of employment are a trial period, and either employer or worker can terminate without notice. However, vacation pay and *aguinaldo* (Christmas bonus; described later) must be paid in addition to wages if the employee has worked more than twenty days in that month's time period. Thereafter, for each month worked, one day's vacation pay is due, up to two weeks of vacation for a full year's work. Many employees, either by custom or through union contracts, receive three weeks' vacation. My understanding is that an employee may work through his or her vacation, provided that the employee receives an additional day's pay for each day worked. (I'm not a labor lawyer, however, so you will want to confirm this point if it arises for you.)

2. **Wages.** Just about every employment imaginable in Costa Rica has an official job description with a corresponding minimum wage. From taxi drivers to physicians, from clerk-typists to college professors, all are listed on a biannual list of minimum wages that requires several pages. Laborers who work with machetes are listed separately from those who mend fences or work with shovels. In addition, various regions of the country have different minimum-wage rates.

    An interesting facet of the wage structure is that a maid, gardener, or chauffeur who lives in your home is considered to be receiving an additional 50 percent of his or her salary as "payment-in-kind." If, for example, you pay a live-in maid a salary of $150 a month, the actual salary is considered to be $225, or 50 percent more when figuring benefits. This is important, because the gross salary (salary plus payment-in-kind) is used to figure the *aguinaldo*, Social Security payments, and severance pay.

3. **Working hours.** The maximum for domestics is twelve hours a day, although almost nobody expects more than eight. The standard is usually an eight-hour day and a five-day week. For regular employees other than domestics, work on Saturday and Sunday is at double-time rates. Often construction workers work a half-day Saturday for a full day's pay. For those working in businesses or industries that traditionally operate seven days a week, the rules are a bit different; check with your local Social Security office. Although the laws are quite specific, *tico* employers often do not follow the laws to the letter, knowing that employees seldom complain. However, I earnestly advise expatriates to follow the rules; you have a high profile in the community, and cutting corners is really a penny-pinching tactic.

4. **Social Security.** An important obligation for employers, one taken quite seriously by the government, is Social Security. This critical institution pays for health care, sick leave, and disability pensions. You, as an employer, must pay 20 percent of a worker's gross salary and must deduct 9 percent of the worker's wages and pay both portions of the tax to the *Caja Costarricanse del Seguro Social.* Make sure your workers understand that you are withholding the taxes from their pay. Otherwise their share of taxes could come out of your pocket. Some people pay both sides of the Social Security payments as a bonus for a good employee.

   Within eight days of hiring a regular employee, you must notify the local Social Security office. Doing so is vital, because should a worker become ill or injured on the job, you could theoretically be liable for medical bills and 50 percent of the employee's salary for the duration of the sickness. When your employee is covered by Social Security, your liability is limited to the first four days' salary; Social Security takes over from there. To prevent abuse of this law, you, as the employer, are entitled to demand a health certificate from the worker (*carnet de salud*) when the employee is hired and every six months thereafter. This is provided at no cost to the employee by the Seguro Social Hospitals.

   Pregnancy is a different situation. Your employee's blessed event will obligate you to some additional employee benefits.

Employees are entitled to a month's rest before the baby is born and three additional months afterward—half the salary to be paid by the employer and the other half by the government. By the way, firing a worker for being pregnant is frowned upon, and you might need to validate your reasons for firing other than pregnancy.

5. **Christmas bonus (*aguinaldo*).** Sometime between December 1 and 20, employees are due an *aguinaldo*. For those who have worked a full year prior to December 1, the bonus is a month's pay. For those who have worked more than the thirty-day trial period but less than a full year, the payment is prorated over the time they have worked. Thus, a person who has worked three months gets three-twelfths of one month's pay. Remember that employees who live in or who regularly receive at least one meal a day get a Christmas bonus based on the payment-in-kind, in addition to their salary, or an additional 50 percent.

6. **Notice and severance pay.** Workers employed more than ninety days and less than one year are entitled to two weeks' notice before being laid off. After a year, one month's notice is required. If you don't or can't give notice, you must pay the employee full wages for the notification period.

    Unless an employee quits, you are obligated to pay severance pay dependent on length of employment: up to three months, none; from four to six months, two weeks' pay; between seven months and one year, one month's pay. Then you must pay an additional month's pay for each year or fraction over six months worked. In no case can this payment be more than the equivalent of eight months' salary.

    Again, remember that this is based on gross pay (including 50 percent payment-in-kind, if applicable). It doesn't matter if the worker immediately finds a new job; you still have to pay.

    A worker can be fired at any time during the first thirty days for any reason, with no obligation other than the *aguinaldo* and wages due. Furthermore, a worker who fails to give notice (*preaviso*) before quitting forfeits the *aguinaldo*.

EMPLOYEE OBLIGATIONS

According to government regulations, workers can be held responsible for damages they have caused, whether intentionally or due to imprudence or "inexcusable neglect." A domestic worker can be discharged without receiving severance if "notorious lack of respect or civil treatment is shown," which should be backed up by witnesses. You had better have good proof, though, because in doubtful cases the Ministry of Labor tends to side with the worker.

When an employee quits or is laid off, it is a good practice to make things crystal clear by having him or her sign a statement (in Spanish) to the effect that all benefits have been paid. Include the severance pay, vacation pay, Christmas bonus, and any salary due up to the time of separation. Have the employee sign the document in front of a witness. Should the employee be quitting voluntarily, be sure to note that in the document.

SALARIES AND WAGE RATES

Tico employers tend to be reluctant to pay higher wages than the law requires, but they are often forced to if they want good help. At times construction workers are in very short supply, so they can demand more than minimum rates. In some parts of the country, workers could earn double what they could make in more depressed areas. Nicaraguan workers (most of them illegal) will usually accept the minimum or less and are resented by *ticos* who have to compete with them for jobs. North Americans who successfully operate their own businesses usually agree that paying decent salaries means happy employees who are loyal and hardworking.

We always pay a little more than our neighbors for two reasons. First of all, we don't want to feel like cheapskates. Secondly, wages are so low in the first place that we feel somewhat embarrassed on payday, as though we're exploiting our employees. Yes, we risk the ire of those who accuse us of "ruining it for everyone," but I can easily dismiss that. I reject the idea that paying our gardener an extra 60 cents an hour will "ruin it" for anyone. Nor can I believe that all this extra money will go to our workers' heads and cause labor unrest among our neighbors' domestic help. We try to be friends with our employees, not bosses. Our maid always gives us both a hug and a kiss on the cheek when we see each other on the village street, just as we do with our good expat friends when we meet.

Unlike the United States, Costa Rica stipulates an individual wage rate for each and every possible job classification and profession, not simply a basic minimum salary no matter what the job. The government's web page (see below) posts specific wage scales for more than 250 occupations; for example: cook's helper, captain of a boat, and bus drivers (there is a different wage scale for a bus driver who also collects fares). The wage rates listed below are accurate only until January 1, 2013, when the new schedule will be posted.

Not only does just about every job classification have a specified minimum wage, but the level of education is considered, having its own minimum wage. For example, minimum wages range from 107,883 colones ($207) a month for domestic workers to 383,359 colones ($737) a month for someone holding a master's degree from a university. Our local librarian went to night school at the university for several years. Once she received her degree in library science, she was entitled to almost double her salary.

Among the highest-paid jobs on the list is journalism, which pays about $1,000 a month, compared with a university professor's salary of colones $850 a month. My impression is that because legislators are sensitive to press criticism, by awarding newswriters the top pay rates, they hope to receive special consideration. Since this is my profession, I feel top pay is perfectly fair. (My publishers might quarrel with that belief.) However, most journalists in the United States earn more money than that every week.

Estimated Minimum Wages until January 1, 2013*

Workers	Monthly	Per hour
Housemaids	$237	$4
Field hands	$305	$5
Semi-skilled workers	$310	$5
Skilled workers	$322	$5
Technicians	$347	$6
University graduates	$524	$9
With graduate degrees	$628	$10

*Actual wages vary, depending on whether domestics are live-in workers, how many hours they work, and other variables.

In addition to the official minimum wages, there are other costs. The employer is obligated to pay 13 percent Social Security taxes, plus withhold 9 percent from the paycheck on behalf of the employee. (Many employers pay the whole tax as a special benefit.) Then there is 3 percent for retirement and 2 percent for workmen's compensation insurance. It's important that these payments are made and that these obligations are met, either by yourself or by a professional manager. Again, accident insurance is also a very good idea.

WORKING IN COSTA RICA

A question often asked is, "How can I get a job in Costa Rica?" The answer is, "It can be done, but it's not easy." The Costa Rican government discourages foreigners from competing with citizens for work. In order to work legally, you'll need a special permit, which involves proving that you are uniquely qualified for a job that can't be done by a *tico*. Foreign companies are entitled to a limited percentage of noncitizen employees, but in practice they seldom fill this quota. The reason is simple: They can hire all the qualified *tico* employees they need, and most foreigners don't want to work for *tico* wages. Twenty dollars a day is considered a generous wage. A bartender earns about $15 a day, a skilled carpenter about $4 an hour.

Since the collapse of high-tech employment and jobs being exported to China and India, many highly qualified and skilled software engineers, technicians, and web specialists find themselves "at liberty" and eager to begin life anew in an interesting setting such as Costa Rica. They are aware that the country's computer technology is riding a wave of expansion as business, industry, and government become computerized and enter the online universe. It's only natural that those recently unemployed and soon-to-be-downsized high-tech people who love Costa Rica will be looking in this direction.

Are there jobs for these highly qualified people? Probably not. You have to realize that Costa Ricans also see the future opportunities in the world of digital employment. Seems as if every other high school student you meet plans to major in computer science. At every one of the many satellite campuses of the universities, the most popular classes involve computers. Students come from miles around to take night classes in *computación*. The good news is that many high-tech jobs have been created through foreign investment. The bad news is that Intel and other corporations are limited to 10 percent of their workforce being foreigners on work permits, and they are committed to hiring as many *ticos* as they can. One exception is in the field of teaching English. Qualified teachers can often find employment, although, again, for minimal salaries. More on this subject can be found in chapter 15, "Costa Rican Schools."

POSSIBLE WORK-IMMIGRATION CHANGES

This is not to say that a large number of foreigners aren't working illegally in the country. Most of them work in real estate sales, property management, and tourism. You'll find them employed as waitresses, bartenders, tour guides, and hotel employees. Most are young and willing to take whatever pay they can get, just to live in Costa Rica. Many work as English teachers, tolerated by the government, ostensibly because they aren't taking work from *ticos*. A few with special skills find work in construction. Often, foreigners working as building contractors don't get hassled by local officials, probably because they hire workers and provide jobs, but basically because they are supervising rather than laboring. Unless foreigners are obviously taking work from *ticos,* their activities are often overlooked. But at the other end of the scale are an estimated 200,000 Nicaraguans working as coffee pickers, unskilled laborers, and at other jobs that Costa Ricans would rather not do. If that figure is accurate, that's a lot of illegal workers in a country of around four million inhabitants!

Let me emphasize: Over the years of updating this book, I've never recommended that people work illegally; I am simply reporting what is the case. The fact is, the Costa Rican government hasn't been overly zealous in enforcing existing laws. My personal opinion (and it's only an opinion) is that the government is not likely to do anything drastic that might affect the status quo for most of those who are technically in violation of immigration rules. Nevertheless, it would be prudent to keep abreast of events should there be any question in your mind. You can do this by reading the *Tico Times* and other online Costa Rican newspapers. (Also, by keeping a very low profile.)

13

Getting to Costa Rica

The quickest and easiest way to get to Costa Rica is by air, of course, but this restricts the amount of belongings you can take—items you may need for a long-term stay. Those who live here full- or part-time always enter with as much luggage as we're allowed. With rising costs of fuel, weight limits on baggage are going down while fares are going up. Our bags are usually packed with items difficult to find in Costa Rica, such as tools, home fixtures, and items from the "wish lists" of our friends in Costa Rica. We bring everything from paperbacks and videotapes to bedding and automobile parts. Customs tend to be rather casual about this, as long as one doesn't go overboard. (Remember, there's only a $500-per-passenger duty exemption.)

A large number of airlines schedule regular service to Costa Rica—including American Airlines, United, Continental, and others—and inexpensive Canadian charter flights fly from Vancouver and Montreal. Foreign lines, such as Mexicana, TACA, Aviateca, COPA, and others, fly from Miami, New Orleans, Houston, San Francisco, and Los Angeles. Some start-up airlines, usually flying out of Miami, occasionally offer "get-acquainted" fares for as little as $40 round-trip from Florida to San José! Obviously, these low-ball tickets don't last very long.

COSTA RICA'S AIRPORTS

Costa Rica's main air facility—totally renovated and ultramodern—the Juan Santamaría Airport, near San José, has streamlined its arrival and departure procedures and is almost a pleasure to use. Customs inspections are relaxed yet professional. Airport taxis to downtown San José are plentiful, and prices are controlled. The standard price to downtown San José is at the time of writing around $20. Cabdrivers readily accept dollars. A real improvement in the taxi situation is that you no longer have to haggle over the fare. As you exit customs, you'll see some windows on your left where you can buy a ticket to wherever your destination. You hand the ticket to a waiting taxi driver, and your fare is paid! Some people will leave a tip, but that's up to you. By the way, airport taxis aren't supposed to go to more than one hotel or address per trip, so if you share a cab with someone, make a deal with the driver, perhaps agreeing on a tip for the extra stop. Also, a bus stops on the main road in front of the terminal, with inexpensive fares to go to downtown San José or to nearby Alajuela. Buses pass by every few minutes.

When returning from Costa Rica, you must pay a departure tax of $26. You'll find two lines in the terminal for paying this tax, and you must pay before going to the ticket counter. You can use colones, dollars, or a combination of either. If you use a credit card, they have to add about $4 to the bill. You'll hear travelers complaining about this tax, but consider that US airports also have hefty charges, which customers often aren't aware of—but are simply added to the price of your ticket.

A popular international airport—Daniel Oduber International, near the northwestern city of Liberia—opened not too long ago. Many of the major airlines, as well as charter flights from the United States and Canada, are making Liberia a major destination for air travelers. For those tourists and residents headed for the popular Guanacaste coast, this means avoiding an overnight stay in San José, coming and going. Of course hotels and tourist facilities in the San José area fiercely resisted the new airport. But travelers to the Pacific beaches love it!

The economy of this western region is already healthy, but increased airline traffic is boosting it even higher as travelers to the Pacific beaches find the Liberia airport extremely convenient. For example, when my wife and I travel to our Pacific Coast home, we used to have a six-hour drive from San José to our house. With the Liberia terminal in place, the drive is just two hours.

DRIVING TO COSTA RICA

For a while, civil wars in Guatemala, El Salvador, and Nicaragua brought tourist automobile travel through these countries to a virtual standstill. But even then some intrepid tourists insisted on driving, merely changing the

route somewhat. They traveled the Pacific coastal route through Guatemala, avoided El Salvador by detouring through Honduras, and then carefully skirted trouble spots in Nicaragua. When we tried to drive through
Guatemala in the 1980s, we returned to Mexico after facing gauntlets of
gun barrels being pointed at our foreheads at every military stop. That was
years ago. Today, the potential problem is with the drug cartel battles taking place in Mexico.

Yet a surprisingly large number of people still routinely make the trip to
Costa Rica through Mexico by automobile! Let's take a look at why they do
this, and why you may or not want to try. I would like to stress that these opinions are strictly my own and not intended as a recommendation. A caveat:
I have a background in Mexico, having lived in Mexico as a youngster and
adult, having written numerous travel articles about Mexico, and having
coauthored the retirement guidebook *Choose Mexico*. Not surprising, I would
feel much more comfortable than would first-time motorists making the
trip, and I admit that I have a tendency to downplay dangers of such a trip.

First of all, according to what we've been told while visiting Mexico
in the past two years, and from what we've read in newspapers and online
news sources, the war between the drug cartels seems to have some mutu-
ally accepted rules, one of them being: "Do not involve civilians!" From
what we've been able to determine, and according to Mexico expatriate
bulletin boards and forums, almost no North Americans have become
casualties. I've only seen a small handful of news media reports of fatalities,
and almost all of them were unintentional or misunderstandings. Many
foreign travelers feel safe on the main highways, especially on the express
toll roads through Mexico. I probably would feel okay, but certainly would
not make a recommendation for others to follow my example. Anyone
interested in the issue of tourist safety can go to the *Mexconnect* bulletin
board and read the opinions and messages from American and Canadian
retirees living in various parts of Mexico. Feel free to post your own queries online and form your own opinions. The forum on *Mexconnect* can be
found at www.tiny.cc/oovwdw. (You will be asked to sign up to access the
forum, but this is free.)

Our Experience

The following information is basically for *after* the drug crisis is over in
Mexico (if that ever happens). My wife and I have driven the route twice

(before the drug cartels were in the picture, of course). The actual driving time from the Arizona border at Nogales was around eight days of no more than eight to ten hours of relaxed driving per day. Not being in a hurry, we spread our last trip over a full month. We stopped to visit friends in Lake Chapala, Mexico, and in Guatemala City. We also detoured to spend a week at the marvelous Mayan ruins in Copán, Honduras. Our memories of this trip are nostalgic and pleasant. We sincerely hope that someday soon, others can enjoy the same route without tension or worries.

Please don't think I'm suggesting that everybody will have a breeze. It's a long trip, with bad roads as well as good ones. Sometimes the accommodations are awful; sometimes they're delightful. If you can speak some Spanish, it would be helpful, but we met many travelers who spoke very little Spanish yet were making out just fine. Some people will enjoy traveling through Mexico and Central America, others will not. Those who won't enjoy this kind of journey are those who probably wouldn't think about going in the first place. You'll know into which category you fall.

Every day on the road was a new adventure, a new challenge, full of photo opportunities and stimulating encounters with other travelers and local people. The most annoying part of the journey was the delay and inconvenience while crossing borders. Frozen-faced officials examine your papers with suspicious eyes, then hand out a sheaf of forms to be filled out in triplicate. Then they rubber-stamp everything in sight. (Oh, how they love rubber stamps!) You go from one official to another for what seems an eternity. Finally, you are allowed to leave the country, only to drive fifty feet into the next country and start the process all over again at the next customs office.

Even if you speak Spanish well, I highly recommend that you hire a *tramitador* for each border crossing, someone to help you through customs, at the busy crossings. (You can generally tell when you need one: when the lines are long and not moving.) You'll usually find kids hanging around who, for a fee, will run your passport and car papers around to the places where they will be rubber-stamped, have stamps affixed, and have signatures scrawled upon them. Which of the kids to hire? I always pick one who appears to be the most aggressive. He will not be shy about elbowing tourists aside to shove his way to the front of the line so that the officials can look at your papers first. The cost is usually $10, but it's well worth it. Get the price fixed before you start. If things appear to be moving smoothly, you may not need to hire a helper.

On the Road

From the US border at Brownsville, Texas, to Costa Rica, the drive is 2,300 miles. From Mexicali the distance is 3,700 miles. Your car should be in good condition, with new tires, a spare, an emergency tool kit, road flares, and flashlights with extra batteries.

Always get out of the car and supervise the gas station attendant while he services the car. Attendants have been known to accidentally put diesel fuel or leaded gas into a car requiring no-lead fuel. And make sure they turn the pump back to zero before they start so that you don't end up paying for gas you don't get. (I've never had this happen in Costa Rica.) You might carry a hand calculator to make sure you are paying the correct amount and getting the right change. Even if you don't know what you are doing, the attendant will think you do, and he won't cheat. A trick that station attendants in Mexico might try to pull on you: When you hand them a 100-peso bill, they quickly switch it for a 50-peso note, to make you think you made a mistake. The cure for this is to carefully hand them the note and say, "*Billete de cien pesos*" ("hundred-peso bill").

Don't forget car insurance. Your US or Canadian policy isn't recognized south of the border, but carry it with you anyway as proof that you have a valid policy, just in case. You can buy a special insurance policy for Central America. Before you cross into Mexico, contact Sanborn's Insurance at (210) 686-0711 (fax 210-686-0732), or write to PO Box 310, McAllen, TX 78505-0310. The website is www.sanbornsinsurance.com. This company can write Central American policies by telephone and will take credit cards. Most people purchase a fifteen-day policy, which should be more than ample time to drive all the way to Costa Rica. Ask for a *Travelog* with detailed directions, maps, and hotel/restaurant listings for Central America (free with insurance).

14

Touring Costa Rica

Every nook and cranny of Costa Rica has something special to offer, something to dazzle the eyes or gratify the other senses. Newcomers are never satisfied until they have seen it all; longtime residents tend to repeat their travels, to see everything again and again. Fortunately, getting around the country is easy. Within a few hours you can visit just about any section of Costa Rica you choose, and you usually have several modes of transportation available to you.

The quickest way to travel about the country is by SANSA, Nature Air, or charter flights. Planes fly regularly, serving San José, Quepos, Golfito, Palmar Sur, Barra del Colorado, Nosara, Tamarindo, and Sámara. Ticket prices used to be inexpensive, but in the past few years, they have become costly. Charter flights cost only a few dollars more than scheduled flights. SANSA offers a discount for residents with *cédulas* (permanent residents), but it's still five to ten times as expensive as bus travel. Flights to anywhere in the country usually take far less than an hour. Check with travel agents or websites for schedules. They can change overnight or be canceled entirely.

Because flights are popular and the planes are small, they are frequently booked solid. Make reservations well in advance. And since regular service can be crowded, "air taxi" or charter flights are popular. Small five-passenger planes will take you anyplace in the country with an airstrip. What's nice is that you can arrange to have a driver awaiting your arrival, who rushes directly to your charter flight, and you don't need to overnight in San José.

What if you are a pilot and would like to rent a plane and fly yourself? Not so easy. Even if you are a certified pilot with a license from another country, you can't rent a Costa Rican plane until you've earned a Costa Rican license. You need to show proof of your total air hours logged in your country as well as log a certain amount of time in Costa Rica. To import an airplane, see chapter 16.

TRAINS AND BUSES

Guidebooks used to rave about the scenic wonders of the country's train system. Especially tempting were descriptions of the spectacular railroad trip from San José to the Caribbean city of Limón. However, since the earthquake of 1991, passenger trains no longer journey to Limón, or anywhere else for that matter. Sad, but true. Some roadbeds and a few ancient bridges slipped downhill—common occurrences during Costa Rican earthquakes—but this time the government decided not to rebuild. The lines were losing money anyway.

It's possible that service to the Pacific port of Puntarenas could be resumed sometime in the future, with a private company taking over the operations. In early 2000 a test run to Puntarenas had people sleeping in line overnight to get tickets. Two hundred disappointed would-be passengers watched the train roll away without them. The train to the Caribbean Coast, however, definitely appears to be history. The cost of repairing the bridges and tracks would be prohibitive.

Buses are another story. In addition to excellent city bus service, eight intercity bus companies provide frequent service to just about anyplace you'd care to go. Unlike the situation in the United States, where monopolistic intercity bus fares sometimes border on extortion, tickets between Costa Rican cities are downright cheap. A four-hour ride from San José to Limón, for example, costs less than $10.

San José has no central bus station; bus lines depart from separate terminals, ranging from a new, full-service terminal to a curbside parking place in front of a small ticket office. For example, to go to Quepos and Manuel Antonio, you take the buses that leave from the "Coca Cola" terminal. (The Coca Cola terminal gains its name in a typical *tico* fashion: There used to be a Coca-Cola bottling plant in the neighborhood.) Buses for Limón, Cahuita, Puerto Viejo, and other Caribbean destinations have their own terminal on Calle Central, six blocks north of the Metropolitan Cathedral. Often reservations need to be made a day or two in advance. The better tourist guidebooks list the bus terminals, destinations, and travel times.

A number of smaller bus companies (often with only one or two buses in the fleet) carry passengers to all imaginable sectors of the country. Few towns or villages in the republic lack bus transportation of some sort. Often while I was negotiating impossible backcountry roads, bouncing through deep potholes, skirting boulders in the trail, and wondering whether my rental car could ever make it back in one piece, a passenger-laden bus would appear from out of nowhere, sound its horn impatiently to move me aside, and then rumble past as it hurried on its way.

These country buses tend to be of an older, rattletrap variety, often comprised of secondhand school buses bought at surplus in the United States. Sometimes the owner-drivers don't bother to change the paint, and the bus finishes its transportation career bouncing along dusty trails in Costa Rica with Maplewood Unified School District still painted on its side. Occasionally, you'll be pleasantly surprised by an air-conditioned vehicle of late manufacture, which makes the backcountry surprisingly luxurious. Of course, there's nothing to guarantee the driver will actually turn on the air-conditioning, which draws power from the engine and consumes more diesel fuel. And since *ticos* open the windows from force of habit, the air-conditioning is redundant.

Since the distance between San José and any destination in the country is not very far, bus trips don't take too long. From San José to Quepos, a popular tourist destination, bus travel time is less than four hours. By air it is only twenty minutes or so, but by the time you get out to the airport an hour early, wait for the plane to leave (often a half hour to an hour late), and then wait for a bus to take you from the airstrip to town, you haven't saved all that much time. Plus you've missed a lot of interesting scenery. However, be aware that different bus lines have varying schedules. For example, travel from San José to Puntarenas takes two hours on one bus line but four hours on another.

I knew Costa Rica had a lot of competing bus companies, but for a while I was astounded at how many different bus lines there appeared to be serving the public. It seemed that the bus lines' names were very creative. Then I discovered that the name painted on a bus's side or on the back wasn't the name of a bus company at all, but rather an imaginative name given to the bus by its driver as an expression of his individuality.

The *Tico Times* once ran a feature article on these names, at which point I realized that the Papa Lolo bus that passed by my house every morning as

I waited for my ride was not owned by Papa Lolo Bus Lines but driven by a driver with the nickname "Papa Lolo." Some buses were named after family members; other names were exercises in imagination. Additional names the article noted were Desert Storm, Krakatoa, *El Príncipe Azul* (the Blue Prince), *Mil Amores* (Thousand Loves), the *Dancing Queen*, and *El Guerrero del Camino* (the Road Warrior). Having mentioned this (one of my favorite stories about buses in Costa Rica), I have to admit that the major bus lines are becoming much more professional, and fewer of them give the driver the autonomy to personalize his vehicle.

A MULTITUDE OF TAXICABS

Costa Rica enjoys an excellent system of taxis, with more than 7,000 cabs zipping along the streets of San José and the suburbs—double what there were a decade ago. Almost all taxis are late-model Japanese imports, usually Toyotas or Nissans. Occasionally you'll see a Volkswagen or a Volvo. By law taxicabs are painted bright red. You can't miss them. In San José you can go practically anywhere in the city from downtown for between $2 and $6. Between 10:00 p.m. and 5:00 a.m., drivers are permitted to charge an additional 20 percent. Drivers don't expect tips, but I always round the bill up to the next 200 colones, and they drive away happy.

All San José taxis are supposed to have meters, and except for the "pirate" cabs, most do. (A "pirate" cab is one without a legal permit, described later.) *Ticos* refer to a taxi meter as a *maría*. Why *maría*? Some years ago Costa Rica's president decided that taxis should have meters rather than have drivers and clients haggling over the price of each ride. So he ordered a batch of taximeters from a company in Argentina for a trial run. The company's name contained the words Santa-María-something-or-other. But with typical Costa Rican bureaucracy, customs officials in Limón refused to allow the contraptions into the country until all the proper papers and forms were filled out in triplicate and stamped. By the time all the red tape and tax stamps had been glued to quadruplicate copies and signatures affixed, the meters—which were mechanical, as opposed to the electronic ones they use today—had rusted in Limón's damp climate and had to be trashed. *Ticos* thought this so funny that they adopted the word *maría* for a taximeter.

Avoid cabs parked in front of hotels or discos. The drivers will tell you that they don't have to use meters because they pay more insurance or some other baloney. The truth is, they charge from two to four times the normal rate. When in doubt, ask, *"¿Hay una maría?"* If the driver claims the meter isn't working, don't enter the cab until you've established a price (provided, of course, that you know about what the price should be). If the driver quotes a ridiculous price or if you haven't any idea of the correct fare, take another cab with a meter. At certain times of the day, especially when it's pouring down rain, drivers are reluctant to turn on the meters because they know they can get all the customers they want and wouldn't want the cab's owner to know exactly how much was taken in.

Often you'll find cabs without meters, known as *piratas,* or "pirates," which are private autos illegally operating as taxis. Usually the fares quoted by these nonmetered cabs are about the same as you'd pay in a legally operated vehicle. The problem with *piratas* is that some of them aren't in safe operating condition. And unless you know what the fare should be and you know enough Spanish to negotiate, I'd recommend waiting for a cab with a meter. All in all, I think Costa Rican taxi drivers are fairly honest. Rarely have I been overcharged, and that was during times of heavy rains or rush hours, when the extra cost was worth it to me.

Although the law says that taxicabs must use meters, bear in mind that any trip over 7.5 miles (twelve kilometers) is exempt. A trip from the airport to San José, for example, should cost between $15 and $20, depending on what part of the city you are going to.

Why are most cabs new? Because one side benefit of owning a taxi is that it can be purchased free of import duties, as long as it is used for three years before selling it as a used car. This means that after three years of generating income, the vehicle can be sold for as much as it cost in the first place!

Up to this point we've been discussing taxicabs around the Central Valley. Taxis aren't only for city folk: You'll find them all over the country, sometimes in places so isolated that they would seem implausible. Not all villages will have a taxi, but most have access to one from a neighboring village or at least someone in the village has a family car he uses to pick up a few extra colones. Today, with the cell phone explosion, you know the village cabdriver will be available anytime his cell phone rings. Away from the city's paved roads, four-wheel-drive taxis are common—and in the rainy season, a must. Four-wheel-drive trucks sometimes serve as taxis, with the truck bed used to transport furniture, appliances, or more passengers. In rural areas, where buses and taxis are rare or nonexistent, private autos and trucks often provide free rides to local people walking from one village to another. I do the same and find that locals appreciate rides—the hospitality enhances their opinion of foreigners.

Taxi Chauffeurs

Driving a car around San José or through the narrow roads in the immediate countryside isn't exactly a relaxing pastime. I sometimes find myself so involved with traffic and confusion that I see very little. My passengers see even less, since they spend a great deal of their time praying, cursing, or shouting at me: "Watch where you're going, you dummy!" For that reason I rarely drive in downtown San José, even though I have my own car. It used to take me ten minutes of sweating and cursing to get from our condo to the center of town, whereas it takes only five minutes of sweating and praying in the average taxi. (My idea of hell would be driving a taxi in San José through eternity!)

There is a better way to explore the Central Valley: Rent a cab! Taxi drivers much prefer the idea of one fare for the entire day, instead of wandering all over town waiting for someone to flag them down. One fare isn't nearly as hard on the cab, since passengers always want to stop, get out, and spend time looking around, giving the taxi and driver a deserved rest.

Not only is it convenient to let someone else drive (someone who knows what he's doing), but renting a cab costs not much more than renting a car for the day. A competent, English-speaking cabdriver will chauffeur you around the Central Valley for five or six hours for about $100. A rental car for one day, with insurance and gasoline, would cost at least $75—and $1 million worth of tension. In other words, after you buy the driver's lunch and give a small tip, you're about even. Most any cabdriver will rent for about $25 per hour, but you're better off making prior arrangements with an English-speaking driver. (It'll cost a little more.)

Taxicab rental will also save you hours of time and frustration when checking out neighborhoods for real estate. The driver can whisk you to a half dozen suburbs in less time than you can stumble onto one. This is also a great idea for sightseeing trips around the Central Valley. Instead of four people paying $30 to $60 per person for a five-hour commercial tour, a cabdriver can show you the same sights, with individual attention, for much less. Some drivers will even take you on longer trips, anyplace in the country you care to go—Monteverde or Manuel Antonio, for example—as long as you also take care of their hotel and meal expenses.

Not all drivers are willing to rent by the hour, and not all can speak English well enough to explain what you are seeing. To find one who does, check with your hotel clerk or a travel agency. Many English-speaking drivers are available and eager to show you around the Central Valley.

COSTA RICAN RENTAL CARS

Renting a car is by far the most convenient way of touring the country. When you get serious about looking for a place to live for a few months or for the rest of your life, renting a car for a week or two allows you to travel about freely in search of your dream location. You don't have to bother with bus schedules; you can check out side streets or country lanes, and you can stop whenever you find a particularly interesting view. With a car, you needn't worry about hotel reservations; chances are, if one hotel is full, another will have room. You can drive around, checking out for sale or for rent signs. You can investigate for yourself instead of being under the control of a salesperson, a rental agent, or others with a vested interest in showing you only their own properties.

At present, automobile insurance is a government monopoly, and it's mandatory that your rental-car insurance be purchased through the government agency. This could change soon, bringing much-needed competition to the field. The way it is now, there's often a hefty $750 deductible in case of an accident with your rental car. Should the car be totaled or stolen, the deductible is usually about $1,500. Since auto theft of rental cars is common, this calls for keeping your rental car in a safe place at night. Nowadays you can pay extra and have full collision insurance, and pay a little more and insure against theft. The insurance isn't cheap, but if you have a gold or platinum credit card (such as Visa or American Express), it should cover the deductible in case of an accident. Check with your credit-card provider to be certain. Be sure to report a mishap to the credit-card company within twenty days, even if the rental agent assures you the other driver's insurance covers the repairs (from sad experience).

Accessories such as antennas, radios, tires, and mirrors aren't covered by rental insurance; if they are stolen, you are liable. The answer to the insurance problem is to keep your car in a guarded parking lot overnight when in the vicinity of San José. Auto-accessory theft is not as common in smaller towns, but in San José and other large cities, be aware.

Important: Unless you purchase full-coverage insurance, before you accept a rental car, check the car for dents, scratches, and blemishes! Make sure the rental-car employee notes each of them on your contract. Unscrupulous employees in some car-rental agencies have been known to work a scam by charging for the same damage over and over. If the damage is there but not duly noted, you could be blamed and may have to pay. Generally, this only happens with smaller rental companies. Discuss the issue before you sign a contract.

Finally, insist on good tires. A sharp rock can penetrate a tire if the tread is thin and the sidewalls weak. If the tire is destroyed, you're liable for that, too. Insist on another car if the tires are not in good shape. If the car-rental agency gives you trouble about this, consider finding another agency.

DRIVING COSTA RICAN ROADS

Your regular driver's license is perfectly legal in Costa Rica for ninety days from the time you enter the country. After that you need a Costa Rican license. For residents or for those awaiting *residente* status, a license is relatively easy to get, although it involves the usual red tape. For example, you will need to present a certificate of health from one of the doctors' offices nearby (which certifies you are still breathing), take a driving test, and the usual bureaucratic hoops to jump through. The license is issued while you wait.

As a tourist, you are permitted to drive with your home country's license as long as your passport indicates you are in the country legally— that is, if your passport shows you haven't been here more than ninety days. If you leave the country long enough to get a fresh stamp on your passport, you'll be okay for another ninety days. Take this warning seriously. Some Ministry of Public Works (MOPT) offices issue driver's licenses to nonresidents; some will not. However, the advantages of having a Costa Rican driver's license are nebulous unless you are a resident or have made application for residency.

Some people believe that with a Costa Rican driver's license, you needn't carry a passport. Not so. If you can't show either a passport or a resident's *cédula* to prove you are in the country legally, you could have a problem. A photocopy of the passport might be acceptable, provided you have a copy of the page showing the date you entered. The original passport is much preferred. Photocopies of your driver's license are not acceptable. In fact, without your original driver's license, car-rental agencies won't even rent you a car.

The first rule of driving in Costa Rica is one that should be followed in any country: Do not leave anything valuable in the car, even out of sight. They say that a favorite trick of thieves is to monitor the car-rental desks at the airport and watch who rents a car and fills the trunk with interesting luggage. They then follow the car to the hotel, and while the passengers are inside at the registration desk, the thieves open the trunk and help themselves to the luggage, extra money, cameras, and so on. Frankly, I've never known anyone who has had this happen, and I think this is a bit far-fetched, but why take chances? If possible, leave someone in the car during that crucial first stop. Once you are outside of San José, the chance of something like this happening is almost nil.

Driving through the Costa Rican countryside isn't difficult; it's just slower. With all that gorgeous scenery, who wants to travel fast? Be especially careful when passing. Make sure you have time to get around safely, and be cautious near hills and curves. Always drive as though you expect trouble. That's just common sense in any country, but particularly so in Costa Rica. Too many drivers have a daring attitude that urges them to pass on hills and curves. For this reason accident rates in Costa Rica are unusually high. Drive defensively, and keep an eye on the speedometer.

Americans, used to high-speed, paved highways, sometimes have difficulty keeping their speed under sixty-five miles per hour; it doesn't seem normal to drive slower. But you must realize that sixty-five miles per hour is about 110 kilometers per hour, a highly illegal speed anywhere in the country. Most Costa Rican highways have an eighty-kilometer-per-hour speed limit. That's only forty-eight miles an hour—not a normal speed for North American drivers, who are used to 65-mile-per-hour limits with most everyone driving 10 miles an hour faster. Depending on the quality of a Costa Rican highway, an eighty-, ninety-, or an occasional 100-kilometer-per-hour speed might be posted..

Watch for oncoming drivers who flash their headlights off and on. That means trouble ahead, usually a radar speed trap or occasionally an accident. Another sign of danger is a tree branch or piece of shrubbery lying across one lane of the pavement. That signifies that an accident, a washout, or some other nasty surprise could await you ahead.

Driving in city traffic anywhere around San José can be frustrating. As you get the knack of it and learn the system, it gets easier, but never easy. Theoretically, finding your way around San José should be simple, because downtown city streets are logically organized on a north-south, east-west grid. *Calles* (streets) run north to south and *avenidas* (avenues) run east to west.

However, nothing in Costa Rica is as simple as it sounds. For one thing, street signs are usually missing. Sometimes they'll be posted on the corner of a building or sometimes on a signpost, but just when you need to know exactly where you are, you'll not find a clue. Furthermore, most downtown streets are one-way, sometimes without arrows to indicate *which* way! You are expected to know. Okay, so you know that Avenida 9 is a one-way street going west, but how do you know the street you are looking at is Avenida 9 when there are neither street signs nor one-way signs? All you can do is watch to see which way traffic is flowing. If no cars are coming either way, you don't dare take a chance.

In the surrounding towns of the Central Valley, traffic is lighter than in San José, but the problem of missing street signs becomes even worse. Some streets are one-way and others two-way, but often there aren't any signs to clue you in as to which is which. An arrow painted on the pavement should indicate which direction is permissible, but often the arrow has faded into history. It's especially disconcerting to be driving along what you believe to be a two-way street and suddenly notice that all the cars parked on both sides of the street are pointing in your direction. Since parking on either side of the street is okay in Costa Rica, you have no way of knowing if they just happen to be facing your direction or if you are traveling the wrong way again.

Away from the cities and major highways, you find bumpy roads that demand slow driving. Going too fast over rocks can cut tires, marooning you several kilometers from a repair shop. You may have to change a tire yourself! When this last happened to me, I stood around looking perplexed until two young men stopped to change the spare for me. They refused to accept money. Next I drove to a sort of auto-repair place where two kids fixed my tire in a jiffy using strips of an old inner tube, some kind of glue, and what appeared to be a steel crochet needle. They didn't even have to take the tire off the rim, as I expected. They charged the equivalent of about $4; that included putting the repaired wheel on the car and stashing the spare in the trunk.

Eventually, if you drive very much in Costa Rica, you are guaranteed to find yourself stalled in an unmoving string of traffic that seems as if it will never start going again. Chances are this is caused by an automobile accident somewhere ahead on the road. It doesn't have to be a horrendous crash; it could just be a fender bender. Then what's the holdup? In case of a collision, no matter how minor, the vehicles mustn't be moved until the police arrive. That really backs up traffic!

What do you do if you are involved in an accident? Call 911 if possible and wait for the police get there. Take some notes, make sketches of what happened, and wait for the police to give a direct order to move your car. This is important, especially when damages are significant, because there could be issues with insurance claims. Supposedly the cops can't make a clear judgment of what happened if they can't observe the position of the vehicles involved.

Allow me to share a recent incident in which an expat was in an accident, being struck by an auto that went through a stop sign and hit his car broadside. He didn't have a cell phone and the guilty driver claimed he didn't either. The American walked down the street to the nearest public phone and called the police. By the time he returned to the scene of the accident, a policeman was writing up a report. But the other driver and friends had changed the position of the autos, making it look as if the *gringo* was in the wrong! So, as awkward as it might seem, hang around to protect your interest! Someone is bound to appear with a cell phone you can borrow.

MAPS AND DIRECTIONS

Maps of Costa Rica are notoriously inaccurate. I've only seen a couple maps that are up to date. Many of them show roads that haven't been traveled in years, having been abandoned long ago. New roads take forever to show up on most maps. The one map I am familiar with and in which I have faith is published by a company called Berndtson & Berndtson. It's rather expensive, but it's printed on a plastic-coated fiber that ought to last forever.

One of my favorite Costa Rican map incidents occurred while I was trying to find my way from Zancudo back to the Panamerican Highway. I had been there several times before, but I was forever getting lost. This time it seemed hopeless. I knew I was about two hours away from the pavement up north, but how to get there? I saw a truck approaching and flagged it down. With my three maps, I approached the driver and asked him to give me a clue as to how to find the sandy trail that headed north.

He puzzled over the maps, shaking his head in despair. "This map is wrong, *Señor*," he said. "This town is not here, it is way over here, and this road has not been used for years." He took a pencil and began tracing what he thought might be the road I wanted. Finally, with a flourish, he marked the last portion of the horrible road that connected with the pavement near Golfito. He explained once again how to find the correct turning points and, as an afterthought, he asked, "But *Señor*, I don't understand why you don't return to San José on the *paved* road instead of such a bad road?"

"Paved road?" I interjected. "These maps don't show a paved road!"

"Of course not. This is a new road and not yet on the maps. Just go two kilometers in the opposite direction and you'll reach the pavement!" (Actually, the road had been there for several years, but mapmakers are notoriously slow updating Costa Rican maps.) A few minutes later we were cruising along the pavement that follows the Panamanian border, with Panama on one side and Costa Rica on the other, headed for the Panamerican Highway!

TRAFFIC COPS AND SPEED TRAPS

I often hear reports of tourists being harassed by Costa Rican traffic cops. No doubt these things happen, as is the case anywhere else in the world. A few bad guys can get on the force. Yet after driving many thousands of miles and receiving numerous traffic tickets (all deserved), I have found the overwhelming majority of Costa Rican traffic police to be courteous and rarely stop someone without due cause. With all the crazy drivers in this country, cops have little reason to stop somebody for "nothing at all." Let's face it: Issuing a ticket for speeding, illegal passing, or no safety belt is not police harassment. In the United States it's known as "law enforcement." Tourists aren't exempt from traffic laws, even if they don't thoroughly understand them. Why should they be?

Yet you'll continually hear *gringos* complain that "the cops only stop rental cars. Why not *tico* cars?" This is partly true, because *ticos* know a little secret: When they see a speed-limit sign of thirty-eight miles per hour (sixty kilometers per hour) near an approaching curve, they slow down. They know there's a good chance that there's a radar gun ahead. Tourists, used to sixty-five-mile-per-hour highways back home, blissfully pass the slowpoke Costa Rican drivers in front of them. And guess what happens?

Paved Costa Rican highways usually are posted at eighty kilometers per hour. This may seem ridiculously slow (forty-eight miles per hour), but you can avoid being stopped if you simply relax and drive the speed limit. *Ticos* know that those occasional long, straight stretches of good pavement are also favorite places for radar guns. Maybe this seems sneaky, but when eighty kilometers per hour is the maximum, you're asking for trouble by going any faster. I've come to love those speed traps; if it weren't for them, all *ticos* would be traveling eighty *miles* an hour! The fine for speeding used to be between $10 and $40 dollars for ordinary violations, or $100 for *velocidad temerario*. That means "frightful and reckless" driving, defined as 120 kilometers per hour and above.

I say "used to be" because in 2010, the country's legislature passed some draconian traffic laws that boosted the fines for speeding to somewhere in the vicinity of $400! The legislature went full out in their war against motorists, raising fines for everything from illegal parking to not using seat belts. The idea was to curb dangerous drivers. However, as often happens, the Supreme Court nullified most of the laws, bringing the speeding fine back to $10. That was only temporary, because the legislature has been busy passing new legislation! As is the custom in all Central American countries, motorists cooperate with each other by giving a flashing headlight warning of a speed trap ahead. So when you see an oncoming vehicle flicking headlights on and off, bring your speedometer down to the proper range, and you'll avoid being "stopped for no reason."

Allow me to offer some advice for when you're stopped by traffic police. (I've had lots of firsthand experience in this department.)

First, **be calm, cool, and courteous.** After all, a ticket is not the end of the world. Until you're officially a resident, a traffic ticket cannot affect your driving record or insurance. Stay cool. I've escaped several well-earned tickets simply by joking with the officers.

Do not get belligerent or raise your voice. Shouting won't help; it only makes things worse. When a cop feels he's being harassed for doing his job, don't be surprised if he retaliates in kind. I suspect this is where many cases of true police harassment originate: A tourist isn't aware that he's done anything wrong and becomes angry and abusive. The cop loses his temper, too.

If the cop suggests that it would be easier to pay him than have to go to some distant place to pay your ticket, just politely decline and calmly wait for the ticket. Often, when the cop suspects you aren't going to give him a bribe, he figures it isn't worth wasting his time with you, and he'll let you off with a warning. Of course, when he seems to have decided to write the ticket, then I make a decision about whether to offer him a moderate sum "to pay the fine for me." But more often than not, I find myself just getting a bawling out.

Example: One day, while driving up the Inter-American Highway toward Liberia, I happened to pass another car on a long bridge. On the other side of the bridge, I was flagged down by a waiting traffic cop. He asked in Spanish if I knew why I was being stopped.

When I replied, "Of course," the cop was surprised, and asked: "Well then, why did I stop you?"

My reply: "Because I passed on a bridge."

"But, don't you know that's against the law?"

I shrugged and said, "Of course."

The policeman looked puzzled as he said, "Then why did you pass on the bridge?"

"Because I didn't know you were here."

Knowing he stood no chance of collecting a "tip" for not issuing a ticket, the cop laughed and motioned for me to get out of his life. It doesn't always work that way, but I feel that's better than apologizing and pleading, and then getting a ticket anyway.

If a cop insists on a bribe when you don't agree, you can pay him, but make a good mental image of him, including his badge number, and report the incident to the **Ministry of Public Works (MOPT)** at 2-227-2188 or at the MOPT office on Calle 9 between Avenidas 22 and 23.

Again, traffic tickets are no big deal. You can pay at any national bank or simply give them to the auto-rental company when you return your rental car. The agency adds the fine to your credit card and pays it for you.

Ticos and expat residents routinely save their tickets and pay them once a year, just before it's time to renew their auto license plates and yearly safety inspection. A final note: If you do get a ticket, be sure to pay it before leaving the country. Why? Because a recent law passed by the legislature blocks anyone from leaving the country until an outstanding traffic ticket is paid. This could be disastrous if this happens while trying to board your airplane for home! Like many laws passed in Costa Rica, this ruling could be ignored, but why take a chance?

I might add that since I've become accustomed to watching the speedometer, I haven't received a speeding ticket in more than nine years, even though I make frequent round-trips to the Nicoya Peninsula—past a dozen speed traps—sometimes with California plates, sometimes in a rental car. Having no speeding tickets in nine years is a lifetime Central American record for me. My secret is simple: I've acquired the habit of watching my speedometer and obeying the speed limit signs.

FINDING HOTELS AND LODGING

The tourist bonanza over the past few years made the hotel situation somewhat tight at times. To compensate, new hotels have been constructed, and *tico* families have converted their homes into bed-and-breakfasts as quickly as they could. Many North Americans have joined this bed-and-breakfast boom, partly financing their retirement by renting out spare bedrooms. In smaller communities, hotels and ecotourism facilities raced to accommodate demand. Today you can often find a room for rent in isolated places where camping was the only choice before. This trend has caught up with demand, at least temporarily, because now there seems to be a slight oversupply of rooms.

The tightest hotel-room market in Costa Rica is during the Christmas–New Year's weeks. Not impossible, just tight. Easter week and spring break are other busy times. During the rush seasons, making reservations before you leave for Costa Rica, even if only for the first couple of nights, is a good insurance policy. After you arrive, you can check around and locate something to suit your taste and/or the size of your pocketbook.

Around San José, hotels come in all sizes and flavors, with expensive rooms costing $100 a night and up and cheap rooms around $30. I looked at one room for under $25 recently, but shivers ran down my spine when I peered into the gloomy-looking space, with dirty linens on the bed, housed in a ramshackle wooden building that looked like a firetrap. For my personal tastes a $40 room would be my bottom choice (of course, I am easily satisfied—even though I do insist on wall-to-wall ceilings). My wife's preferences fall into the $65 range or above.

If you're on a budget—as long-term travelers usually are—don't expect too much in the way of luxury. You may find an affordable rate for a room with a private bath, only to discover that the shower is plumbed for cold water only. When a hotel advertises hot water, you'll often find one of those rinky-dink electric heaters attached to the showerhead. This contraption, known as a "suicide shower," has a lever that can be set to one of three positions: hot, warm, and off. The position that says "off" is often the only setting that works all the time. This encourages short but exhilarating showers (ideal for anyone considering celibacy). The secret is allowing the water to flow at its lowest possible volume, in the hope of coaxing warmth from the heating element. You'll usually get a satisfactory stream of warm water.

Should you be stranded out in the country, unable to find a place to stay, your ace in the hole is the local *pulpería*. This is the Costa Rican equivalent of a country "general store." It also serves as the social center of the community or village. Drinks and snacks are sold, as neighbors congregate to exchange news and tidbits of gossip as well as purchase necessary items ranging from matches to machetes. The proprietor of the *pulpería* can sometimes find you a room with a local family. This is a unique opportunity to see how country folk live in Costa Rica, but don't expect luxury. A *pulpería* is also an excellent place to inquire about real estate. If anything is for sale or rent in the neighborhood, the proprietor will know, and she might even know the bottom-line price as well as the asking price.

15

Costa Rican Schools

Because of Costa Rica's high literacy rate and extensive education system, a higher percentage of people speak English here than in any other Latin American country. English is a required course in grade school and high school. However, don't expect every *tico* you meet to understand your English; being exposed to English doesn't make them bilingual. *Ticos* forget high school English just as quickly as you forgot your high school Spanish. The fact that most Costa Ricans know at least a smattering of English makes it a little easier for those newcomers who are struggling with Spanish conversation. When a certain word eludes you, you simply toss in the English word and forge ahead with your discourse, knowing there's a good chance the listener will understand either the word or its context. Fluency and learning are greatly enhanced when you don't have the tension of pausing and searching your memory for the proper word. Tension is an enemy of language acquisition.

I'm continually surprised at the number of North Americans who live in Costa Rica for years and never bother to learn any more Spanish words than those needed to deal with the gardener or the gas-station attendant. Learning a language isn't easy, but those who do take the trouble to at least try to learn Spanish find that they are highly respected by their *tico* friends and neighbors. This opens the door to interaction with a whole new set of friends and acquaintances.

SPANISH-LANGUAGE SCHOOLS

An excellent way to study Spanish and to learn about Costa Rica at the same time is to enroll in one of the country's many Spanish-language schools. Language acquisition is big business here. There are at least twenty schools just in San José offering intensive Spanish classes. Throughout the country you'll find schools and individuals who are eager to give you private, one-on-one Spanish lessons. Some schools keep the class size to three or four students, ensuring each person maximum attention from the teacher.

Most schools offer programs that include homestay living arrangements with a Costa Rican family. By interacting with a local household, you might learn how Costa Ricans cook, where and how they shop, and how to deal with servants, as well as other everyday routines of life that can be so different from back home. Combining classroom study and a homestay with a Costa Rican family puts you in a round-the-clock Spanish-speaking environment, speeding up the learning process. Some schools include tours of farms, factories, archaeological sites, museums, conservation projects, national parks, and other places of ecological and cultural importance as part of the curriculum. Some schools will pick you up at your door every morning and return you to your family homestay in the afternoon.

An important observation about homestays comes from a former student, who says: "It's best to find a situation where you are the only guest in the home. When three or four students stay in the same house, you'll find yourselves talking to one another in English instead of to your hosts in Spanish."

No matter where you are in Costa Rica, there'll often be a language school nearby. You can study Spanish in downtown San José, on the beach in Quepos, in the cloud forest at Monteverde, sometimes even in a typical rural village. The sheer number of schools makes it impractical to list them here. Also, the varying quality of instruction makes it impossible for this book to make recommendations; we just don't know enough about them to vouch for their quality. The *Tico Times,* various tourist publications, and the Internet are full of information about *tico* language schools. Your best source for recommendations is from those who have attended a language school in Costa Rica.

YOUR CHILDREN IN COSTA RICAN SCHOOLS

A remarkable difference between Latin American children and their North American counterparts is their behavior toward one another and toward authority. *Gringo* kids are typically boisterous, full of energy, and extremely competitive. On the other hand, Latin American children, especially *ticos,* tend to be polite, calm, and well behaved. Bullying other students is all but unknown. Both in the family and in school, cooperation is approved and competition discouraged. Classroom discipline is no problem for the teachers, which makes *tico* kids a delight to work with. (I can say this from experience, as one who has taught language classes both in the United States and in Costa Rica.)

Your children can select from three types of Costa Rican schools: 1) private English-only schools, 2) private bilingual schools, or 3) free public schools. The farther you live from the Central Valley, the more limited your choices. When you live in an area where private schools are too far away to commute, your choices could be a public school or homeschooling.

Most foreign residents I've interviewed about their children's progress in private schools heartily endorse the educational and cultural experience their kids were enjoying. Tuition costs vary from the most expensive private school, with tuition and fees of about $7,500 per year, to some of the more inexpensive bilingual schools that offer tuition as low as $100 a month, last time I checked. Again, it's way beyond my scope of expertise to even try to make recommendations. You'll need to interview your neighbors and interview the school personnel.

Private Schools

Most North American parents prefer an American-accredited school with a curriculum equal to that offered stateside. Around the San José area, you'll find a choice of twenty or thirty English-only or bilingual private schools. Some present classes half in Spanish, half in English; others are basically English-language schools. Some offer classes from prekindergarten through high school, others just the first three to seven grades. English-only schools are popular with Costa Rican families who can afford the tuition. They want their children to learn English, and these schools are essential for those preparing for US universities.

At the end of this chapter, you'll find a partial list of well-known private schools that cater to North American students. Tuition varies from moderate to expensive, and selections will depend on the location of the school facility and the distance from your new home.

Public Schools

For the most part, Costa Rica's public schools are patronized by expatriate children living too far from the larger population centers to attend a conventional private school. Despite the fact that Costa Rica spends an inordinate amount of money on education, schoolrooms and facilities can be crude and rustic when compared with the average US or Canadian classroom. Often library books are scarce or nonexistent, and the quality of the teachers varies widely.

The daily hours of a public school day are usually shorter than those at private schools. Also, when a teacher is absent, classes are canceled and children are sent home early. This is partly due to an irrational government policy of assigning teachers to schools based on need, without considering where a teacher's home is located. Schools often provide housing for teachers during the week, and they go home on weekends. Understandably, teachers look for any possible excuse to cancel Friday-afternoon classes so that they can get an early start on the trip to their hometowns.

Depending on where you live, your only alternatives could be home-schooling or a Spanish-only public school (sometimes both). Parents of kids enrolled in public schools give mixed reviews. Some children are immediately befriended and accepted by the other children and love their teachers. Others feel lonely and ignored. None reported their kids being mistreated, bullied, or teased because they are different—common problems in US schools. Much depends on a combination of the individual child's ability to adjust and the particular situation in the school (the attitude of the teachers, the friendliness of other students, etc.).

I knew a couple from Holland whose three children attended an all-Spanish classroom located in a small village on the Guanacaste coast. The youngest (in second grade) absolutely adored the school, the teacher, and her classmates. The next eldest (fourth grade) hated school as much as her sister loved it. The older brother, who has Down syndrome, enjoyed school so much that his parents had trouble making him come home after classes. The students his size encouraged him to play soccer (which he loves), and they treated him with extraordinary kindness and respect.

The bottom line is that not all children can adapt to a public-school setting in Costa Rica, and some could do poorly. It seems to be an either/or situation that becomes apparent rather quickly. They either love it or they hate it. Whatever you do, don't force the issue if the child is not happy with public school.

Costa Rican Homeschooling

Some families choose homeschooling as an alternative to expensive private schools or to supplement the public school curriculum. To be honest, while children benefit immeasurably from immersion in the Spanish language and Costa Rican culture, a public school can't provide the background needed to be accepted at a North American university. Homeschooling can be crucial here. Also some children will not like public schools; homeschooling could be their only alternative. A poll among parents with school-age children indicated that 30 percent of the parents responding described themselves as homeschoolers. Those attending conventional schools were divided between 25 percent in public schools and 75 percent attending private schools.

Sharon Wallace, from Ciudad Colón, has homeschooled three children over the years and sent them away to be accepted at universities in the United States and France. She has this to say about homeschooling in Costa Rica: "The nitty-gritty is that homeschooling isn't recognized as a legal entity, yet the government takes a typical laissez-faire attitude. The official word is that kids must be in an educational program until age sixteen, but this is not enforced. In fact, local schools are delighted to not have the burden of more students in an already crowded environment. So, like almost everything here, it's considered tacky to butt into someone else's business.

"We've been homeschoolers in Costa Rica for more than thirty-five years. Parents all use a wide range of techniques. Among them are: online classes, standard curriculum, various mixed media courses, supplementary classes, mentor situations, and none of the above (aka: 'unschoolers.') My husband and I are unschoolers, meaning no prescribed course of study; instead we facilitate the kids' interests. And it's worked out beautifully for us. It's interesting that many of us who are totally sold on homeschooling also work as volunteers in local public schools, teaching English, helping set up computer access, teaching CPR (I did that), and whatever is needed."

One common objection to homeschooling is that children miss the social interaction of being in a traditional classroom. However, homeschooling parents in Costa Rica typically get together on a regular basis, bringing the children into social groups, doing ad hoc classes in creative writing, book reviews, science, drama, art, and other subjects. Since the

Costa Rican school day is a half-day, at any given time half the schoolkids are available for an out-of-the-classroom social life.

CHILDREN LEARNING SPANISH

Whether your children go to public or private schools, you will be astounded at how quickly they become fluent in Spanish (while you struggle and can't seem to get anywhere). It's nothing short of miraculous how kids can absorb a language simply by sitting in a classroom and listening to strange words and mixing with children using these same words. With most adults, it's too late to simply "pick up" the language; you're going to have to work at it.

My favorite example of this instant-learning process comes from Hilary Aeschliman, originally from Kansas City. Her daughter Stephanie had been placed in a very rustic village school on Costa Rica's Guanacaste coast. She started class not knowing a word of Spanish. After a few weeks, they needed to purchase Stephanie another school uniform. Hilary says, "We went to this little village store, but despite my Spanish lessons, I couldn't understand a thing the owner was saying. We were just talking in circles—my husband and I in English, the lady who was running the shop spoke only Spanish. We exchanged plenty of smiles and *lo siento*'s, but neither had a clue to what the other was saying. After about fifteen minutes we gave up.

"As we were leaving, I said, 'Well that wasn't very productive. I have no idea what she was trying to tell us.'

"At that point, Stef piped up and explained, 'She said that the lady who makes the uniforms is in Nicoya today and for us to come back next week. She'll be here Monday and Tuesday.'

"I could have strangled her!"

ATTENDING THE UNIVERSITY

Students from abroad are welcome at Costa Rica's many universities. There are four public universities and nine listings for private institutions. The largest school is the University of Costa Rica (UCR), with about 35,000 students, located in San Pedro, on San José's northeastern edge. Tuition for *tico* students is less than $100 a semester; foreign students are charged considerably more, with rates available on request. The other large school is Universidad Nacional. It has about 13,000 students and has several campuses scattered about the country, as does UCR.

Most satellite campuses are rather basic, with instruction geared to *ticos* who can't afford to take time off from work to study in the San José area. Many classes are held in the evening and offer studies in computers or bookkeeping or preparatory classes for entering a full university setting. I doubt that many *gringos* could benefit from attending one of these schools.

Private universities offer programs ranging from MBAs to degrees in theology, tropical agriculture, and conservation. Most accept and welcome foreign students, charging tuition of as low as $100 per class and $5,600 for an MBA degree.

EXCHANGE-STUDENT OPTION

If you're convinced that you'd like to relocate to Costa Rica but just aren't ready for it right now, an interesting idea is to send your offspring here for a school term as an exchange student—or maybe just for a class during summer vacation. This gives the youth a head start in learning the language as well as a great cultural experience. And you will have an interpreter when you do decide to make the move. You can contact the Iberoamerican Cultural Exchange Program and inquire about their various exchange-student programs in Costa Rica. The address is 13920 Ninety-third Avenue NE, Kirkland, WA 98034; (206) 821-1463; fax (206) 821-1849.

Christen Kemp, at the time a Spanish and international business major at the University of Tennessee at Knoxville, tells of her experience as an exchange student in a Costa Rican university where she studied Spanish under ISEP (International Student Exchange Program) for a year. The Universidad Nacional is one of few schools offering an optional fee-paid ISEP Spanish program outside the United States and is designed to provide study opportunities beyond those offered typically only through reciprocal exchange.

Christen says, "I studied at the university's campus in Heredia, and, though it's not the nicest school in Costa Rica, it was better than I had expected. Some foreign students who studied at other universities claim their schools are better. Apparently Universidad Nacional enrolls many *ticos* who can't afford the tuition to attend the better schools. The tuition for *ticos* is of course much lower than that for foreign students.

"Technology at this university is not up to US standards. There are only a few computers in the library, and students line up to use them. I found it easier to go to one of the many Internet cafes around town. An hour's Internet connection costs only a dollar. And then there's McDonald's, where you can use the Internet if you buy a Value Meal.

"Registering for classes was quite confusing. They don't use a computer system, so you end up making several trips to classes and the registrar's office. Another big difference is that the teachers are on *tico* time. In my first class, the teacher was always about forty-five minutes late. The students told me that teachers can be up to an hour late, and, unlike in the United States, where a class meets for an hour three days a week, at this school a class was held once a week for three to four hours. It's hard to keep focused for that long, but the teachers were actually pretty good. I had an excellent literature teacher from Chile. You do not buy books for your classes. Instead your teacher places a packet of photocopies at a designated copy shop and you go there each week and make copies. They are really cheap, like ten colones each.

"Living with a *tico* host family is awesome. This was probably the best part of my education in Costa Rica. Being introduced to and actually accepted into a traditional family and being part of their religious-holiday celebrations was an unexpected gift.

"There are many advertisements for families looking for students. The exchange program from the University of Tennessee paid my family $300 a month. For this I received a nice room, three full meals a day, and all my clothes and linens washed and ironed (sheets, pajamas—everything was ironed!). The family had a maid from Nicaragua whom they paid $100 a month to cook and clean five days a week."

TEACHING ENGLISH

If you look on the Internet, you'll find a dozen or so Costa Rican forums and bulletin boards where folks exchange information about living or retiring in Costa Rica. Very common on these forums are requests for job information from young people who want to live in Costa Rica so bad they'll work for any amount of money. The most frequent question is, "How can I get a job teaching English in Costa Rica?" Many queries come from those who assume that just because they speak English, they are competent to teach

English. This obviously can't be true, or else people wouldn't waste time in universities earning teaching credentials and studying classroom techniques or the latest ESL (English as a Second Language) methods. Believe me, as a credentialed ESL teacher myself and one who passed courses in these techniques, I can vouch for the awesome magnitude of facing a class of eager faces and hoping they will learn more from today's lesson than I will. (Even though I have university training in ESL, have taken all the requisite classes, and have even coauthored textbooks in language acquisition, I am the first to admit that I am not a very good teacher. I have neither the temperament nor the patience.)

That's not to say that you can't find a teaching position without an ESL degree. Mike Curls, who taught ESL at two schools in the San José area, points out that it's not essential to be an experienced English teacher. But you should have some teaching background, he says. "Myself, I have a degree in business administration (accounting major) and teaching experience from the Air Force. I was a classroom instructor in resource management school with extensive background training." By the way, many local colleges offer classes in teaching English to foreigners. It will go a long way toward your finding a job if you have some experience before you move to Costa Rica.

How to find one of these jobs? Something that ought to be obvious is that you won't find a teaching position while in the United States or Canada. You'll have to apply in person, in Costa Rica, ready to go to work. Every day schools receive job queries from people 6,000 miles away; the schools routinely ignore them. Why waste time corresponding with someone who may or may not ever come to Costa Rica—who is very likely just daydreaming about an adventure that will never happen? You'll have to be on the ground, ready to go to work.

Claudia Jenkins taught ESL in Costa Rica and points out an exception to the rule of applying in Costa Rica. "One way for an experienced ESL teacher—or one with a master's degree or at least an ESL certificate—to get a job with a Costa Rican language school might be to go to the annual springtime TESOL conference, which is held in different parts of the United States and sometimes other countries. While there, I showed copies of my résumé to two school administrators from the Centro Cultural Costarricense-Norteamericano. They wanted me to start teaching in ten days! I couldn't do it because I was a full-time teacher and only looking for something during my summer vacation. Later I did teach at that school for a ten-week bi-semester."

Claudia also points out an enormous drawback to teaching English in Costa Rica: the pay. She says, "At that time [in 1990] my net pay in Costa Rica was $2 per hour. My hourly pay in California at the same time was more than ten times that amount! Fifteen years later, the school was paying $4 an hour. And it's mostly part-time work." Claudia was a volunteer ESL teacher for an expatriate-sponsored library in Nosara and did teacher training for volunteer college students who come to Nosara every winter to teach classes for university credit.

Mike Curls reports on today's salaries, saying, "The pay is not adequate if someone needs to live on the salary. The Pro English school where I work pays $5.75 per hour, but most classes are two hours a day, two days a week ($23 a week). Where I taught in Cartago, they paid by class size. For example, a class of six to nine students paid $114 a month; twelve or more students paid $142 per month."

Why such low wages? Obviously because of the excess of applicants for the jobs. This is one of the few jobs foreigners can obtain without a work permit being absolutely necessary. Technically, one would think that schools would demand work papers, but they get around this by hiring their teachers as *servicios profesionales* (independent contractors). Technically, they aren't really working for the school. Mike Curls says he is aware of a couple of schools requiring working papers at the moment.

Claudia Jenkins says, "Teaching adults at a private school in Costa Rica is simply a wonderful experience. The students pay a lot of money, by local standards, for the classes, so they are motivated to learn. Since *ticos* like to *quedar bien,* even the most disinterested adult student would never be disruptive in class!"

A few Americans and Canadians earn extra money by tutoring in English in their homes. Sometimes a lack of formal training isn't that much of a handicap because the students merely want an opportunity to practice their fluency in one-on-one conversations.

LIST OF PRIVATE SCHOOLS

A full list of private schools is far too long for this book, and I have no way of evaluating them. Below are a few of the more popular and prestigious schools that have come to my attention. As in any educational situation, you'll need to ask other parents for recommendations and personally interview school personnel before making any decisions.

- **Country Day School** is a prestigious institution in Escazú, with classes from prekindergarten through the twelfth grade. It is Costa Rican accredited and has 650 students, with classes all in English. There is also a Country Day School in Flamingo. Tuition is moderately expensive. Tel. (506) 2-289-8406; fax (506) 2-228-2076; www .cds.ed.cr.

- **Costa Rica Academy** is another popular school and charges similar tuition. It is accredited by Costa Rica and in the United States by the Southern Association of Colleges and Schools. It's located in Ciudad Carrari, west of San José, on the way to the airport. Tel. (506) 2-253-1231; fax (506) 2-225-9762.

- **Lincoln School** in Moravia is the largest, on the northeast side of San José, with 1,600 students. Tuition is somewhat less than the abovementioned schools. Tel. (506) 2-247-0800; fax (506) 2-247-0900; www.lincoln.ed.cr.

- **Escuela Britanica** teaches half in English and half in Spanish, kindergarten through eleventh grade. It's located in Santa Catalina on San José's west side and has 800 students. Tuition is very affordable. Tel. (506) 2-220-0719.

- **American International School** is located in Cariari. This is a co-educational day school and college-preparatory school, with classes from prekindergarten through twelfth grade. Tel. (506) 2-239-0376.

- **Marian Baker School** in San Ramón de Tres Rios offers a US- and Costa Rican–based curriculum to prepare students for colleges and universities in the United States and Costa Rica. Tel. (506) 2-273-3426; fax (506) 2-273-4609; www.mbs.ed.cr.

16

Importing Your Belongings

Importing an automobile is one of the first things newcomers consider. Public transportation in Costa Rica is more than adequate, and many folks here do perfectly well without an automobile, yet having your own wheels is a luxury some refuse to forgo. Since car monthly rentals are exorbitant, before long the savings involved in owning your own car will become quite evident. The equivalent of a year's car rental would purchase a nifty, slightly used, four-wheel-drive vehicle.

There are places in Costa Rica where it just isn't practical to visit without a vehicle. True, buses make it just about anywhere you can imagine—some places I'd hesitate to take a four-wheel-drive vehicle—but after you get there, then what do you do? If you have to walk a few kilometers to the nearest store or restaurant, you might not be a happy camper. Without a set of wheels, your choice of hotel accommodations is governed by where the bus stops—if there is a bus. With your own transportation you can shop around for the best place to stay, and then use your wheels to select the best restaurants or hunt out the nicest beaches (which are usually a long way from a bus stop).

BUY OR IMPORT YOUR VEHICLE?

Chapter 13 gives details on driving your vehicle down from the United States. That's an option for the hardy, one not to be undertaken lightly, but in our experience, it can be fun, too. If you choose not to drive, you are left with the alternatives of buying a vehicle in Costa Rica or shipping one down from the north. There are advantages to both options. Which option is better depends on several conditions in effect at the time you need a vehicle.

There are two schools of thought about buying vehicles in Costa Rica. One claims that cars here are maintained in excellent shape because they are so expensive; folks protect their investments with loving care. The other school of thought is that Costa Rican roads are so full of bumps that cars age quickly beyond their years.

No matter which school of thought you favor, take my advice: Never buy a refurbished taxicab! Taxis in Costa Rica go through absolute hell, driving all day and all night, cruising over rough streets—stop and go, stop and go—the worst kind of wear. I know a mechanic in San José who restores taxicabs for a living. He has a great body-and-paint man and has a skilled upholsterer on his staff. I've seen vehicles limp in looking hopeless and strut out looking brand-new. I've studied these cars in minute detail, and I swear, each looks showroom fresh! How can you tell if a car is a rebuilt taxi? You need to find an expert mechanic you trust and have him inspect the vehicle.

This is sometimes easier said than done. I happen to have a good friend who is also a great *tico* mechanic, and several years ago I asked him to find a trustworthy four-wheel drive for me. He had a mechanic search Heredia and Alajuela for reliable vehicles and found five to recommend. I bought the first one I looked at, which was his first choice, too.

Import Taxes on Autos

Customs duties are responsible for the sky-high prices of new and used cars in Costa Rica. At one time taxes were more than 100 percent of the vehicle's value. They are a bit lower now but are still about 60 percent (sometimes more) of the appraised value, depending on age. Tax rates keep changing as the Congress and Ministry of Customs vacillate on how to apply customs duties. Decisions change every year or so.

I know, this sounds like highway robbery (excuse the metaphor), but the government presents two arguments for high customs duties. One, of course: They need the money. *Ticos* dodge as many taxes as they can, but they can't avoid customs on that new Mercedes because it's collected before they get their hands on the steering wheel. The other justification is that high prices discourage people from adding more vehicles to already overcrowded streets and highways. This strategy doesn't seem to be working—at least not the last time I tried to drive along Paseo Colón.

It doesn't do any good to argue about the value of your vehicle with the customs people, because they go by a printed list of market values. If your vehicle is in bad shape, they may deduct for that. But you wouldn't be bringing a piece of junk here in the first place. My recommendation is to contact a customs agent who knows how to get things done and can tell you exactly what you'll need to pay in taxes.

SHIPPING YOUR VEHICLE

Cars can be shipped from either Atlantic or Pacific ports to Costa Rica. But the cheapest and fastest way is from Florida or New Orleans. The cost varies widely, depending on the shipping line and availability of space. From California, costs are higher: I paid $1,300 from San Francisco a few years ago. From Florida, the destination port is Limón; from California it's Puerto Caldera (near Puntarenas). The shipping line will prepare the documents stateside and take care of details once you deliver the car. Don't fail to ask for full-coverage insurance; it's not terribly expensive. You will also need to obtain a smog certificate from the state of origin of the car before shipping it to Costa Rica.

Once the car arrives at the port, you have the option of picking it up at the port or waiting until it arrives at the main customs house in San José. In either event, you then have the decision of taking possession and going through customs yourself or hiring a Costa Rican customs agent to handle the paperwork for you. If you speak a bit of Spanish, you can do it yourself, but I'd advise asking a *tico* friend to walk you through the hurdles of red tape and forms in triplicate. The friend needn't be an expert, just someone who speaks good Spanish and who can ask which line you must stand in—and which line after that.

SHIPPING YOUR HOUSEHOLD GOODS

Although many will disagree, I wouldn't bother shipping household goods and belongings to Costa Rica, unless they were items I couldn't replace or couldn't live without. Just about anything you can think of to import into Costa Rica can be purchased for less than what you would pay in the United States or Canada, including import duties and shipping.

Another idea is that you can make a trip to Golfito or to the Panamanian border and buy your appliances—duty-free in Golfito and $500 per person duty-free at the border (a couple gets $1,000, and they can do this every six months). I've been told that the government decided that automatic washers and dryers are no longer luxury goods; they've reduced, if not eliminated, import taxes on them. This brings prices down to US levels.

Many of you will go ahead and import everything but the proverbial kitchen sink. If so, you will need a shipper in the United States to make sure things are packed properly and stowed away on a ship. Shipping from Florida or New Orleans is much less expensive than from the West Coast. When your cargo arrives, you will need a customs broker to handle things on this end. You can get your personal items out of customs yourself, but I'm convinced that an experienced hand, someone who knows whom, when, and where to schmooze, will save you aggravation.

A problem with cargo ships is they are seldom on schedule. This makes it difficult to arrange a definite date to meet the ship and usher your belongings through customs. You'll have to wait until the unpredictable day when the ship finally docks in Costa Rica. When we shipped our car from San Francisco, we were told it would arrive within a three-day spread. Would it surprise anyone that the ship was fifteen days late? We called every day, and they promised it would be there within two more days, God willing. (God was most unwilling during those two weeks.) By the way, shipping from San Francisco was three times more expensive than it would have been from Tampa.

Packing your goods correctly will save them from damage when tossed around in the loading process. Labeling them properly will help keep duty down. Marking boxes "used household goods" and "not for sale" will also help. Some people take grease pens and mark *usado* on the items themselves to make it clear that they aren't going to be sold.

Duty assessed can be rather erratic, depending on the mood of the customs official, so this is where your suave customs representative can earn his pay. I will say that I've always been treated with respect when dealing with customs, with one exception: I was bringing in a computer that the customs official wanted to mark on my passport as my exempted duty. After a shouting match (which I won), we both apologized.

You are entitled to import a certain amount of items for personal use tax-free (as well as $500 per person of normally taxable goods). The amount of duty you pay on additional items can be minimal or very high according to a highly involved and subjective combination of import duty, consumption tax, sales tax, and other miscellaneous charges. These are multiplied by the value of the item (a combination of estimated cost plus freight plus insurance). Depending on the article, there could be a 37 percent tax or, sometimes, no tax at all.

I've heard about different experiences from people who've brought a lot of belongings into the country by automobile, and they've been mostly favorable. My own experience is that when entering Costa Rica from Nicaragua with the back of our station wagon stuffed to the max with household goods, power tools, and who knows what, the only inspection we got was from a Costa Rican guard, who asked whether we had electronic items such as TVs or VCRs. When we said no, he waved us on without even looking. Maybe we were lucky. By the way, two things you don't want to get caught bringing in without proper papers are arms and munitions!

BRINGING AN AIRCRAFT TO COSTA RICA

(The following information was supplied by Peter Todd, manager of Helicorp S.A. Maintenance at Tobias Bolanos Airport in Pavas.)

There are two options the private owner has regarding bringing an aircraft to Costa Rica.

As a tourist: You have the same privileges as the local aircraft do for three months. No duties, no taxes, no local insurance required. At the end of three months, you will have to take the aircraft out of the country for at least three months. You may then bring it back again for another three months.

Import the aircraft into Costa Rica: To do this, you will need the following: Either in Costa Rica or in the United States you will need to get a DAR (Designated Airworthiness Representative) to issue an Export Airworthiness Certificate naming Costa Rica as the importing country. For the DAR to do this, the aircraft will need to have had an "Annual Type" inspection within the last thirty days and be airworthy.

When this is done, you will have to de-register the aircraft from the United States. This can be done from Costa Rica, and the FAA will issue a letter confirming this. The AOPA can assist with this function. Once this is done you may start the registration proceedings in Costa Rica. This is fairly simple and should only take about two weeks if you have your ducks lined up. The DGAC (Dirección General de Aeronáutica Civil) will inspect your aircraft, review the documents, and issue you a TI number and local certificates.

You will also have to pay the import taxes, which are about 20 percent based on market value. I have been told that the taxes are in reality pretty reasonable, but things can change! You will also have to purchase the local liability insurance from the government insurance agency, INS.

Some other items for aviators coming to Costa Rica: There is no night VFR here, and you have to file a flight plan no matter where you go. There are four international airports in Costa Rica: the main ones in Alajuela and Liberia, and two smaller ones in Pavas and Limón. Your FAA private license will get you a *tico* private license just by showing it. For a commercial license you will have to take the test. I have heard conflicting stories about it being available in English and Spanish.

BRINGING PETS TO COSTA RICA

Those of you who refuse to relocate anywhere without your faithful furry companions will be pleased to know that there is no legal problem bringing them to Costa Rica. You will, of course, have a certain amount of paperwork.

You begin the process with a visit to your local veterinarian for a complete examination of your pet to make sure that your companion is free of all infectious and/or contagious diseases and that all vaccinations are up to date against rabies, distemper, hepatitis, parvovirus, and leptospirosis. The rabies shots should be at least thirty days but less than one year old at time of departure. The examination report will identify the pet's name, breed, sex, and color, as well as the owner's name and address. This health certificate must be signed by a licensed veterinarian. The papers are supposed to be good for ten days after issue by the consulate, but some customs people say thirty days is okay. Many travelers report that they weren't even asked for papers when they arrived in Costa Rica, but it makes sense to shoot for the ten-day deadline if possible.

I have a friend who doesn't bother with papers going in either direction; she just tucks her toy poodle into her large handbag and marches aboard the airplane. That's taking a chance, but she claims that if there's a problem, she has a thirty-day grace period to straighten things out. (Presumably, little Fifi could be incarcerated in a doggy jail in the meantime.)

I highly recommend getting all the proper documents, with precisely crossed *i*'s and correctly dotted *t*'s—or whatever.

Some unusual animals, especially endangered species, require special papers, from both the US and Costa Rican governments. Another friend's son insisted on bringing his huge pet Tasmanian monitor lizard (the size of an alligator), and although he had the proper papers, the freaked-out customs inspectors at the San José airport refused to allow the large reptile to enter until a veterinarian certified that it wasn't venomous.

Yet another friend, Pam, wanted to bring Oliver, her daughter's blue and gold macaw, into the country (akin to carrying coal to Newcastle). After three months of paperwork in both the United States and Costa Rica, paying fees and duty and such, Pam made a special trip back to the States, only to spend a lot more time cutting through red tape. "The only hassles I ran into were in the States!" she said. "When I arrived in Costa Rica, the customs guy peeked into the large carrier, glanced at my paperwork, and sent me on my merry way, never asking to see the health certificate or declaration papers that cost me so much time, effort, and worry!"

Once you have your pet's papers, you still have to figure out how to get the animal to Costa Rica. I find it difficult to give advice in this area because airlines keep changing their policies. Some airlines (and maybe all) are currently refusing to carry pets in the cargo holds in summer because of possible heat danger to the animals. Some airlines are refusing to accept animals, period; others are more pet-friendly. The last I heard, Delta was the most friendly, still allowing small animals to be carried into the passenger cabins (although they could balk at accepting a large Tasmanian reptile). With the current uncertainty about rules and regulations, you'll need to check individual airlines to find the right carrier. I'll try to post current info on my web page for the book update (www.discovery .press.com/update).

To leave the country, your pet needs an exit permit, just like human *residentes*. For this you'll need a health certificate from a Costa Rican veterinarian (well, actually, *you* don't need it, your *pet* does). The vet usually accepts your original papers as valid and fills out the proper Costa Rican exit permit without having to personally inspect the animal. The vet can do all the paperwork, obtain the proper stamps, and pay fees. Some people arrange this by fax; the vet or an assistant then meets them at the airport with the necessary permits. Call your vet or contact the Departamento de Zoonosis, Ministerio de Salud, Apartado 10123, San José; (506) 2-223-0333, ext. 331.

Contrary to the situation in some Latin American countries, pet food is readily available at most Costa Rican supermarkets and sometimes in the local *pulpería*. Veterinarians are numerous, with at least a dozen practicing in the San José area. Some will even make house calls. Actually, many villages are without a small-animal veterinarian because most vets specialize in treating large animals such as horses and cattle. They have little experience taking care of pets, and some don't like to be bothered with them. Those vets with small-animal practices are often reluctant to travel an hour or more to your beach-village home just to give a distemper shot to Fido or to neuter Miss Pussycat. Expats sometimes bring their pets together and have a "veterinarian party." They'll have a dozen animals ready for the vet to work on when he arrives for his monthly visit. The party guests enjoy themselves, sharing *bocas* and sipping cocktails, while the unfortunate *animalitos* are experiencing the business end of needles—and possibly losing some precious parts of their anatomy.

IMPORTING FIREARMS

Over the years, I've had numerous inquiries about bringing handguns into the country. Technically, it can be done. However, the government strongly discourages the practice and erects legal and red tape barriers that make it somewhat impractical. This doesn't mean you cannot legally purchase a handgun in Costa Rica. Under certain circumstances you can even obtain a permit to carry one. The following is some information extracted from the *Tico Times*.

First of all, you must be a legal resident to own a handgun and/or apply for a concealed carry permit. Nonresidents can own a gun when it's registered in the name of their corporation, but nonresidents cannot get a concealed weapons permit.

To buy a new gun, you'll need to fill out a form, giving the name of the gun shop, the serial number, and other descriptions of the purchase. (For some reason you can buy a used gun and take it with you, provided you report it to the Armament Administration within ten days.) Next you take a written test, and a firearms practice test that requires you to hit a target seven out of ten shots. You must pass a psychological exam given by a government-certified psychologist and undergo a criminal background check by the OIJ (Judicial Investigation Police), and then you must provide two photographs of yourself. Finally, you receive papers and official seals that entitle you to purchase your handgun.

All of this sounds very reasonable, but my impression is that many people skip the formal application and simply buy a used gun and never follow through with the official process.

I urge you to consider the philosophy of handguns in Costa Rica; that is, carrying concealed weapons is not part of Costa Rica's peaceful *pura vida* culture. Because burglaries while residents are home are rare, few *ticos* even bother to keep weapons in their homes. Furthermore, in instances of disputes involving a handgun, the law often comes down against the shooter, even though a US court would consider justified self-defense in similar circumstances. Just carrying a weapon raises a suspicion of aggressive intent.

Commonly, in many sections of the United States, juries of your peers will listen to your plea of self-defense with sympathetic ears, taking the word of the survivor over the silence of the deceased. In Costa Rica, you plead your case in front of three judges who take a dim view of foreigners packing guns and shooting each other. A few years ago, when an American bar owner in Playas del Coco was attacked by a belligerent customer with a knife, he fired a gun in obvious self-defense. Yet the bar owner was held in prison for almost two years before a decision of self-defense was reluctantly rendered. In the meantime, his business deteriorated and his finances were devastated, and, if I'm not mistaken, he was forced to return to the United States after his release.

17

Becoming a Resident

Because the rules for entering Costa Rica are so liberal, most people who live in the country for six months or less at a time do not feel it is worth the effort of applying for residency. My wife and I fall into this category. We seldom live in our Costa Rican home more than three months at a time, and when we do, we leave the country for a seventy-two-hour stay in Nicaragua or Panama before returning and receiving another visa.

Although the laws seem clear—you are entitled to one visa extension—many people have spent years in Costa Rica, leaving every ninety days and "renewing" their visas at the border. For years, many haven't even bothered doing that, since the fine for having an expired visa used to be a ridiculous amount, about $6 a month. However, several years ago the government did away with the fines and began cracking down on those overstaying their visas. Several persons have been picked up and deported for having expired visas. So far, the seventy-two hours outside the country seems to be acceptable. Generally tourists who do get deported are those who are somewhat undesirable in the first place.

But be aware that at some point, the Ministry of Immigration could become serious and begin enforcing regulations. Once your application is in, you don't have to worry about leaving while your residency is being processed. I must emphasize that I am in no way encouraging people to do this "ninety-day turnaround" to get around the rules. I am merely reporting the situation at the time of this writing. If you are going to stay in Costa Rica year-round, you would be well advised to consider applying for residency. (This is discussed in detail in chapter 12.)

Even though Costa Rica's rules have tightened somewhat, they are still exceedingly liberal compared with those in most other countries. In the United States, for example, if you stay even one day over your visa, you might *never* be permitted to return!

It's embarrassing to contrast the openness of Costa Rica's immigration with the way the United States treats Costa Ricans when they want to vacation in Disneyland or Las Vegas, or visit friends and relatives who have immigrated to the States. To receive a temporary visa, a Costa Rican must visit the embassy, hat in hand, pay a nonrefundable application fee of $160, and prove beyond the shadow of a doubt that he or she has every intention of returning to Costa Rica and has no possible motive for staying in the United States. It must be a humiliating experience to be denied a visa because your job doesn't pay a salary high enough to convince an embassy employee that you're sufficiently trustworthy to visit Disneyland and return. A large percentage of those requests are turned down with no explanation. A few years ago, the daughter of a Costa Rican vice president was rejected because a clerk doubted her character, assuming that because she was wearing flashy clothes and loaded with jewelry, she had to be a prostitute looking for employment abroad.

Compared with US immigration rules, Costa Rica's are very liberal. To become a legal resident, all you need to do is prove you have a sufficient income and do not have a serious criminal record. From time to time the Costa Rican congress considers raising income requirements, thinking that they may be unrealistically low. In my opinion, it is unlikely they will take any action. If they do, I will report it on my *Choose Costa Rica* update website at www.discoverypress.com/update.

From time to time the government declares an immigration amnesty for those who've been in the country illegally for a certain amount of time—say, two years or longer—and they can apply for permanent residence. People who are operating successful businesses are sometimes permitted to apply for residence papers. Those who qualify under amnesty rules are particularly lucky because they don't have to certify that they won't work for a living and therefore aren't restricted from holding jobs. It has been some time since amnesty was last offered. Then, in October 2012, the government made an announcement that "foreigners legally residing in Costa Rica for an acceptable number of years, and wanting to become citizens" may apply for citizenship. Exactly what this means is not totally clear. The question of whether the applicants will have to renounce their US or Canadian citizenships or can maintain dual citizenship is not clear. This could be critical in making decisions of this nature, because giving up

US or Canadian citizenship isn't a trivial matter. (We will keep you posted via our website, www.discoverypress.com/update.)

I'm not recommending that anyone overstay his or her visa or try to ignore Costa Rican laws. I'm simply reporting how the laws are being enforced at this time and how they are being applied toward foreigners who have the wherewithal to support themselves, who invest much-needed capital in the country, and who won't be taking jobs from Costa Rican citizens. Those who are indigent or who get into trouble may not find the laws applied quite so gently. For those who contemplate staying in Costa Rica more than six months at a stretch, it isn't very difficult to obtain legal residency, so why not bite the bullet and make it legal?

COSTA RICAN RESIDENCY

The government fully recognizes the economic value of foreign residents living in Costa Rica, bringing dollars to spend and deposit in banks. People from North America and Europe create jobs by investing money, building homes, starting businesses, and hiring Costa Rican employees.

For people like my wife and I, who can be satisfied with living half the year in Costa Rica and the other half in our home country, there's no clear advantage to becoming a legal resident. We can own property or a business and can travel about the country with nothing more than a tourist visa. On the other hand, there are restrictions and obligations on *pensionados* and *rentistas*—not ponderous ones, but they involve a certain amount of red tape. For example, if you aren't retired, you must prove that a certain amount of monthly income has been deposited in a Costa Rican bank. On a regular basis, you must provide police certification of good conduct, and once you obtain residency, you must live in Costa Rica for at least four (nonconsecutive) months of the year in order to hold on to your *residente* status.

For those who will be staying pretty much full-time in Costa Rica or who plan on entering into business and working as a manager in the business, the resident option is no doubt the best way to go. Once you have the papers and fulfill the residency obligations, you are completely legal and can enjoy all the rights of a Costa Rican, except voting. Becoming a legal resident of Costa Rica doesn't affect your US or Canadian citizenship in any way.

Categories of Residents

Immigration and applications for residency are handled by the Costa Rican Immigration Department. There are dozens of types of residency, but most North Americans use three classes of legal immigrant residents: Residente Pensionado, Pensionado Rentista, and Rentista Inversionista. After a stipulated number of years of residency under one of these categories, you may apply for permanent residency, and then you have fewer restrictions; for example, you can work without permission from the government.

Residente Pensionado

This category pertains to retired people with $1,000 or more guaranteed income per month. Social Security, or a military or government pension, is usually sufficient to qualify for this status. Those with a State or Province pension fund, or other guaranteed source, can also qualify as a *Residente Pensionado*. For this category, a total of at least $12,000 a year must be converted from dollars to colones in a Costa Rican bank and proof of this shown to the government every year. No law says that you have to spend all of it; you have only to prove that you've brought that amount of dollars into the country. Some people deposit the full amount at the beginning of the year to get the requirement out of the way.

For a married couple, the person without retirement income is considered a dependent, and no extra income is required (that is, only one pension per family). Children under the age of eighteen (or under twenty-five if in school) are also considered dependents. Social Security is sufficient proof of income. This is the option most retired people go for.

Pensionado Rentista

This category is for those who are not old enough to retire or who do not have a pension, yet who want residency in Costa Rica. Applicants must prove $2,500 a month guaranteed income. The best way to acquire this residency status is to deposit $150,000 in an interest-bearing dollar account in a Costa Rican bank. The bank then pays you $2,500 each month from this account for a period of five years. Deposits in state-owned banks are government guaranteed without limit, and most bank interest in Costa Rica is not taxed by the Costa Rican government. Younger people and those who want to go into business often choose this option.

Rentista Inversionista

People who are serious about going into business prefer this category. The requirement: A $200,000 investment in your business (with government approval). You must spend at least six months a year in the country. The investment can also be $50,000 in an approved tourism or export business; $100,000 in a reforestation project also can qualify you for residency.

You understand, of course, that you needn't become a resident to own or operate a business in Costa Rica: You can actually do so on a tourist visa. However, owners without residency are ostensibly restricted to management duties and not permitted to work at ordinary tasks in the business. This is not always enforced, especially if the person working isn't displacing a Costa Rican worker. But those who are serious about going into business usually either have residency or will eventually apply for residency.

When it comes to investment in a business or a reforestation project, please exercise extreme caution. As mentioned elsewhere in this book, Costa Rica is teeming with sharks just waiting for fish like you and me. Reforestation investments are highly promoted as lucrative investments. You should be cautious of overly optimistic claims; teak promoters have poor track records in fulfilling their promises. Consult a good lawyer first. Some, but not all reforestation investments are hoaxes; you need to do your homework to filter out the scammers.

What Do You Get with Residency?

As a resident with any of the aforementioned three statuses, you have the following benefits and requirements:

1. You have all the rights of citizenship except voting.

2. You can own and manage businesses, but you cannot earn a salary from a Costa Rican employer. You can pay yourself dividends, however. Once your residency is permanent, you can work for anyone.

3. You must reside in Costa Rica the equivalent of at least four months a year, not necessarily contiguous months. Once you have permanent residency, you are expected to visit Costa Rica once a year for at least one day.

4. You must renew proof of stable and permanent income annually until you have full residency.

To make an application, you can either do it yourself or hire an experienced attorney to go through the red tape for you. The process requires a moderate deposit of money to cover fees, stamps, and forms. Once you accumulate the necessary documents, it could take from a few months to a year before approval comes through, depending on the thoroughness of your preparation and who is assisting you. Meanwhile your residency status is legal and won't be challenged.

Ask around the North American community for recommendations of a good lawyer or an experienced *tramitador* (a person who knows which lines to stand in and knows whom to see to get your papers processed promptly). But be careful: Hiring someone who doesn't know what he or she is doing not only takes a lot more time but could be a waste of money if the person does not or cannot follow through.

Association of Residents of Costa Rica

Personally, I am convinced that one of the most important moves you can make toward obtaining residency is joining ARCR (Association of Residents of Costa Rica) and letting them handle the red tape. Yes, some individuals have done the paperwork on their own, but you'll hear sad tales of woe from those who have tried it without knowing what they were doing or who chose a lawyer with little experience in maneuvering through the maze of bureaucracy. An ARCR membership entitles you to apply for residency through the group, attend social events and meetings, and other benefits. Further benefits are as follows: The association can make sure your annual papers are up to date, translate and notarize your documents, renew the required Costa Rican ID card, help you get a driver's license and other special permits, and assist you in many other ways before your move. The organization will also do English-to-Spanish translations and authenticate a photocopy of your resident's *carnét* so that you can leave your original at home.

Members with residency are eligible to receive doctor and hospital care in the National Health Services System, under terms of a special contract. This relieves you of the obligation of standing in line each month to make your payments. The organization pays it on a three-month basis and sends you proof of payment for the current month, which entitles you to medical service. You can also obtain all other types of insurance, a Miami PO box to receive your mail, and many other services. The association also publishes a newsletter six times a year. For more information write ARCR, Apdo. 1191–1007, Centro Colón, San José, or call (506) 2-233-8068. The ARCR has a comprehensive website at www.arcr.net.

Paperwork

In any event, the process of getting your resident papers is best started by you, right in your home country. It's much easier to get these at home than by mail from Costa Rica. The four main items you need are listed below, and in all cases processing must be done through your local Costa Rican consulate. They charge about $40 per document.

Income certification is the first and most important step; it's often complicated and difficult. Rules and proof of income differ between Residente Pensionados and Pensionado Rentistas. Social Security or other government pension money is the easiest to prove. Ask for a statement from the pension source confirming that you have at least $1,000 a month guaranteed pension, and have that notarized at a Costa Rican consulate in your country. If the pension is nongovernmental, you'll need notarized letters that the pension is for life and two letters from bank officials testifying to the soundness of the company's pension plan.

The guarantee of income for *rentistas* is $2,500 monthly in interest and dividends from banks or investment houses. The decision on whether your income qualifies is made on a case-by-case basis. You'll need statements establishing that this income is guaranteed for at least five years, and you'll need to renew these guarantees every succeeding five years. The Costa Rican consulate can help you with this. Again, it's important to have the notary certification and authentication of the documents done by a consulate in your home country.

You need to provide a **birth certificate.** This is needed for you and each of your dependents. Also a **marriage certificate** (proof of previous divorce is not necessary), as well as a **police certificate of good conduct**. Obtain this at your last place of residence, and make it the last document you receive. Have the police certify a set of fingerprints as well; ask the Costa Rican consulate for the necessary forms. Make the good-conduct verification your last step because it's only valid for six months from the time of certification. If you get this document first and then spend a lot of time with the other papers, it could expire before your application gets under way. I know of people who've had to return to the United States to get another conduct certification because theirs was more than six months old. You'll also need certificates of good conduct for dependents over eighteen.

Note, too, that if you are traveling with children, some special rules apply. Apparently, these rules apply more for Costa Rican citizens than for tourists, and even though they don't seem to be strictly enforced, it's important that you be aware of them. When a child traveling without both parents stays beyond thirty days, the child falls under the jurisdiction of the *Patronato Nacional de la Infancia,* a children's welfare organization. In order for a child to leave the country without both parents, it might be necessary to have a permit notarized by the Patronato offices on Nineteenth Street and Sixth Avenue in San José. I've never heard of any tourist being hassled for this, but if just one parent is traveling with a child for long periods, it might be a good idea to have a notarized statement of permission from the other parent. And remember, just having your documents notarized is not enough.

The documents must be taken to the Costa Rican consulate in your country to verify the notary's validity and certification. The notary isn't merely verifying your signature but also that the documents are valid and that they belong to you. Not following each step correctly is responsible for the many delays and obstacles you often hear people complain about.

Other details can be taken care of in Costa Rica at the time you make a formal request for residency. Several certified copies of your passport are required, and you'll fill out a questionnaire of personal information. As a retiree, you'll have to sign a statement that you won't work for pay while in Costa Rica (without authorization) and that you'll spend at least four months a year in Costa Rica. (As stated earlier, the months needn't be consecutive.)

From here on, it's filling out forms, standing in line, waiting for stamps and signatures, standing in more lines to put a deposit in the bank, going hither and yon to stand in still more lines—most of which can be done by your surrogate, the *tramitador.*

18

Will You Love Costa Rica or Hate Costa Rica?

This chapter could well have appeared in the very front of the book. However, it might have discouraged potential expatriates from considering what Costa Rica has to offer for relocation before visiting and seeing for themselves. The bottom line is this: *Costa Rica is not for everyone!*

Readers are hereby encouraged to reflect upon their own personalities as a way to ascertain if they might "fit in" and adapt to any foreign culture. After that, consider this particular foreign country, with its own distinctive customs and sometimes bewildering worldviews.

Allow me to explain: My own love affair with Latin America began as a teenager, when my family moved to Mexico City. My father, a veterinarian, accepted a position with the US Department of Agriculture on a project to eradicate hoof-and-mouth disease in the Mexican countryside. The job ended after a few years, but my family's residency in Mexico endured another thirty years.

From the beginning, my parents became active in Mexico's sizable British/American expatriate community. We entertained at our home and were often invited to dinner parties and social events where we mingled with other expatriates living in the Mexico City area. As an interested teenager, I listened to folks comparing their experiences in this foreign environment. I found it interesting that some expats seemed to totally *detest* living away from "back home" in North America or Britain. They had absolutely nothing good to say about life in Mexico. Yet, for various reasons, they would not (or could not) return to their homes up north. I estimated that 20 percent of our expatriate acquaintances felt that way. I was both puzzled and annoyed by their constant negativity.

The disappointed expatriates detested their maids and gardeners, convinced they were stealing everything they could carry away. Expat housewives would deliberately leave money or jewelry in plain sight, hoping to confirm their suspicions. They detested the ugly iron bars over their windows and the outside doors. All storekeepers were short-change artists. Mexican neighbors were snobbish and impossible. Mexican police demanded bribes whenever the *gringo* driver was going even a few miles over the speed limit, or was simply driving on the sidewalk after a cocktail party.

The other side of the coin: Another 20 percent of foreign residents were exactly the opposite. These happy campers adored *anything* and *everything* about Mexico! They refused to see anything wrong. They accepted the "*mañana* attitude" as humorous and inevitable. Instead of fretting about security and employee theft, they locked valuables away and used common-sense precautions to prevent crime. When the maid slipped a thick steak and cupcakes into her handbag, the American housewife thought it was charming, picturing how the woman's happy family would enjoy the treats. When a favorite piece of jewelry could not be found, it wouldn't occur to her that one of the household staff could be responsible. When the gardener didn't show up the day after (or maybe two days after) a holiday, they sympathized with him. "You wouldn't expect someone to work with a hangover, would you?"

The happy campers prided themselves for having an attractively designed set of wrought-iron door and window bars. When a cop stopped their car for a traffic infraction, the driver would smile pleasantly as he handed over his driver's license along with a folded $5 bill, thankful that one could get by so cheaply for a well-earned punishment. (Had he been driving on the sidewalk, he would make it a $20 bill.)

The other 60 percent of the expatriates resigned themselves to accepting the good, the bad, and ugly of relocation in a foreign country. When they didn't like or failed to understand the customs, they didn't continually fret and whimper. They would research neighborhoods to find recommended and safe places to live and immediately begin making friends with residents. They learned to laugh at the ridiculous and feel blessed when things went well. When something went wrong, they felt fortunate that it wasn't much worse. They continually reminded themselves of the conditions "back home" that convinced them to become expatriates. Whether it was freezing winters, expensive living, idiotic politicians, or simply bore-dom—they felt fortunate that they were able to leave all of that behind.

This negative-positive phenomenon isn't confined to Mexico or Costa Rica. We've found these divisions in all expatriate communities we've vis-ited throughout Latin America (as well as Spain and Portugal) as we inter-viewed British and North Americans living abroad. Once, in the south of Spain, we visited an expat couple from England who owned a beautiful sixteenth-century-style home on the crest of a hill with a view of the Medi-terranean, overlooking an ancient Moorish castle. It was absolutely breath-taking. After listening to a boring list of dislikes and complaints about living in Spain, we tried to change the subject to their gorgeous view. The man shrugged and said, "It's like new wallpaper. After a while you get used to it and it becomes invisible!"

Each person's dream of life in a foreign setting will vary widely. It should be no surprise that idyllic pictures of life in Costa Rica will rarely correspond precisely with reality. That dream of a romantic tropical beach home, swaying palm trees, and the sound of gentle surf—can morph into a high-maintenance, poorly built structure, full of mildew and land crabs, a leaking roof, and in the distance, loud laughs of tourists and shouts of muscular surfers arguing over wave territory.

Then, there's that quiet and peaceful Costa Rican home, perched on a lovely forested mountain slope, with a magnificent view of the volcano across the valley. Without friends and neighbors to share the view, the place becomes altogether *too* peaceful! Boring, actually. After while, the spectacular view becomes ordinary, "Just like wallpaper!"

Other disappointed expatriates continually complain about Costa Rica's cost of living. They had envisioned the country as a thrifty person's retirement paradise. They assumed that rent, groceries, utilities—prices in general—would be a fraction of what they were "back home." "After all, this *is* a 'banana republic,' right? Wages are low, why shouldn't *prices* be low?" They are horrified to realize they could have stayed in Alabama or even rural California and enjoyed a cost of living almost as low as in Costa Rica. They feel cheated. Every time the government mandates a change in the dollar-colon exchange rate or an increase in minimum wages (which happens every January and July), they get depressed.

They also complain about Costa Rican taxes. The road in front of their home is seldom repaired, and when it is repaired, the road often ends up in worse shape than before the work was done. "What in the world does the government *do* with our tax money?" They seem to forget that property taxes on their home in Fort Worth were more than $7,000, instead of the $350 for a similar home in Costa Rica.

We will end this book with an observation recently posted to a Costa Rican bulletin board by a five-year resident of Costa Rica (obviously one of the 60-percent retirees). He said, "When making an international move, many people invest time and effort learning about real estate, health care, transportation and the locations of great restaurants, but they often fail in understanding and learning about Costa Rica's culture."

Welcome to Costa Rica! Here's hoping you will become one of the 60 percent!

Appendix

EMBASSY OF COSTA RICA IN THE UNITED STATES

2112 S St. NW, Washington, DC 20008; (202) 234-2945; fax (202) 265-4795.
Tomas Dueñas, ambassador.

COSTA RICAN CONSULATES IN THE UNITED STATES

Arizona

Phoenix (area of coverage: Arizona): Andrew P. Burke, Honorary Consul, 7373 E Doubletree Ranch Rd., Ste. 200, Scottsdale, AZ 85258; (480) 951-2264; fax (480) 991-6606

California

Los Angeles (areas of coverage: Arizona, Hawaii, Nevada, Southern California, and Utah): Percy Calvo Cartín, Consul, 1605 West Olympic Blvd., Ste. 400, Los Angeles, CA 90015; (213) 380-7915; fax (213) 380-5639
San Francisco (areas of coverage: Alaska, Idaho, Montana, Northern California, Oregon, and Washington): Manuel Escoto, Honorary Consul, PO Box 7643, Fremont, CA 94537; (510) 790-0785; fax (510) 792-5249

Colorado

Denver (area of coverage: Colorado): Tito Chaverri, Honorary Consul, 3356 South Xenia St., Denver, CO 80231-4542; (303) 696-8211; fax (303) 696-1110

District of Columbia

(Areas of coverage: all US territory): Alejandro Cendeño, Consul General, 2112 S St. NW, Washington, DC 20008; (202) 328-6628; fax (202) 265-4795

Florida

Miami (area of coverage: Florida): Oscar Camacho, Consul General, 1600 NW Forty-second Ave., Miami, FL 33126; (305) 871-7485

Tampa (area of coverage: Florida): Erica Salgado, Consul General, 14502 North Dale Mabry Hwy., Ste. 200, Tampa, FL 33618; (813) 969-3837; fax (813) 969-3357

Georgia

Atlanta (area of coverage: Georgia): Emilia Trejos, Consul General, 1870 The Exchange, Ste. 100, Atlanta, GA 30339; (770) 951-7025; fax (770) 951-7073

Illinois

Chicago (areas of coverage: Illinois, Indiana, Iowa, Kentucky, Michigan, Minnesota, Missouri, North Dakota, Ohio, South Dakota, and Wisconsin): Juan Salas Araya, Consul, 185 North Wabash Ave., Ste. 1123, Chicago, IL 60601; (312) 263-2772; fax (312) 263-5807

Louisiana

New Orleans Temporary (areas of coverage: Alabama, Arkansas, Louisiana, Mississippi, New Mexico, Oklahoma, and Tennessee): 1514 Martens Dr., Ste. 210, Hammond, LA 70401; (504) 581-6400 or (985) 549-5454

Massachusetts

Boston (area of coverage: Massachusetts): 175 McClellan Hwy., East Boston, MA 02134; (617) 561-2444; fax (617) 561-2461

Minnesota

St. Paul (area of coverage: Minnesota): Anthony L. Andersen, Honorary Consul, 2424 Territorial Rd., St. Paul, MN 55114; (651) 481-3616; fax (651) 645-4684

New York

New York City (areas of coverage: Connecticut, Maine, Massachusetts, New York, New Jersey, Pennsylvania, and Rhode Island): 80 Wall St., Ste. 718, New York, NY 10005; (212) 509-3066; fax (212) 509-3068

Puerto Rico

San Juan (area of coverage: Puerto Rico): Avenida Ponce de Leon, Edificio 1510, Oficina P1, Esquina Calle Pelaval, San Juan, Puerto Rico 00909; (787) 723-6227; fax (787) 723-6226

Texas

Houston (area of coverage: Texas): Sergio Valverde, Consul General, 3000 Wilcrest, Ste. 112, Houston, TX 77042; (713) 266-0484; fax (713) 266-1527
San Antonio (area of coverage: Texas): Marta Rojas, Consul, 6836 San Pedro, Ste. 116, San Antonio, TX 78216; (210) 824-8474; fax (210) 824-8489

COSTA RICAN CONSULATES IN CANADA

Embassy of Costa Rica, 135 York St., Ste. 208, Ottawa, ON K1N 5TA Canada; (613) 562-2855; fax (613) 562-2582

British Columbia

Vancouver: Antonio Arreaga, Honorary Consul, Suite 430–789, West Pender Street, Vancouver, BC V6C 1H2 Canada; (604) 681-2152; fax (604) 688-2152

Ontario

Ottawa (areas of coverage: all Canadian territory): 325 Dalhouise St., Ste. 407, Ottawa, ON K1N 7G2 Canada; (613) 562-2855; fax: (613) 562-2582
Toronto: Peter Alexander Kircher, Honorary Consul, 164 Avenue Rd., Toronto, ON M5R 2H9 Canada; (416) 961-6773; fax (416) 961-6771

Quebec

Montreal: Roy Thompson, Consul General, 1425 René Levexque-West, Ste. 602, Montreal, QC H3G 1T7 Canada; (514) 393-1057; fax (514) 393-1624

Index

About the Authors

John Howells and his wife, Sherry, know Latin America well. John lived with his family in Mexico as a youth and has traveled extensively throughout Central and South America, Spain, and Portugal, publishing several guidebooks about living, retiring, and investing in these foreign locations. His thirty-plus-year love affair with Costa Rica and Central America uniquely qualifies him as an expert on what it is like to be an expatriate in this charming little country known as "the Switzerland of the Americas." John and Sherry divide their time between Costa Rica and California. Teal Conroy, John's granddaughter, also an author, joined the writing team to produce this tenth edition of *Choose Costa Rica*.